Sir Edward Bulwer Lytton

Caxtoniana

A Series of Essays on Life, Literature and Manners

Sir Edward Bulwer Lytton

Caxtoniana

A Series of Essays on Life, Literature and Manners

ISBN/EAN: 9783742822383

Manufactured in Europe, USA, Canada, Australia, Japa

Cover: Foto ©Andreas Hilbeck / pixelio.de

Manufactured and distributed by brebook publishing software (www.brebook.com)

Sir Edward Bulwer Lytton

Caxtoniana

COLLECTION

OF

BRITISH AUTHORS.

VOL. 693.

CAXTONIANA BY SIR E. BULWER LYTTON, Bart.

IN TWO VOLUMES.

VOL. II.

CAXTONIANA:

A SERIES OF ESSAYS
ON
LIFE, LITERATURE, AND MANNERS.

BY
SIR E. BULWER LYTTON, BART.
AUTHOR OF "THE CAXTONS," ETC.

COPYRIGHT EDITION.

IN TWO VOLUMES.
VOL. II.

LEIPZIG
BERNHARD TAUCHNITZ
1864.

CONTENTS

OF VOLUME II.

		Page
ESSAY XXII.	Motive Power	1
— XXIII.	On certain Principles of Art in Works of Imagination	119
— XXIV.	Posthumous Reputation	157
— XXV.	On some Authors in whose Writings Knowledge of the World is eminently displayed . . .	185
— XXVI.	Readers and Writers	295
— XXVII.	On the Spirit of Conservatism	301
L'envoi .	. . . .	320

ESSAY XXII.

MOTIVE POWER.

MOTIVE POWER.

A LITTLE while ago, as I was walking down Parliament Street, I suddenly found myself face to face with a man who, in the days of my early youth, had inspired me with a warm regard and a lively admiration. Though he was some years older than myself, we had been for a short time very intimate; but after we had once separated, I saw no more of him till thus, towards the evening of life, we two, who had parted company in its morn, recognised each other at the first glance; and, after exclaiming, "Is it you?" halted mute, like men to whom startling news is abruptly told. The past, as when we last separated, the present as we now met, brought before us in the extreme of contrast; the long, gradual, stealthy interval between the dates annulled; so that, in uttering those words, "Is it you?" each saw himself as he was in youth, and simultaneously felt the change time had wrought in his own life by reading the work of time in the face of the other. But such reflection was, as it were, the flash of the moment, and with the next moment it passed away. As I was then hurrying down to the House of Commons, somewhat fearful lest I should not be in time to vote on a question worn so threadbare that it was not likely the patience of members would allow it to be long rediscussed, my old acquaintance kindly turned back from his own way to accommodate himself to mine; and, when we parted at the doors of Westminster Hall, much to my surprise he had invited me to visit him in the country, and, perhaps still more to his surprise, I had accepted the invitation.

Sir Percival Tracey (so let me call the person I have just introduced to the reader) was one of those men to whom Nature gives letters of recommendation to Posterity, which, from some chance or another, never reach their destination.

It has been said by a man of a genius and a renown so great as to render his saying the more remarkable, that if we could become thoroughly acquainted with the biography of any one who has achieved fame, we should find that he had met with some person to fame unknown, whose intellect had impressed him more than that of any of the celebrated competitors with whom it had been his lot to strive. He whom I call Percival Tracey might serve to illustrate whatever truth may be found in that bold assertion. At the time of life in which I had been among his familiar associates, I can remember no one of the same years who has since become distinguished, so strongly impressing the men who were distinguished then with respect for his superior capacities, and a faith in his ultimate renown. Yet, if I disclose his real name, in him this later generation would only recognise one of those wealthy and well-born gentlemen of whom little or nothing is known to the public, except that they are — well-born and wealthy.

Deprived of both parents in early childhood, Percival Tracey was left to the guardianship of his maternal uncle, the Duke of ———. Sent to a public school, illustrious less for learned boys than famous men, he there acquired one of those brilliant reputations which light up the after-paths of ambition; for it is a wondrous advantage to candidates for power and renown to enter on the arena of life with the *esprit de corps* of coevals already enlisted in their favour; an advantage so great, that I venture to doubt whether any system of wholly private education, however theoretically admirable, can compensate to an able and ambitious man, whom such education had formed, for the loneliness in which, at the onset of his career, he stands among his own generation — no young hands thrilling to applaud, no young voices whispering "he was one of us!" all disposed to cavil at the claims of a stranger whose talents revive no recollections of early promise — whose successes recall no sympathies of boyish friendship — whose honours, if his labours win them, will add no name to the *Libro d'oro* of the never-forgotten School!

Cambridge was the university selected for the completion of Tracey's academical studies, whether from family associations or by his own desire. On leaving school, somewhere about the age of sixteen, he was accordingly placed in the house of a tutor, who had acquired the highest mathematical honours which the University of Cambridge can confer. There he contracted a taste, and developed an aptitude, for the Positive Sciences, which might have enabled him to confirm at college the reputation he had gained at school. But just as he was about to commence his first term at Trinity, he was attacked by a fever, in reality caused by a rash feat in swimming, but which his guardian insisted on imputing to an over-fatigue in study. The

Duke of —— was in his own way an exceedingly clever man — a man of the world — into which world he had entered as an aspiring cadet, before, by the death of his elder brother, he had become a contented duke. His Grace was no Goth; he held book-learning in the greatest possible respect. But while he allowed that book-learning lifted up into station the poor and the humbly born, he had a vague notion that book-learning tends to divert from their proper sphere of action the wealthy and the highborn: and in Percival Tracey he hoped to find the zealous champion, and perhaps ultimately the redoubted chief, of that party for which his Grace felt a patriot's preference. Hailing, therefore, in Percival's unlucky fever, an excuse for distracting him from unhealthful studies, the Duke, instead of immuring his brilliant ward in the cloisters of a college, sent him forth to perform what was anciently called "The Grand Tour," and in polite acquaintance with courts and capitals, learn by how little knowledge mankind are governed. At the end of three years Percival Tracey returned to England, and entered London society as a young man in possession of vast estates entirely at his own disposal, and with the command of a considerable capital accumulated by the savings of a long minority. He was the representative of a family which, in point of antiquity, of illustrious connections, and the political influence derived from territorial possessions, might vie with the noblest in England. The advantages he took from Nature were as brilliant as those he had received from Fortune. His frame, at once light and vigorous, was the faithful index of a constitution capable of enduring any of those fatigues, more exhausting than

bodily labour, by which study or ambition tasks the
resources of life. He was sufficiently good-looking to
be generally considered handsome; but not so outrageously good-looking as to acquire that kind of reputation for beauty which elevates the rank of a woman,
but disparages that of a man. For I presume that
any woman, however sensible, would be rather admired
for her outward attractions than her intellectual powers;
and I am sure that no sensible man, who possesses
that pride which Milton calls "an honest haughtiness,"
would not feel very much ashamed of such a reputation. In fact, if Percival Tracey was handsome, it
was not from mere regularity of feature, nor lustre of
colouring, but from an expression of countenance which
seemed to take sweetness from the amenities of his
heart, and nobleness from the dignity of his mind. In
his prodigal culture, graceful accomplishments felicitously combined with severer studies; so that the one
seemed as naturally to grow up amidst the other as
the corn-flowers grow amidst the corn. He excelled
in all the bodily sports and exercises which young
Englishmen of his rank esteem as manly, to a degree
which won their pardon for his display of those elegant
ornaments of character which they are apt to neglect
as effeminate. Endowed with a vivid sense of beauty,
and an exquisite felicity of taste, he was more than
an amateur of the Fine Arts, more than a connoisseur;
he was an artist. Professional painters discovered
amazing beauties in his paintings — had he himself
been a professional painter, they would doubtless have
paid him the higher compliment of discovering amazing
faults. He was an excellent linguist; and wrote or
spoke most of the polite languages in Europe with the

correctness and fluency of an educated native. Yet with all this surface of graceful accomplishment no one ever called him superficial. On the contrary, it was the habit of his mind to search into the depth of things. Hence his confirmed attachment to the Positive Sciences; and I believe, indeed, the only MSS. he was ever induced to publish (and those anonymously) were some papers in a scientific journal, which were held, at the time, to throw much light upon a very abstruse subject, and spoken of highly by professed philosophers. But his authorship was undetected, and the papers themselves, in the rapid progress of scientific discovery, have no doubt been long since forgotten. Hence, too, the tendency of his faculties was not towards the creative, but towards the critical directions of intellect. He had sufficient warmth of imagination to appreciate the works on which imagination bestows a life more lasting than the real, yet that appreciation did not lead him to imitate, but rather to analyse, what he admired. Fond of metaphysics, he prized most that kind of poetry in which metaphysical speculation lights up unsuspected beauties, or from which it derives familiar illustrations of recondite truths. Thus in his talk, though it had the easy charm of a man of the world, there was a certain subtlety, sometimes a certain depth, of reasoning, which, supported by large stores of comprehensive information, imposed upon his listeners, and brought into bolder relief the vantage-ground for political station which his talents and his knowledge took from the dignity of his birth and the opulence of his fortune. In short, at the date I now refer to, the practised observers of the time, and the acknowledged authorities in opinion, glancing over the foremost figures in the young generation, pointed to Percival Tracey and said, "See the Coming Man!"

Secretly, as I learned more intimately, and yet more admiringly, to know the object of a prediction which all appearances might justify — I doubted whether the prediction would be realised. The main reason of my doubt was this: because even then, in the prime of his dazzling youth, Percival Tracey lacked that enthusiasm without which even a great intellect is seldom impelled into the doing of great things.

Perhaps from one of the very excellencies of his mental organisation he was indifferent to ambition, and not covetous of fame. All that culture which he had so liberally bestowed on the natural fertility of his mind, was rather in compliance with his own tastes than for any definite object in connection with what the world could give or what the world might say. He had little of that vanity which makes men restless — much of that self-esteem which tends to keep men still. Partly from the speculative bias to which his fondness for philosophical studies inclined his thoughts — partly from the *vis inertiæ* which is the property of bodies so solidly fixed on this earth as are great wealth and great station — he said "*Cui bono*" to any effort that imposed a violence on tastes and dispositions, which, in themselves serene and peaceful, were shocked by strife, as the ears of a master in music are shocked by discord.

He had abundant energy and perseverance in the accumulation of his mental stores, simply because he was thus rendered more complete and more happy in himself; and he was averse to all gladiatorial vying and contest with others, inasmuch as the passions engendered by ambition serve rather to render the intellectual being less harmoniously completed, and the moral being less felicitously calm. His mind thus resembled one of those fountains which feed themselves through invisible conduits from an elevated source, but overflow into no running streams; — ever fresh and ever full, they soar, but they do not spread. Yet, at the time I speak of, Percival Tracey had a vague consciousness that he ought to do something — some day or other. But as that consciousness disquieted his enjoyment of the present, he never nourished it by meditation. Day after day he put off the doing of the destined something to that morrow which is the vanishing point in so many of our fancy landscapes. One day he took it into his head to set out on a tour in the East, a region of the globe which he had not hitherto visited. The eve before his departure he said to me, "When I come back, I suppose I must make up my mind to enter Parliament — why do you smile?"

"Because you know there will shortly be a vacancy for the county which your forefathers represented for centuries, and you are going to the East in order to get out of the way of requisitions and deputations from the North."

"Well, I own that the House of Commons does not attract me at present; as no doubt it will by-and-by. Infancy has its whooping-cough — middle age its politics."

"If politics be a disease, I don't think you are likely to catch it. It is a complaint which shows itself early, and the Englishman who has no twinge of it in youth has not that sort of constitution on which it ever takes hold in middle life."

"Hem," answered Tracey, "perhaps you are right there: — Metaphor apart, I do not fancy that I could ever take much interest in politics, unless the country were actually in that danger which one-half the country always say that it is, when the leaders of the other half govern it. But still I ought to do something; — speech-making and voting are not the only occupations of life — what do you think I could best do?"

"The best thing you could do at present is to leave off saying 'Cui bono' when anything whatever is to be done."

Tracey laughed gaily — we shook hands and parted, nor met again till the Percival Tracey whom I had last seen at the age of thirty was close upon his sixtieth year.

As I had been unable to fix the precise day for my visit, so it had been left to my option to come without previous notice any day in the following week which my avocations and engagements would permit. It was a bright summer afternoon in which I found myself free, with two or three days before me equally at my command, should I wish so far to prolong my visit. After a journey by the railway of some hours, I arrived at the small station which Tracey had told me was the nearest one to his house — and I heard to my surprise that I was then six miles distant from his park gates. "How is it," I asked the station-master, "that your Company do not accommodate so large a proprietor as Sir Percival Tracey with a station nearer to his residence?"

"Sir," answered the official, "it is not the fault of

the Company; — when they asked his consent to the
line, which passes for several miles through his estate
— in the plan submitted to his inspection, a station
was marked close to his gates. He made it a peremp-
tory condition that there should be no such station —
no station nearer to him than this one."

"I should think he must have repented that whim
by this time," said I.

"No," answered the station-master, smiling. "It
was only the other day that the Company again offered
Sir Percival the station he had before declined, and
again he refused it."

I inquired no farther, entered the chaise which was
waiting for me, and, traversing a country singularly
beautiful, but singularly primitive, with large wastes
of heath land and common, backed sometimes by many-
coloured hills clothed with wandering sheep, sometimes
by masses of hanging wood, intersected by devious rivulets breaking into rocky falls, I arrived at last at
my friend's lodge. The opening into the glades of the
park so caught my eye that I descended from the
chaise, and, ordering my servant to go on before and
announce my visit, I walked leisurely along the sward,
under the boughs of trees that might have sheltered
the ringdove from the falcons of Saxon earls. The
heat of the day had declined; the western sun was
tempered by the shades of the forest hills, amidst
which it was slowly sinking. It had been my first
escape into the country that summer; and the change
from the throng and reek of London was in itself delight. Perhaps on such holiday occasions there is more
pure and unalloyed enjoyment of nature when it is
wholly dissociated from the sense of property — when

we do not say to ourselves, "This is my land, these my groves, these my flocks and herds." For with the sense of property come involuntarily the cares of property. And in treading his own turfs the observer looks round to see what has been neglected or what has been improved in his absence; he casts not a poet's but a farmer's eye on the ewe nestled under the oak tree. "Heavens! Has it got the fly?" and the kine that pause from grazing, "Why! Have they got the mouth-complaint?" But that is not all. Even when one is undisturbed by the master's cares, the pleasure of gazing, after absence, on what is one's own, what one remembers in childhood, in youth, what is associated with events of hope and fear, sorrow or joy in one's own past life, is not that absolute sympathy and fusion with outward objective nature herself, into which she quietly steals us when we have no personal history connected with the scenes we behold. For where our own individual existence obtrudes itself upon our contemplation, the Genius of the Place is no longer the joyous Universal Pan, but rather the pensive ghost of our former selves: and Nature, instead of gently subjugating our own mind, and weaning us from the consciousness of our own careworn life, separate and apart from herself and her myriads, rather wakes up reflections which subject her to their dominating intellectual influences, and deepen the sense of our own fate and place in her world.

Somewhat suddenly, the features of the park changed; the wilder beauties of woodland, with many a dell and hillock, and sweeps of profitless fern and gorse, gave way to a broad lawn, separated from the park by a slight fence; and the house of the owner rose before me. My first impression at its sight was that of surprised disappointment. I had, not unnaturally, presumed that I should see an ancient stately pile in keeping with the long descent and vast possessions of its lord. But the house before me seemed small for the character of the ground immediately round it, and was evidently modern. As I drew nearer to it, however, the first impression of disappointment wore off. And for that kind of architecture which suits best with what we call a villa, I have seldom seen any structure more pleasing to the eye from justness of proportion and elegance of appropriate enrichments. The columns of its lofty portico were of the *rosso antico* marble, and the sky-line of the roof was playfully relieved by statues and vases of exquisite workmanship. Still the house was certainly small for the habitual residence of an owner so wealthy. It could not have accommodated the guests, nor found room for the establishment, of a man disposed to be hospitable on the scale of sixty thousand a-year; it would have been a small house for a social squire of five thousand. When I was about a hundred yards from the stone balustrade in front of the building, one of the windows on the ground-floor was thrown open, and my host sprang out with the bound of a boy. He still, indeed, preserved the lightness of frame which had rendered him in youth so peerless in all active sports. And as he came towards me, I muttered to myself the lines which I remembered to have applied to him more than thirty years before —

> "'Tis he; I ken the manner of his gait;
> He rises on the toe — that spirit of his
> In aspiration lifts him from the earth."

After we had shaken hands and exchanged the customary salutations, Tracey said to me, "Shall we look into the garden? It wants a good hour yet to our dinner-time, for to-day we do not dine till eight. I had a presentiment that you would come to-day."

"Eight o'clock is not then your usual hour? I am afraid I have put you out of your ways."

"Reassure yourself; we have no usual hour for dinner so long as the summer lasts. Yesterday we dined at three on the banks of the lake which I hope to show you; the day before, we resolved to enjoy a moonlight sail on the sea, which is eighteen miles off, and did not dine till ten. . . . . We live a strange forester kind of life here, and have no habits which do not vary with a whim or the weather."

By this time he had led me to the garden-side of the house, which was not seen from the road, and at this side the building was of a much gayer and more fanciful character than that of the entrance front. It was enriched yet more profusely with urns and statues; with the lively additions of gilded balconies filled with flowers, and admitted of reliefs in colour, which, though not uncommon in Italy, I had never before seen introduced into the facades of our English homes. But what chiefly pleased me was a very long colonnade, terminating in a lofty Belvidere tower, which extended from the body of the house. Seeing that this colonnade was glazed between the pillars, and catching sight of some plants within, I supposed at first that it was a conservatory; but Tracey told me that it was never heated to a degree beyond the temperature maintained in the sitting-rooms, and contained only those plants which could thrive in an atmosphere not insalubrious to English lungs. "It serves," said he, "as a lounge in winter or wet weather, and answers the purpose of the peristyles or porticos attached to the old Roman villas. It also holds my aviaries, and constitutes my statue gallery, as well as a museum for such classical antiquities as I have collected in my travels. In short, I endeavour to store within it whatever may suggest pleasant thoughts when one wanders there alone, or agreeable subjects for conversation when one is there with companions. You will find its walls inscribed with quotations from favourite authors in all languages. Perhaps this will strike you at first as pedantry or affectation. But when you have made acquaintance with the place, I am sure that you will recognise the charm of being greeted by beautiful thougths every time you pause, tired with your own thoughts, or willing to lead some languid or over-disputatious talker into trains of idea, for ever fresh yet for ever soothing."

Turning from the house, my eye now rested on a garden, which seemed to me a perfect model of art, whether from the harmony with which colours were assorted in the parterres, or the delicacy of proportion observed in the numerous sculptured ornaments which decorated the terraces — the whole taking life and movement from the play of many fountains; and the confines of the artistic scenery fusing themselves in the natural landscape beyond, as the green alleys, stretching from the last of the gradual terraces, lost themselves in the depth and mystery of the closing woods. Just then a ringdove was winging its flight along one of these vistas, and simultaneously to both

our lips came the quotation from Keats's wondrous
'Ode to the Nightingale' —

> "To leave the world unseen,
> And with thee fade away into the forest dim!"

A poet's verse remembered and repeated by two companions in a breath, why or wherefore they can scarcely explain, is a link in sympathy which brings them both insensibly nearer together. Hitherto we had walked somewhat apart; the next moment we were arm-in-arm. There was, however, a pause in our conversation till we found ourselves seated near one of the fountains. Then, rousing myself from my reverie, I asked my host if he had built the house and planned the gardens.

"Yes," he said, with a smile; "whatever we owe to our ancestors, one likes best what one has done one's self. The fact is, however, that when, many years ago, I resolved to settle in England, but to renounce London, I found that, with three family seats, I had not one home in which I could live according to my tastes. Tracey Court, in the north of England, has been the usual residence of our family for several generations: it is an enormous pile, which necessitates an immense establishment. Now I have a special dislike to live begirt with dependants for whom I have no use, and to incur constraints for which there is no object. At Tracey Court, which is the centre of my principal estates in England, my predecessors had always maintained as much formal state, and indulged in as much wearisome ostentation, as if they had had the misfortune to be born German princes instead of English country gentlemen. There, they kept up what they called the political influence of the family. I could not have lived at Tracey Court, but what I must either have perpetually put myself out of my way for things in which I had no interest, and for persons with whom I had no sympathy, or I should have been the object of universal dislike; and I am not so stoical a philosopher as to be callous to unkind glances and indignant whispers every time I cross my threshold. Besides, Tracey Court, though grand in its way, is gloomy, the scenery rude, the climate harsh: I love to surround myself with cheerful images. In Ireland I have a large rude old castle in the midst of a county in which it rains nine months in the year. Universal hospitality, too, is still more the curse of Irish castles than of English manor-houses. I might have shut my windows against the rains, but not my doors against the neighbourhood, to say nothing of invading tourists. I had visited the castle in my youth — I had no desire to visit it again;" here, I observed that my friend sighed, and then, as with an effort, went on more rapidly. "Thirdly, I have what is considered the jointure-house for widowed Traceys — a pretty place enough, not too large, on the banks of the Thames. There I first took up my abode. But it is only twelve miles from town — a railway station close to its garden-wall. So near London, the fidget of London travelled in the atmosphere with the smoke, and irritated my nerves. I wished to forget London, and London at twelve miles' distance would not be forgotten. Then I bethought me of this place, which was the earliest possession of my family, but at which for more than two centuries they had never resided — for a very good reason, there was on it no residence; the manor-house had been burned down in the troubled

reign of Charles I. Here there were no hereditary
duties of hospitality — no troubles of political influence
— small comparative cares of property; for in this
county I am not one of the wealthiest proprietors — the
rental I derive from my lands here does not exceed
£6000 a-year. But the acreage is happily very large
in proportion to the rental, so that I have no near
neighbours. The farmers are old-fashioned primitive
agriculturists, and allow their hedges to grow six yards
high and spread four yards thick, all lush with convol-
vulus and honeysuckle. Here you can ride through
the green lanes which make the beauty of England
and the reproach of husbandry. The climate is enjoy-
able — its springs and autumns delicious, its winters
mild, its summers only too hot for those who do not
take exercise. In a word, the air and the scenery
pleased me. I built a house here according to my
own fancy — not one that would please a formal
architect — not purely Greek, Roman, Italian, but
such as seemed to me to blend the general characteristics of the bright classic life with the necessities
of English climate and the comforts of modern usage.
I resolved beforehand that I would construct a residence on a scale proportioned to the rental of the
estate on which it was built — in short, that I would
here escape from the toils and troubles which embitter
the expenditure of £60,000 a-year, and, so far as my
personal income is concerned, live somewhat within
the £6000 a-year which I possess in this county. If
I lived alone, and if my tastes as artist did not corrupt
my theories as philosopher, I should contract my expenditure into much narrower limits. But I have an
aunt — a sister of my mother — who was born in a

second wedlock, and is very little older than myself.
When I came back to England I found her a lone
widow, and as she had given up all jointure and settlement for the purpose of paying her husband's debts,
her natural home was with me. She had been accustomed to a certain mode of living; I could not ask her
to submit to privations. For this reason, and for other
reasons more personal, I have fixed my expenditure at
the highest rate which, to my mind, is compatible with
ease; for in all walks of life there is quite as little case
in an over-large shoe as there is in a tight one."

"I congratulate you, my dear Tracey," said I,
somewhat sarcastically, "on having assessed your expenditure at a sum which does not necessitate very
rigorous privations. Six thousand a-year, which you
speak of so modestly as a kind of genteel poverty, is,
I suspect, when net and clear, as in your case, somewhat above the average income enjoyed by peers
under the rank of earl. I agree with you that a
gentleman who does not care for ostentation may contrive, by the aid of philosophy, to live very comfort-
ably on £6000 a-year. But still you have the remaining £54,000 yearly on your hands; and I presume
that you do not get rid of that burden by hoarding it
in the Three per cents."

"Nay," answered Tracey, slightly colouring, "if
hoarding be a pleasure, I think it is a sinful one; and
sins are like thistles — despite the best husbandry,
they will spring up; but it is only in the worst husbandry that one does not try to get rid of them. The
surplus of my income is spent somehow — I hope
usefully. I endeavour to know as little as I can the

precise details in which it disappears. But, hark! there rings the half-hour bell."

"Do you live here, with no other companion but your aunt?" I asked, as we walked back towards the house.

"Oh, no; that would be loneliness twice over. We have always a few friends staying with us. I have so arranged my house, that, thank heaven, it cannot hold many acquaintances. But let me tell you whom you will meet here. First, as to my aunt, Lady Gertrude, her you have met before, but many years ago: I will leave you to discover for yourself those changes which Time makes in us all. Secondly, you will find, in a gentleman named Caleb Danvers, who condescends to act as my librarian and secretary, a prodigy of learning and memory, with a touch of quaint humour. Thirdly, I shall introduce to you, in Patrick Bourke, a young Irish artist, full of promise and enthusiasm. Some young artist or other is always in the house. I like the society of artists; and, from pure selfishness, I secure to myself that luxury by a pretence of liberality. Every year I select some young painter or sculptor, and, after a short probation in this retreat, I send him to Italy to finish his studies. Fourthly and fifthly, you will make acquaintance with a young couple, Henry and Clara Thornhill. They have not been long married, and are still in love with each other; but he, ungrateful man! is not in love only with her as she is with him — he is in love also with his profession, which is the army. He is at present nothing more than a captain in the line, but is in daily hopes that Europe will be desolated by some horrible war, which may result in his becoming a

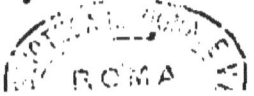

field-marshal. For the rest, a fine young fellow, a
relation of mine — a relation near enough to count
on being one of my heirs. But he is, at present, less
bent upon killing me than some half a million or so of
unsuspecting foreigners."

By this time we were within the house. My host
conducted me to the rooms which he devoted to my
use, and which, though small, constituted the ideal of
a bachelor's apartment — the bedroom opening, on
one hand, to a bath-room; on the other to a pretty
study, the writing-table placed at the window. Did
Tracey remember my love to be near the light whenever I read or scribble? — probably enough; for he
had a happy memory where he could give pleasure.
The walls of the room were made companionable by
dwarf bookcases, which, as I afterwards discovered,
were enriched with those volumes one is always glad
to reperuse. When Tracey left me, I sat for some
minutes musing. Was this man, for whom such high
destinies in fame had been predicted, wholly without
regret for the opportunities he had thrown away? In
the elegant epicurean life which he had planned, and
seemed to carry out for himself, should I not detect
some disguised disappointment? And if not, had a
being who, whatever his faults, had been in youth
singularly generous and noble-hearted, really degene-
rated into a bloodless egotist, shunning all the duties
which could distract him from the holiday into which
he sought to philosophise away existence?

I could not satisfactorily unravel the problem
which my conjectures invented, and addressed to my
fancy; and I went down-stairs just as the dinner-bell
rang, resolved to gather, from the talk of my fellow-

guests, some hints that might enlighten my comprehension of the character of the host.

On entering the drawing-room, I found there already assembled all whom I had been prepared to meet. I had scarcely renewed a very slight and ancient acquaintance with Lady Gertrude before dinner was announced. She took my arm, and we were soon seated side by side at a round table in the prettiest dining-room I ever saw. The shape of the room was octagon, with a domed ceiling, beautifully painted in the arabesques and festoons which gave so fanciful a decoration to the old Roman villas. On the walls were repeated the same imageries as we see in Pompeian houses, but in tints more subdued, and more suited to the taste in colour which we take from our colder climate, than the glaring contrasts in which Pompeian artists indulged. The arabesques formed panels for charming pictures, the subjects of which I soon perceived to be taken from the more convivial of Horace's odes. In these paintings there was a certain delicacy of sentiment, conjoined with an accuracy of costume and a fidelity of scene and manners, in which I recognised at once the learning and the taste of my host. I pointed to them with a gesture which asked, "Are they not the work of your hand?" — "Nay," he answered, at once interpreting the gesture; "they were painted by a young friend of mine, now in Rome. I did but give him the general idea, sketched in crayons. I am fond of classical subjects, but not of mythological ones. I think that it is the mistake of artists, and perhaps of poets, who wish to be classical, to imagine that they must be mythological. We have no associations with Venus and Apollo, but we have associations

with the human life of which poets who believed in
Venus and Apollo have left eternal impressions on our
minds. For this world, I like the classical type of
thought rather than the Gothic; for the classical type
brightens and beautifies all that is conceived by our
senses. But for all that is to set me thinking on the
world to come, I prefer the Gothic type. Classical
imagery would shock me in a chapel; Gothic imagery
would offend me in a dining-room. I keep the two
trains of idea apart. I dislike to confound the sensuous with the spiritual. I dedicate this room to
Horace, because of all poets he is the one who imparts
a sentiment at once the most subtle and the most
hearty to that happy hour in the twenty-four in which
we live back our youth at the sight of our old
friends."

These remarks calling forth a reply from me, the
conversation at first threatened to become, as it generally does the first day a stranger is introduced into a
small family-party, somewhat too much of a dialogue
between the host and the stranger. But in a short
time other tongues were drawn into talk, and I, in my
turn, became a listener. There was this notable distinction between the kind of conversation which I had
just left behind me in London, and that which now
interested my attention: in London dinners, no matter
how well informed the guests, talk nearly always turns
upon persons — here, talk turned upon things. The
young painter talked well; so did Clara Thornhill.
Now and then the Librarian threw in an odd, quaint,
out-of-the-way scrap of erudition, delivered so like a
joke that it made us merrier if it failed to make us
wiser. Tracey himself was charming, never allowing

one subject to become tedious, and lighting up all subjects with a gaiety which, if it was not wit, was very much what wit might be, if something of ill-nature were not at the bottom of all the good sayings by which wit epigrammatises the epics and the dramas of human life.

We all left the dining-room together, men and women alike, according to the foreign fashion; we passed, not into the drawing room in which we had assembled before dinner, but into a library of such dimensions that I could not conceive how it could possibly belong to the house. Lady Gertrude laughed at my astonishment, and explained away its cause.

"You could not have guessed at the existence of this room," said she, "on seeing the exterior of the house, for it is screened from sight by the glazed colonnade behind which it extends. The fact is, when Percival built this house, he did not feel so sure that it would become his habitual residence as to transport hither the vast library he inherited, or has collected. It was not till we had been here two years that he determined on doing so; and as there was no room for so great a number of volumes in the building, and any large visible extension of the house would have spoilt its architectural symmetry, this gallery was run out at the back of the colonnade; and a very happy afterthought it was: it has become the favourite sitting-room. On one side (as you will see when we come to the centre of the room) it opens on the colonnade or statue gallery, and on the other side the view from the windows commands the most picturesque scenery of the park and the hills beyond, a striking contrast to the dressed ground of the gardens."

"And," said the Painter, "to my mind much more pleasing, for in all highly-dressed ground the eye becomes conscious of a certain monotony which is not found in the wilder landscapes, where the changes of prospect, which Nature is perpetually making, are more visible: I mean, that in these gardens, for instance, the most striking objects are the sculptured ornaments, the parterres, the fountains — the uniformity of art and plan; but in a natural landscape every varying shadow is noticed."

Here we had got into the middle of this vast gallery, and I caught sight, through an arched recess, from which the draperies were drawn aside, of the plants and statues in the adjoining colonnade. Tracey, who had lingered behind in conversation with Mrs. Thornhill, now joined us, and, passing his arm through mine, drew me into the colonnade, which was partially and softly lighted up. Some of its glazed compartments were left open, giving views of the gardens, with their terraces and fountains hushed in the stillness of the summer night. The rest of the party did not join us. Perhaps it was thought that such old friends, after so long a separation, might have much to say to each other which they would not wish to say before listeners. Nevertheless, we two walked for some minutes along the corridor in silence, Tracey leaving me to make acquaintance for myself, and unassisted by comment of his own, with the statues and antiquities, the inscriptions, the orange-trees, the aviaries, which made the society of the place. At length we paused to contemplate the gardens, and stepped out into the starlight. Then said Tracey, "I often think that we do not sufficiently cultivate the friendship of Night. We separate the night by too sharp a line from the day. We close her out from us by shutters and curtains, and reject her stars for our lamps. Now, since I have lived here, I have learned that Night is a much more sociable companion than I before suspected. In summer I often ride out, even in winter often ramble forth, when my guests have been for hours in their beds. I take into my day impartially all the twenty-four hours. There are trains of thought set in motion by the sight of the stars which are dormant in the glare of the sun. And without such thoughts, Man's thinking is incomplete."

"I concede to you," said I, "the charm of Night; and I have felt the truth which you eloquently express; more especially, perhaps, when travelling alone in my younger days, and in softer climates than our own. But there arrives a time when one is compelled to admit that there is such a thing as rheumatism, and that even bronchitis is not altogether a myth. All mortals, my dear Tracey, are not blessed with your enviable health; and there is a proverb which warns us against turning night into day."

TRACEY. — "I suspect that the proverb applies to those who shut out the night the most — to students, wasting night in close chambers; to the gay folks of capitals, who imagine that it is very imprudent to breathe the fresh air after twelve o'clock, but perfectly safe to consume all the nitrogen, and exhaust all the oxygen, in the atmosphere of ball-rooms. The best proof that night air in itself is wholesome (I mean, of course, where the situation is healthy), may be found in the fact, that even delicate persons can, with perfect impunity, sleep with their windows open. And I see that practice commended in the medical journals. The unhealthful time to be out is just before and just after sunset; yet that is precisely the time which the fashionable part of our population seem to prefer for exercise. Of course, however, I can only pretend to speak from experience. I do not study at night; the early hours of day seem to me the best for brain-work, and certainly they must be so for the eyesight. But I never discover that outdoor exercise at night injures my health; at my age, I should soon know if it did. My gamekeeper tells me he is never so well as at that part of the year when he is out half the night at watch over his preserves.* Be this as it may, I rejoice to find that I, at least, can safely follow out, in so pleasant a detail, the general system on which I planned the philosophy of my life in fixing my home remote from capitals, and concentring into confines as narrow as fate will permit, my resources of thought and of happiness."

"Your system?" said I; "that interests me; what is it?"

TRACEY. — "How many men we see, who, having cultivated their minds in capitals, retire into the country, and find themselves, after the novelty of change has worn away, either without amusement and object, or involuntarily deriving amusement and object from things that really belong, not to the pure country life, but to the life of the capital which they have left in body, but where they still are in mind. One rich man

* Of course I am not responsible for any opinions of Sir Percival Tracey's, with many of which I disagree; but as this whim of his about night perambulations is captivating and plausible, so I think it due to the health of my readers to warn them against subscribing to it without the approval of their medical advisers.

places his pleasure in receiving distinguished guests — viz., a certain number of inane persons with sonorous titles, variegated by wits à la mode, who import into the groves the petty scandals they learned at the clubs, or leading politicians who cannot walk in your stubbles without discharging on you the contents of a blue-book on agricultural statistics. Another man, not so rich, or not so desirous of putting the list of his guests into the 'Morning Post,' thinks he has discovered a cure for ennui in the country by luxuriating there in the vanities of an ambition which he could not gratify in the town. He can be a personage in a village — he is nobody in a capital. He finds to his satisfaction that the passions are hardy plants, and will thrive as well in the keen air of a sheepwalk as in the hothouse of London. Vanity and avarice proffer to him the artificial troubles which he calls 'natural excitements.' He cannot be an imperious statesman, but he may be a consequential magistrate; he cannot be a princely merchant, but he can be an anxious farmer, and invest the same fears of loss, and the same hopes of gain, in oats and turnips, which the merchant embarks in the vessels that interchange the products of nations. He says, 'How much better is the country life to the town life,' only because his vanity finds at quarter-sessions and vestries the consideration which would fail it in courts and senates; and his avarice has excitement and interest in the Short Horns on his home farm, and none in the Bulls and Bears on Exchange. How many other men, settling in the country, only vegetate there, having no living interest except in what passes in the city they have left; the only hour of the day to which they look forward with eagerness, and in which they expand into intellectual being, is that in which they seize on the daily newspaper, and transport themselves in thought from Arcady to Babylon. Now, when I resolved to live in the country, I wished to leave wholly behind me, not merely the streets and smoke of London, but the trains of thought which belong to streets and smoke. I did not desire to create for myself, in a province, those gratuitous occasions of worry; the anxiety and trouble, the jealousy, envy, and hate, which the irritations of the *amour propre*, and the fever of competition for gain, or fame, or social honours, engender in the life of capitals, but which in that life are partially redeemed, and sometimes elevated, by a certain nobleness of object. But in the country life they only make us unamiable, and we cannot flatter ourselves that they serve to make us great. The severest of philosophers might be contented to take on himself all the anxieties and troubles which weighed on the heart of a Pitt. He might feel no shame to have indulged in all the outbreaks of rage which gave thunder to the eloquence of Fox. He might consent to have on his conscience the sins of polemical wrath, of malevolent satire, of the vindictive torture and anguish inflicted by truculent genius on presuming rivals or disparaging critics. He might be haunted by no avenging furies if, as a Milton, he had stung to death a Salmasius, or, as a Pope, libelled with relentless hate the woman who had ridiculed his love. For the career of active genius is a career of war — '*Ma vie, c'est un combat*,' said Voltaire. What aspirant for a fame which other aspirants contest does not say the same? Suffering and rage, wounds given and wounds received, are the necessities of war; and he who comes out of the war, a hero, is, after all, a grander creature than he who shrinks from the war, a sage. But to undergo an equal worry, and feel an equal acerbity of temper in provoking little battles for little triumphs; to ride the whirlwind of a keyhole and direct the storm of a saucer; in a word, to enter upon country life, looking round for excitements in ambition, vanity, or the fidgety joys of a restless nervous temperament, is but to take from a town life the cares that disquiet the heart; leaving behind all those grander intellectual rivalries which, at least, call into play powers that extract reward out of the care, glory out of the disquiet, which must ever accompany the contest between man and man.

"Therefore, my resolve, on fixing my abode in the country, was to make myself contentedly at home with Nature — to place my enjoyments in her intimate companionship — to gratify my love for art in such adornments as might yet more please my eye in her beauty, or blend the associations of her simple sensuous attraction with those of the human beings who have loved and studied her the most, and given to her language the sweet interpretations of human thought — the sculptor, the painter, the poet, the philosopher who explores her through science, or serenely glasses her in the calm of contemplation. And among these links between man's mind and nature, we may place as one of the most obvious, man's earliest attempt to select and group from her scattered varieties of form, that which — at once a poem and a picture — forms, as it were, the decorated border-land between Man's home and Nature's measureless domains — THE GARDEN.

"As we walk along these terraces, which no doubt, many a horticulturist would condemn as artificial, either I mistake, or all that Art has done here, unites yet more intimately Nature with the Mind of Man. For this seems to me the true excuse for what is called the artificial style of gardening — viz., that the statue, the fountain, the harmonies of form and colour into which even flower-beds are arranged, do bring Nature into more familiar connection with all which has served to cultivate, sweeten, elevate the Mind of Man. All his arts, and not one alone, speak here! What images from the old classic world of poetry the mere shape of yon urn, or the gleam of yon statue, calls forth! And even in those flower-beds, — what science has been at patient work, for ages, before the gracious forms by which Geometry alone can realise the symmetries of beauty, or the harmonies of hue and tint which we owe to research into the secrets of light and colour, — could have thus made Nature speak to us in the language of our choicest libraries, and symbolise, as it were, in the most pleasing characters, whatever is most pleasing in the world of books."

In these lengthened disquisitions Tracey had not been uninterrupted. I had, from time to time, interposed dissentient remarks, which, being of little consequence, I have wellnigh forgotten, and it seems to me best, therefore, to preserve unbroken the chain of his discourse. But here, I repeated to my host the Painter's observation on the monotony of dressed ground in comparison with scenery altogether left to Nature, and asked Tracey if he thought the observation true.

"I suspect," he answered, "that it is true or false, very much according to the degree to which the spectator's mind has been cultivated by books, and reflections drawn from them. My friend the Painter is very young, and the extent of his reading, and, of course, the scope of his reflections, have been hitherto circumscribed. I think that artistic garden-ground does, after a time, more than wildly natural landscape, tire upon the eye not educated in the associations and reminiscences which preserve an artistic creation from monotony to the gaze of one who draws fresh charms from it out of his own mind — a mind which has accustomed itself to revive remembered images or combine new reflections, at every renewed contemplation of that art which comprises the æsthetic history of man's relationship with nature. Now, our Painter, habituated, very properly, to concentre his own thoughts on his own branch of art, observes, as something ever varying, the shadow that falls from the rude mountain top on the crags and dells of the old forest-land on the other side of the park, and does not observe that, as the sun shifts, it must equally bring out into new variations of light and shadow these lawns and flights of stairs; because he is not a painter of gardens, and he is a painter of forest scenery. Had he been a painter of gardens, he would have discovered variety in the garden, and complained of monotony in the forest-land. So let any man who has not cultivated his mind in the study of poems or pictures, be called upon to look every day at Milton's 'Paradise Lost,' or Raffaele's 'Virgin,' he will certainly find in either a very great sameness; but let a man who, being either a very great poet, a very great painter, or a very profoundly educated critic on poetry or painting, look every day at the said poem or the said picture, and he will always find something new in what he contemplates — the novelty springing out of the fertility of perception which proceeds from the lengthened culture of his own taste. In short, there is nothing same or stale in any object of contemplation which is intimately allied to our own habits of culture; and that which is strange to those habits, becomes, however multiform and varying its charms to another may be, insipid and monotonous to ourselves, just as the world of ambition and of cities, with its infinite movement and play, to those whose lives are one study of it, is to me 'weary, stale, flat, and unprofitable,' as all its uses seemed to Hamlet."

Here our talk ended. Re-entering the library, we found Clara Thornhill at the piano, singing with exquisite spirit, and in the sweetest voice —

"Under the greenwood tree,
Who loves to lie with me," &c.

And so in song and music the rest of the evening wore away.

The next morning the sun shone into my windows so brightly that I rose at an earlier hour than I had been accustomed to do for months, and strolled into the gardens, interesting myself in considering the Painter's charge against dressed ground and Tracey's ingenious reply to it. The mowers were at work upon the lawns. Perhaps among rural sounds there is none which pleases me more than that of the whetting of the scythe — I suppose less from any music in itself, than from associations of midsummer, and hay-fields, and Milton's 'Allegro,' in which the low still sound is admitted among the joyous melodies of Morn. As the gardens opened upon me, with their variety of alleys and bywalks, I became yet more impressed than I had been on the day before, with the art which had planned and perfected them, and the poetry of taste with which the images of the sculptor were so placed, that at every turn they recalled some pleasing but vague reminiscence of what one had seen in a picture, or in travel; or brought more vividly before the mind some charming verse in the poets, whose busts greeted the eye from time to time in bowery nook or hospitable alcove, where the murmur of a waterfall, or the view of a distant landscape opening from out the groves, invited pause and allured to contemplation.

At last, an arched trellis overhung with vine leaves led me out into that part of the park which fronted the library, and to which the Painter had given his preference over the grounds I had just quitted. There, the wildness of the scenery came on me with the suddenness of a surprise. The table-land, on which the house stood on the other side of the building, here abruptly sloped down into a valley through which a stream wound in many a maze, sometimes amidst jagged rocklike crags, sometimes through low grassy banks, round which the deer were grouping. The view was very extensive, but not unbrokenly so; here and there thick copses, in the irregular outline of natural groves, shut out the valley, but still left towering in the background the wavy hill-tops, softly clear in the blue morning sky. Hitherto I had sided with Tracey; now I thought the Painter right. In the garden, certainly, man's mind forms a visible link with Nature; but in those scenes of Nature not trimmed and decorated to the book-lore of man, Thought takes a less finite scope, and perhaps from its very vagueness is less inclined to find monotony and sameness in the wide expanse over which it wanders to lose itself in reverie.

Descending the hillside, I reached the stream, and came suddenly upon Henry Thornhill, who, screened behind a gnarled old pollard-tree, was dipping his line into a hollow where the waves seemed to calm themselves, and pause before they rushed, in cascade, down a flight of crags, and thence brawled loudly onward.

As I know by experience how little an angler likes to be disturbed, I contented myself with a nod and a smile to the young man, and went my own way in silence; but about an hour afterwards, as I was winding back towards the house, I heard his voice behind me. I turned; he showed me, with some pride, his basket already filled with trout; and after I had sufficiently admired and congratulated, we walked slowly up the slope together. The evening before, Captain Thornhill had prepossessed me less than the other members of the party. He had spoken very little, and appeared to me to have that air of supreme indifference to all persons and things around him, which makes so many young gentlemen like — so many young gentlemen. But this morning he was frank and communicative.

"You have known Sir Percival very long, I think?" said he.

"Very long. I knew him before I had left Cambridge. In my rambles during a summer vacation, chance brought us together; and though he was then one of the most brilliant oracles of the world of fashion, and I an unknown collegian, somehow or other we became intimate."

"I suppose you find him greatly altered?"

"Do you mean in person or in mind?"

"Well, in both."

"In person less altered than I could have supposed; his figure just the same — as erect, as light, and seemingly as vigorous. In mind I cannot yet judge, but there is still the same sweetness, and the same cheerfulness; the same mixture of good-tempered irony and of that peculiar vein of sentiment which is formed by the combination of poetical feeling and philosophical contemplation."

"He is a very fine fellow," returned Henry Thornhill, with some warmth; "but don't you think it is a pity he should be so eccentric?"

"In what?"

"In what? Why, in that which must strike everybody; shirking his station, shutting himself up here, planning gardens which nobody sees, and filling his head with learning for which nobody is the wiser."

"His own friends see the gardens and enjoy them; his own friends may, I suppose, hear him talk, and become the wiser for his learning."

"His own friends — yes! a dozen or two individuals; most of them undistinguished as — as I am," added the young man, with visible bitterness. "And, with his talents and fortune, and political influence, he might be, or at least might have been, anything; don't you think so?"

"Anything is a bold expression; but if you mean that he might, if he so pleased, have acquired a very considerable reputation, and obtained a very large share of the rewards which ambitious men covet, I have no doubt that he could have done so, and very little doubt that he could do so still."

"I wish you could stir him up to think it. I am vexed to see him so shelved in this out-of-the-way place. He has even given up ever going to Tracey Court now; and as for his castle in Ireland, he would as soon think of going to Kamtschatka."

"I hope, at all events, his estates, whether in the north or in Ireland, are not ill-managed."

"No, I must say that no estates can be better managed; and so they ought to be, for he devotes enormous sums to their improvement, as well as to all public objects in their district."

"It seems, then, that if he shirks some of the pomps of wealth, he does not shirk its duties?"

"Certainly not, unless it be the duty which a great proprietor owes to himself."

"What is that duty?"

The young man looked puzzled; at last he said —

"To make the most of his station."

"Perhaps Sir Percival thinks it is better to make the most of his mind, and fancies he can do that better in the way of life which pleases him, than in that which would displease; but he is lucky in stewards if his estates thrive so well without the watch of the master's eye."

"Yes, but his stewards are gentlemen — one, at Tracey Court, is a Mr. Aston, an old schoolfellow of Sir Percival, who was brought up to expect a fine property at the death of an uncle; but the uncle unluckily married at the age of fifty, and had a large family. Sir Percival heard he was in distress, and gave him this appointment; it just suits him. The

Irish steward, Mr. Gerrard, is also a capital fellow, who travelled in the East with Sir Percival. Being half Irish himself, Gerrard understands how to make the best of the population; and being half Scotch, he understands how to make the best of the property. I have no doubt that the estates are better managed in Sir Percival's absence than if he resided on them, for you know how good-natured he is. A bad tenant has only to get at his heart with a tale of distress, in order to renew his lease for whipping the land on his own terms."

"So then," said I, "we have come at last to this conclusion, that your wise relation, knowing his own character, in its merits and its failings, has done well in delegating to others, in whose probity and intellect he has a just confidence, the management of those affairs which he could not administer himself with equal benefit to all the persons interested. Is not that the way in which all states are governed? The wisdom of a king in absolute governments, or of a minister in free ones, is in the selection of the right persons for the right places; thus working out a wise system through the instrumentalities of those who best understand its details."

"Yes; but, talking of ministers, Sir Percival makes nothing of his political influence; he shuns all politics. Can you believe it? — he scarcely ever looks into the leading article of a newspaper!"

"To a man who has been long out of the way of party politics, there is not the interest in leading articles which you and I take."

"I rather think that Sir Percival does not like to

be reminded of politics, for fear he might be induced to take an interest in them."

"Ah, indeed! Why do you think so?"

"Because, three years ago, Lady Gertrude was very anxious that he should claim the old barony of Ravenscroft, which has been in abeyance for centuries, but to which the heralds and lawyers assured him there could be no doubt of his proving his right. Lady Gertrude was so intent upon this that at one time I thought she would have prevailed. He looked into the case, invited the lawyers here, satisfied himself that the proof was clear, and then suddenly forbade all steps to be taken. Lady Gertrude told me that he said to her, 'For my family this honour is nought, since the title, if revived, would again die with me; but for myself it is a temptation to change, to destroy the mode of life in which I am happiest, and in which, on the whole, I believe I am morally the least imperfect. If I once took my seat in the Lords, a responsible legislator, how do I know that I should not want to speak, to act, to vie with others, and become ambitious if successful — and fretful if not?'"

"So he declined. Well, after all, a life most in harmony with a man's character is that in which he is probably not only the happiest, but the best man. Ambition is but noble in proportion as it makes men useful. But, from your own account, Tracey's private life is useful already, though its uses are not obtrusive. And for public life, three parts of the accomplishments, and perhaps of the virtues, which make his private life beautiful, would not be needed."

I uttered these defensive suggestions on behalf of my host somewhat in rebuke of the young relation

whose criticisms had called them forth, though in my
own mind I felt a sort of melancholy regret that
Percival's choice of life should be in walks so cool and
sequestered, and the tenor of his way so noiseless.
And did not his own fear to be tempted into more
active exertions of intellect, if once brought under the
influence of emulative competition, indicate that he
himself also felt a regret, on looking back to the past,
that he had acquired habits of mind to which the
thought of distinction had become a sensation of pain?

When our party assembled at breakfast, Tracey
said to me, "I had no idea you were so early a
riser, or I would have given up my ride to share your
rambles."

"Are you too, then, an early riser?"

"Yes, especially in summer. I have ridden twelve
miles with Bourke to show him the remains of an old
Roman tower which he has promised to preserve a few
ages longer — in a picture."

Here the entrance of the letter-bag suspended conversation. The most eager for its opening was young
Thornhill; and his countenance became at once overcast when he found there was no letter for him; as
mine, no doubt, became overcast when I found a large
packet of letters forwarded to me. I had left town
long before the post closed; and two or three hours
suffice to bring plenty of troublesome correspondents
upon a busy Londoner. My housekeeper had forwarded them all. I think Lady Gertrude was the
only other one of our party for whom the postman
sped the soft intercourse from soul to soul. When I
looked up from my letters, Henry Thornhill had already glanced rapidly over the panorama of the world,

displayed in the 'Times' newspaper, and, handing it to the Librarian, said disdainfully, "No news."

"No news!" exclaimed Caleb Danvers, after his own first peep — "no news! Why, Dr. ——'s great library is to be sold by auction on the 14th of next month!"

"That *is* interesting news," said Tracey. "Write at once for the catalogue."

"Any further criticism on the Exhibition of the Royal Academy?" asked the Painter, timidly.

"Two columns," answered Mr. Danvers, laconically.

"Oh," said the Painter, "that is interesting too."

"I beg your pardon, Mr. Danvers," said Lady Gertrude, "but will you glance at the foreign intelligence? Look to Germany; — anything about the Court of ——?"

"The Court of ——? yes, our minister there is convalescent, and going to Carlsbad next week."

"That's what I wanted to know," said Lady Gertrude. "My letter is from his dear sister, who is very anxious about him. Going to Carlsbad — I am glad to hear it."

Meanwhile Clara, who had possessed herself of the supplementary sheet, cried out, joyously — "O dear Henry, only think — Ellen has got a baby. How pleased they will be at the Grange! A son and heir at last!"

"Tut," growled Henry, breaking an egg-shell.

"So," said Tracey, "you see the 'Times' has news for every one except my friend here, who read in London yesterday what we in the country read to-day; and Captain Thornhill, who finds nothing that threatens to break the peace of the world to the promotion of himself and the decimation of his regiment."

Henry laughed, but not without constraint, and muttered something about civilians being unable to understand the interest a soldier takes in his profession.

After breakfast, Tracey said to me, "Doubtless you have your letters to answer, and will be glad to have your forenoon to yourself. About two o'clock we propose adjourning to a certain lake, which is well shaded from the sun. I have a rude summer pavilion on the banks; there we can dine, and shun the Dogstar. Clara, who happily does not know that I am thinking of Tyndaris, will bring her lute, Aunt Gertrude her work, Bourke his sketch-book; and the lake is large enough for a sailing excursion, if Henry will kindly exchange, for the day, military repose for nautical activity."

All seemed pleased with the proposal except Henry, who merely shrugged his shoulders, and the party dispersed for the morning.

My letters were soon despatched, and my instincts or habits (which are, practically speaking, much the same thing) drew me into the library. Certainly it was a very noble collection of books, and exceedingly well arranged. Opening volume after volume, I found that most of those containing works of imperishable name were interleaved; and the side-pages thus formed were inscribed with critical notes and comments in my host's handwriting.

I was greatly struck with the variety and minuteness of the knowledge in many departments, whether of art, scholarship, or philosophy, which these annotations displayed, and the exquisite critical discrimination and taste by which the knowledge was vivified and adorned. While thus gratifying my admiring curiosity, I was accosted by the Librarian, who had entered the room unobserved by me.

"Ay," said he, glancing over my shoulder at the volume in my hand — "Shakespeare; I see you have chanced there upon one of Sir Percival's most interesting speculations. He seeks first to prove how much more largely than is generally supposed Shakespeare borrowed, in detail, from others; and next, to show how much more patently than is generally supposed, Shakespeare reveals to us his own personal nature, his religious and political beliefs, his favourite sentiments and cherished opinions. In fact, it is one of Sir Percival's theories, that though the Drama is, of all compositions, that in which the author can least obtrude on us his personality, yet that of all dramatists Shakespeare the most frequently presents to us his own. Our subtle host seeks to do this by marking all the passages of assertion or reflection in Shakespeare's plays which are not peculiarly appropriate to the speaker, nor called for by the situation — often, indeed, purely episodical to the action; and where in such passages the same or similar ideas are repeated, he argues that Shakespeare himself is speaking, and not the person in the dialogue. I observe in the page you have opened, that Sir Percival is treating of the metaphysical turn of mind so remarkably developed in Shakespeare, and showing how much that turn of mind was the character of the exact time in which he lived. You see how appositely he quotes from Sir John Davies, Shakespeare's contemporary — who, though employed in active professional pursuits, a lawyer — nay, even an Attorney-General and a Serjeant; a Member of Parliament, nay, even a Speaker, and in an Irish House of Commons — prepared himself for those practical paths of life by the composition of a poem the most purely and profoundly metaphysical which England, or indeed modern Europe, has ever produced: at this day it furnishes the foundation of all our immaterial schools of metaphysics. You will see, if you look on, how clearly Sir Percival shows that Shakespeare had intently studied that poem, and imbued his own mind, not so much with its doctrines, as with its manner of thought."

"Tracey was always fond of metaphysics, and of applying his critical acuteness to the illustration of poets. I am pleased to see he has, in the tastes of his youth, so pleasing a resource in his seclusion."

"But it is not only in metaphysics or poetry that he occupies his mind; you might be still more forcibly struck with his information and his powers of reasoning if you opened any of the historians he has interleaved — Clarendon, for instance, or our earlier Chronicles. I cannot but think he would have been a remarkable writer, if he had ever acquired the concentration of purpose, for which, perhaps, the idea of publishing what one writes is indispensably necessary."

"Has he never had the ambition to be an author?"

"Never since I have known him; and he never could conceive it now. You look as if you thought that a pity."

"Well, is it not a pity?"

"Sir," quoth the Librarian, taking snuff, "that is not a fair question to put to me, who have passed my ife in reading books, and cherishing a humane compassion for those who are compelled to write them. But permit me to ask whether a very clever man, himself a voluminous writer, has not composed a popular work called the 'Calamities of Authors'? — did you ever know any writer who has composed a work on the 'Felicities of Authors'? Do you think, from your own experience, that you could write such a work yourself?"

"Rhetorically, yes; conscientiously, no. But let us hope that the calamities of authors lead to the felicities of readers."

Thus talking we arrived at the Librarian's own private sanctuary, a small study at the end of the library, looking on the wilder part of the park. Pointing to doors on the opposite side of a corridor, he said, "Those lead to Sir Percival's private apartments — they are placed in the Belvidere Tower, the highest room of which he devotes to his scientific pursuits; and those pursuits occupy him at this moment, for he expects a visit very shortly from a celebrated Swedish philosopher, with whom he has opened a correspondence."

I left the Librarian to his books, and took my way into the drawing-room. There I found only Clara Thornhill, seated by the window, and with a mournful shade on her countenance, which habitually was cheerful and sunny. I attributed the shade to the guilty Henry, and my conjecture proved right; for after some small-talk on various matters, I found myself suddenly admitted into her innocent confidence. Henry was unhappy! Unreasonable man! A time had been when Henry had declared that the supremest happiness of earth would be to call Clara his! Such happiness then seemed out of his reach; Clara's parents were ambitious, and Henry had no fortune but "his honour and his sword." Percival Tracey, *Deus ex machinâ*, had stepped in — propitiated Clara's parents by handsome settlements. Henry's happiness was apparently secured. Percival had bestowed on him an independent income, had sought to domiciliate him in his own neighbourhood by the offer of a charming cottage which Tracey had built by the sea-side as an occasional winter residence for himself; had proposed to find him occupation as a magistrate — nay, as a commanding officer of gallant volunteers — in vain —

"He was all for deeds of arms;
Honour called him to the field."

The trophies of Miltiades would not suffer him to sleep.

Henry had been moving heaven and earth to get removed into a regiment which was ordered abroad, not exactly for what we call a war, but for one of those smaller sacrifices of human life which are always going on somewhere or other in distant corners of our empire, and make less figure in our annals than they, do in our estimates. Such trivial enterprises might at least prepare his genius and expedite his promotion.

"Mox in reluctantes dracones," &c.

Percival, who was in secret league with Clara against this restlessness for renown which it is to be fervently hoped the good sense of Europe will refuse to gratify, had done his best, by a pleasant irony and banter, to ridicule Henry out of his martial discontent. In vain — Henry only resented his kinsman's disapproval of his honourable ambition, and hence his regret that Sir

Percival did not "make the most of his station." Surely, did he do so, a word from a man of such political importance in point of territory would have due effect on the Horse Guards. Henry thought himself entitled not only to a chance of fighting, but to the dignity of Major. All this, by little and little, though in her own artless words, and in wifelike admiration of Henry's military genius as well as ardour, I extracted from Clara, who (all women being more or less, though often unconsciously, artful in the confidences with which they voluntarily honour our sex) had her own reason for frankness; she had seen Sir Percival since breakfast, and he had sought to convince her that it would be wise to let Henry have his own way. The cunning creature wished me to reason with Tracey, and set before him all the dangers to limb and life to which even a skirmish with barbarians might expose a life so invaluable as her Henry's. "I could see him depart without a tear, if it were to defend his country," said she, with spirit. "But to think of all the hardships he must undergo in a savage land, and fighting for nothing I can comprehend, against a people I never heard of — *that* is hard! it is so reckless in him — and, poor dear, his health *is* delicate, though you would not think it!"

I promised all that a discreet diplomatist under such untoward circumstances could venture to promise; and on the Painter entering the room, poor Clara went up-stairs, trying her womanly best to smile away her tears.

Left alone with the artist, he drew my attention to some pictures on the wall which had been painted by Sir Percival, commended their gusto and brilliancy of execution, and then said, "If our host had begun life on fifty pounds a-year, he would have been a great painter."

"Does it require poverty in order to paint well?"

"It requires, I suppose, a motive to do anything exceedingly well; and what motive could Sir Percival Tracey have to be a professed painter?"

"I think you have hit on the truth in his painting, and perhaps in his other accomplishments: all he wants is the concentration of motive."

"Is it not that want which makes three-fourths of the difference between the famous man and the obscure man?" asked the Painter.

"Perhaps not three-fourths; but if it make one-fourth, it would go a long way to account for the difference. One good of a positive profession is, that it supplies a definite motive for any movement which the intellect gives itself the trouble to take. He who enters a profession naturally acquires the desire to get on in it, and perhaps in the profession of art more ardently than in any other, because a man does not take to art from sheer necessity, and without any inclination for it, but *with* a strong inclination, to which necessity gives the patient forces of labour. I presume that I am right in this conjecture."

"Yes," said the Painter, ingenuously. "So far back as I can remember, I had an inclination, nay a passion, for painting; still I might not have gone through the requisite drudgery and apprenticeship; might not have studied the naked figure when I wished to get at once to some gorgeous draperies, or fagged at perspective when I wanted to deck out a sunset, if I had not had three sisters and a widowed mother to think of."

"I comprehend; but now that you have mastered the fundamental difficulties of your art, and accustomed yourself to hope for fame in the fuller and freer developments of that art, do you think that you would gladly accept the wealth of Sir Percival Tracey, on the condition that you were never to paint for the public, and to renounce every idea of artistic distinction? or, if you did accept that offer for the sake of your sisters and mother, would it be with reluctance and the pang of self-sacrifice?"

"I don't think I could accept such an offer on such conditions even for them. I am now, sir, utterly unknown — at best one of those promising pupils, of whom there are hundreds; but still I think there is a something in me as painter, as artist, which would break my heart if, some day or other, it did not force itself out."

"Then you would not lose your motive for becoming a great painter, even did you succeed to the wealth and station which you say deprive Sir Percival of a motive, supposing that, in accepting such gifts of fortune, you were *not* required to sacrifice the inclination you take from nature?"

"No, I should not lose the motive. Better famine in a garret than obscurity in a palace!"

Our conversation was here broken off by the entrance of Lady Gertrude. "It is just time for our expedition," said she. "I think it is about to strike two, and Percival is always punctual."

"I am quite ready," said I.

"And I shall be so in five minutes," cried the Painter; "I must run up-stairs for my sketch-book."

"Oh, I see what is keeping my nephew," said Lady

Gertrude, looking out of the window; and as I joined her she drew my attention to two figures walking slowly in the garden; in one I recognised Tracey, the other was unknown to me.

"He must have come by the early train," said Lady Gertrude, musingly. "I wonder whether he means to stay and go with us to the lake."

"You mean the gentleman in black?" said I; "I think not, whoever he may be, for, see, he is just shaking hands with Tracey like a man who is about to take leave. By his dress he seems a clergyman."

"Yes, don't betray me — Percival's London almoner. My nephew has employed him for seven years, and it is only within the last year that I discovered by accident what the employment is. He comes here when he likes — seldom stays over a day! One of those good men who are bored if they are not always about their work; and indeed he bores Percival by constantly talking of sorrow and suffering, which Percival is always wishing to relieve, but never wishes to hear discussed. You don't know to what a degree my nephew carries his foible!"

"What foible?"

"That of desiring everybody to be and to look happy. A year ago, his valet, who had lived with him since he came of age, died. I found him another valet, with the highest character — the best servant possible — not a fault to find with him; but he had a very melancholy expression of countenance. This fretted Percival; he complained to me. 'Dolman is unhappy or discontented,' he said. 'Find out what it is; remedy it.' I spoke to the poor man; he declared himself most satisfied, most fortunate in obtaining such a place. Still he continued to look mournful. Percival could not stand it. One day he thrust a bank-note into the man's hand, and said, 'Go, friend, and before sunset look miserable elsewhere.'"

I was laughing at this characteristic anecdote, when Percival entered the room with his usual beaming aspect and elastic step. "Ready?" said he; "that's well: will you ride with me?" (this addressed to myself). "I have a capital sure-footed pony for you."

"I thought of giving your friend a seat in my pony-chaise," said Lady Gertrude.

Percival glanced at his aunt quickly, and replied, "So be it." I should have preferred riding with Tracey; but before he set off he whispered in my ear, "It makes the dear woman happy to monopolise a new-comer — otherwise——" He stopped short, and I resigned myself to the pony-chaise.

"Pray," said Lady Gertrude, when we were fairly but slowly in movement along a shady road in the park, — "pray, don't you think it is very much to be regretted that Percival should be single — should never have married?"

"I don't know. He seems to me very happy as he is."

"Yes, happy, no doubt. I believe he would make himself happy in a dungeon; and——" Lady Gertrude rather spitefully whipped the ponies.

"Perhaps," said I, as soon as I had recovered the first sensation of alarm, with which I am always seized when by the side of ladies who drive ponies and whip them — "perhaps," said I — "take care of that ditch — perhaps Percival has never seen the woman with whom it would be felicity to share a dungeon?"

"When you knew him first, while he was yet young, did you think him a man not likely to fall very violently in love?"

"Well, 'fall' and 'violently' are two words that I should never have associated with his actions at any time of life. But I should have said that he was a man not likely to form a very passionate attachment to any woman who did not satisfy his refinement of taste, which is exquisitely truthful when applied to poems and statues, but a little too classically perfect for just appreciation of flesh and blood, at least in that sex which is so charming that every defect in it is a shock on the *beau ideal*."

"Nevertheless," said Lady Gertrude, after acknowledging, with a gracious smile, the somewhat old-fashioned gallantry conveyed in my observations — "nevertheless, Percival has loved deeply and fervently, and, what may seem to you strange, has been crossed in his affections."

"Strange! Alas! in love nothing is strange. No one is *loved* for his merits any more than for his fortune or rank; but men, and women too, are *married* for their merits, and still more for their rank and their fortune. I can imagine, therefore, though with difficulty, a girl wooed by Percival Tracey not returning his love, but I cannot conceive her refusing his hand. How was it?"

"You see how I am confiding in you. But you are almost the only friend of his youth whom Percival has invited as his guest; and your evident appreciation of his worth at once opens my heart to you. In the course of that lengthened absence from England — on the eve of which you took leave of him nearly thirty

years ago — Percival formed a close friendship with a
fellow-traveller in the East: Percival considers that to
the courage, presence of mind, and devotion of this
gentleman, a few years younger than himself, he owed
his life in some encounter with robbers. Mr. Garrard
(that is this friend's name) was poor and without a
profession. When Percival was about to return to
Europe, he tried in vain to persuade Mr. Garrard to
accompany him — meaning, though he did not say so,
to exert such interest with Ministers as he possessed,
to obtain for Gerrard some honourable opening in the
public service. The young man refused, and declared
his intention of settling permanently at Cairo. Percival, in the course of his remonstrances, discovered
that the cause of this self-exile was a hopeless attachment, which had destroyed all other objects of ambition in Gerrard's life, and soured him with the world
itself. He did not, however, mention the name of the
lady, nor the reasons which had deprived his affection
of hope. Well, Percival left him at Cairo, and travelled back into Europe. At a German spa he became
acquainted with an Irish peer who had run out his fortune, been compelled to sell his estates, and was living
upon a small annuity allowed to him either by his
creditors or his relations; a man very clever, very accomplished, not of very high principle, and sanguine
of bettering his own position, and regaining the luxuries to which he had been accustomed, through some
brilliant marriage, which the beauty of his only daughter might enable her to make. Beauty to a very rare
degree she possessed — nor beauty alone; her mind
was unusually cultivated, and her manners singularly
fascinating. You guess already?"

"Yes. Percival saw here one with whom he did not *fall* in love, but for whom he *rose into love*. He found his ideal."

"Exactly so. I need not say that the father gave him all encouragement. Percival was on the point of proposing when he received a letter from Mr. Gerrard (to whom he had written, some weeks before, communicating the acquaintance he had made, and the admiration he had conceived); and the letter, written under great excitement, revealed the object of Gerrard's hopeless attachment. Of Irish family himself, he had known this young lady from her childhood — and from her childhood loved her. He had been permitted to hope by Lord ——, who was at that time in a desperate struggle to conceal or stave off his ruin, and who did not scruple to borrow from his daughter's suitor all that he could extract from him. Thus, when the final crash came, Lord ——'s ruin involved nearly the whole of Gerrard's patrimony; and, of course, Lord —— declared that a marriage was impossible between two young persons who had nothing to live upon. It was thus that Edmund Gerrard had become an exile.

"'This intelligence at once reversed the position of the rivals. From that moment Percival devoted himself to bless the life of the man who had saved his own. How he effected this object I scarcely know; but Lord —— gave his consent to Gerrard's suit, and lived six years longer with much pomp and luxury in Paris. Gerrard settled with his wife in Percival's Irish castle, and administers Percival's Irish estates, at a salary which ranks him with the neighbouring gentry. But Percival never visits that property — I do not think he would trust himself to see the only woman he ever loved as the wife of another, though she is no longer young, and is the mother of children, whose future fortunes he has, doubtless, assured."

"What you tell me," said I, with emotion, "is so consistent with Tracey's character that it gives me no surprise. That which does surprise me is, not the consent of the ruined father, but the consent of the accomplished daughter. Did Percival convince himself that she preferred his rival?"

"That is a question I can scarcely answer. My own belief is, that her first fancy had been caught by Gerrard, and that she had given him cause to believe that that first fancy was enduring love; but that, if her intimate acquaintance with Percival had continued longer, and had arrived at a stage at which his heart had been confessed to her, and her own heart frankly wooed, the first fancy would not have proved enduring love. But the acquaintance did not reach to that stage; and I have always understood that her marriage has been a very happy one."

"In that happiness Tracey is consoled?"

"Yes, now, no doubt. But I will tell you this, that as soon as all obstacles to the marriage were removed, and Gerrard on his way from the East, Percival left Germany and reached Lausanne, to be seized with a brain fever, which threatened his life, and from the effects of which it was long before he recovered. But answer me candidly one question, Do you think it is too late in life for him to marry yet?"

Poor Lady Gertrude asked this question in so pleading a tone of voice, that I found it very difficult to answer with the candour which was insisted on as the condition of my reply. At length I said, bravely —

"My dear Lady Gertrude, if a man hard upon sixty chooses to marry, it becomes all his true friends to make the best of it, and say that he has done a wise thing. But if asked beforehand whether it be not too late in life for such an experiment, a true friend must answer, 'Yes.'"

"Yet there have been very happy marriages with great disparity of years," said Lady Gertrude, musingly, "and Percival is very young for his age."

"Excellent after-reflections, if he do marry. But is he not very happy as he is? I know not why, but you all seem to conspire against his being happy in his own way. One of you wants him to turn politician, another to turn Benedict. For my part, the older I grow, the more convinced I am of the truth of one maxim — whether for public life or for private— 'Leave well alone.'"

By this time we had arrived into the heart of a forest that realised one's dreams of Ardens; a young man would have looked round for a Rosalind, a moralising sage for a Jaques. Many a green vista was cut through the mass of summer foliage, and in full view before us stretched a large wild lake; its sides, here and there, clothed with dipping trees or clustered brushwood. On the opposite margin, to which, in a neck of the lake, a rustic bridge gave access, there was a long and picturesque building, in the style of those quaint constructions of white plaster and black oak beams and rafters, which are still seen in Cheshire, but with ruder reliefs of logwood pilasters and balconies; a charming, old-fashioned garden stretched before it, rich in the genuine English flowers of the Elizabethan day; and scattered round, on inviting spots, were lively-coloured tents and awnings. The heron rose alarmed from the reeds as we drew near the water; but the swans, as if greeting the arrival of familiar friends, sailed slowly towards us. Tracey had already arrived at the cottage, and we saw him dismounting at the door, and talking to an old couple who came out to meet and welcome him.

"I believe," said Lady Gertrude, "that Percival's secret reason for building that cottage was to place in it those two old servants from Tracey Court. They had known him there when he was a boy, and are so attached to him that they implored him to let them serve him wherever he resided. But they were too old and too opinionated to suit our moderate establishment, which does not admit of supernumeraries, so he suddenly found out that it would be very pleasant to have a forest lodge for the heats of summer, built that house, and placed them in it. The old woman, who was housekeeper at Tracey Court, is, however, as I hope you will acknowledge, a very good cook on these holiday occasions; and her husband, who was butler there, is so proud and so happy to wait on us, that —. But no doubt you understand how young it makes us old folks feel, to see those who remember us in our youth; and to whom we are still young."

Our party now assembled in front of the forest lodge, and the grooms took back the ponies, with orders to return before nightfall. Tracey carried me over the lodge, while Henry Thornhill and the Painter busied themselves with a small sailing vessel which rode at anchor in a tiny bay.

This rustic habitation was one for which two lovers might have sighed. Its furniture very simple, but picturesquely arranged, with some of those genuine relics of the Elizabethan age, or perhaps rather that of James I., which are now rarely found, though their Dutch imitations are in every curiosity-shop. As in the house we had left there was everywhere impressive the sentiment of the classic taste, so here all expressed the sentiment of that day in our own history which we associate with the poets, who are *our* most beloved classics. It was difficult, when one looked round, to suppose that the house could have been built and furnished by a living contemporary; it seemed a place in which Milton might have lodged when he wrote the 'Lycidas,' or Izaak Walton and Cotton have sought shelter in the troubled days of the Civil War, with a sigh of poetic regret as they looked around, for the yet earlier age when Sidney escaped from courts to meditate the romance of 'Arcadia.'

"I have long thought," said Tracey, "that if we studied the secrets of our English climate a little more carefully than most of us do, we could find, within a very small range, varieties of climate which might allow us to dispense with many a long journey. For instance, do you not observe how much cooler and fresher the atmosphere is here than in the villa yonder, though it is but five miles distant? Here, not only the sun is broken by the forest-trees, but the ground is much more elevated than it is yonder. We get the bracing air of the northern hills, to which I have opened the woods, and here, in the hot relaxing days of summer, I often come for days or weeks together. The lodge is not large enough to admit more than two, or at most three other visitors, and therefore it is only very intimate friends whom I can invite. But I always look forward to a fortnight or so here, as a time to be marked with the whitest chalk, and begin to talk of it as soon as the earliest nightingale is heard. Again, on the other extremity of my property, by the sea-side, I have made my winter residence, my Tarentum, my Naples, my Nice. There, the aspect is due south — cliffs, ranged in semicircle, form an artificial screen from the winds and frosts. The cottage I have built there is a sun-trap. At Christmas I breakfast in a bower of geraniums, and walk by hedgerows of fuchsia and myrtle. All this is part of my philosophical plan, on settling down for life — viz., to collect all the enjoyments this life can give me into the smallest possible compass. Before you go, you must see my winter retreat. I should like to prove to you how many climates, with a little heed, an Englishman may find within a limit of twenty miles. I had thought of giving Bellevue (my sea-side cottage) to the Thornhills, and delighted in the thought of becoming their guest in the winter, for aunt Gertrude does not fancy the place as I do, and wherever I go I cannot live quite alone, nor quite without that humanising effect of drawing-room scenery, which the play-writers call 'petticoat interest.' But when a man allows himself to be selfish, he deserves to be punished. Henry Thornhill disdains Bellevue and comfort, and insists on misery and bivouacs."

"Ah, my dear Tracey," said I, mindful of my promise to Clara, "Henry Thornhill is much too fine a young fellow to be wasted upon ignoble slaughter, and still more ignoble agues and marsh fevers. I hope you do not intend to gratify his preposterous desire to plant laurels at the other end of the world, and on soil in which it may be reasonably doubted whether any laurels will grow —"

Tracey's brow became clouded. He threw himself on a seat niched into the recess of a lattice window, looked out at first abstractedly, and then, as the cloud left his brow, observantly.

"See, my dear friend," said he — "see, how listlessly, for a mere holiday pleasure, that brave lad is running up the sails. Do you think that he would be thus indifferent if he were clearing decks for a fight — if responsibility, and honour, and duty, and fame were his motive powers? No. If he stayed at home inactive he would be miserable the more Clara and I tried to make him happy in our holiday way. That which a man feels, however unphilosophically (according to other men's philosophy), to be an essential to the object for which he deems it noble to exist — that the man must do, or at least attempt; if we prevent him, we mar the very clockwork of his existence, for we break its mainspring. Henry must have his own way. And I say that for Clara's sake; for if he has not, he will seek excitement in something else, and become a bad man and a very bad husband."

"Hem!" said I; "of course you know him best; but I own I do not see in him a genius equal to his restlessness or his ambition; and I think his wife very superior to himself in intellect. If, besides giving him your sea-side villa, you gave him a farm, surely he might become famous for his mangol-wurzel; and it is easier for all men, including even Henry Thornhill, to grow capital wurzel than it is to beat Hannibal or Wellington."

"Pish!" said Tracey, smiling, "you ought to know mankind too well to think seriously what you say in sarcasm. Pray, where and what would England be if every sharp young fellow in the army did not set a Hannibal or a Wellington before his eyes; or if every young politician did not haunt his visions with a Pitt, a Fox, or a Burke? What Henry Thornhill may become, Heaven only knows; but if you could have met Arthur Wellesley before he went to India, do you think you would have guessed that he would become the hero of England? Can any of us detect beforehand the qualities of a man of action? — Of a man of letters, yes; to a certain degree, at least. We can often, though not always, foresee whether a man may become a great writer; but a great man of action — no!! Henry has no literature, no literary occupation, nor even amusement. Probably Hannibal had none, and Wellington very little. *Bref* — he thinks his destiny is action, and military action. Every man should have a fair chance of fulfilling what he conceives to be his destiny. Suppose Henry Thornhill fail; what then? He comes back, reconciled to what fate will still tender him — reconciled to my sea-side villa — to his charming wife — reconciled to life as it *is* for him. But now he is coveting a life which *may* be. A man only does that which fate intends him to do, in proportion as he obeys the motive which gives him his power in life. Henry Thornhill's motive is military ambition. It is no use arguing the point — what man thinks, he is."

I bowed my head. I felt that Tracey was right, and sighed aloud, "Poor little Clara!"

"Poor little Clara!" said Tracey, sighing also,

"must, like other poor dear little loving women, take her chance. If her Henry succeed, how proud she will be to congratulate him! if he fail, how proud she will be to console him!"

"Ah, Tracey!" said I, rising, "in all you have said I recognise your acute discernment and your depth of reasoning. But when you not only concede to, but approve, the motive power which renders this young man restless, pray forgive so old a friend for wondering why you yourself have never found some motive power which might, long ere this, have rendered you renowned."

"Hush!" said Tracey, with his winning, matchless smile — "hush, look out on yon woods and waters. Has not the life which Nature bestows on any man who devoutly loves her a serener happiness than can be found in the enjoyments that estrange us from her charms? How few understand the distinction between life artificial and life artistic! Artificial existence is a reverence for the talk of men; artistic existence is in the supreme indifference to the talk of men. You and I, in different ways, seek to complete our being on earth, not artificially, but artistically. Neither of us can be an insincere mouthpiece of talk in which we have no faith. You cannot write in a book — you cannot say in a speech — that which you know to be a falsehood. But the artificial folks are the very echoes of falsehood; the noise they make is in repeating its last sounds. An artist must be true to nature, even though he add to nature something from his soul of man which nature cannot give in her representations of truth. Is it not so?"

"Certainly," said I, with warmth. "I could neither

write nor speak what I did not believe to be, in the main, truthful. A man may or may not, according to the quality of his mind, give to nature that which clearly never can be in nature — viz., the soul or the intellect of man; but soul or intellect he must give to nature — that is, to everything which external objects present to his senses as truthful — or he is in art a charlatan, and in action a knave. But then Truth, as Humanity knows it, is not what the schoolmen call it, One and Indivisible; it is like light, and splits not only into elementary colours, but into numberless tints. Truth with Raffaele is not the same as truth with Titian; truth with Shakespeare is not the same as truth with Milton; truth with St. Xavier is not the same as truth with Luther; truth with Pitt is not the same as truth with Fox. Each man takes from life his favourite truth, as each man takes from light his favourite colour."

"Bravo!" cried Tracey, clapping his hands.

"Why bravo?" cried I, testily. "Can the definition I hazard be construed into a defence of what I presume to be your view of the individual allegiance which each man owes to truth as he conceives it? No; for each man is bound to support and illustrate, with all his power, truth as truth seems to him, Raffaele as Raffaele, Titian as Titian, Shakespeare as Shakespeare, Milton as Milton, Pitt as Pitt, Fox as Fox. And the man who says, 'I see truth in my own way, and I do not care to serve her cause;' who, when Nature herself ever moving, ever active, exhorts him to bestir himself for the truth he surveys, and to animate that truth with his own life and deed, shrugs his shoulder, and cries 'Cui bono?' — that man, my dear Tracey, may talk very finely about despising renown, but in reality he shuffles off duty. Pardon me; I am thinking of you. I would take your part against others; but as friend to friend, and to your own face, I condemn you."

To this discourteous speech Tracey was about to reply, when Lady Gertrude and Clara Thornhill entered the room to tell us that the boat was ready, and that we had less than two hours for aquatic adventure, as we were to dine at five.

"I am not sorry to have a little time to think over my answer to those reproaches which are compliments on the lips of friends," said Tracey to me, resting his arm on my shoulder; and in a few minutes more we were gliding over the lake, with a gentle breeze from the hills, just lively enough to fill the sail. Clara, bewitchingest of those womanliest women who unfairly enthral and subdue us, while we not only know that their whole hearts are given to another, but love and respect them the more for it, — Clara nestled herself by my side. And I had not even the satisfaction of thinking that that infamous Henry was jealous. He did indeed once or twice pause from his nautical duties to vouchsafe us a scowl; but it was sufficiently evident that the monster was only angry because he knew that Clara loved him so well that she was seeking to enlist me on her side against his abominable ambition of learning the art of homicide.

"Well," whispered Clara to me — "well, you have spoken to Sir Percival!"

"Alas, yes! and in vain. He thinks that for your sake Henry must fulfil that dream of heroism, which perhaps first won your heart to him. Women very naturally love heroes; but then they must pay the tax for that noble attachment. Henry must become the glory of his country, and a major of a regiment in active service. My dear child — I mean, my dear Mrs. Thornhill — don't cry; be a hero's wife. Tracey has convinced me that Henry is right; and my firm belief is that the chief motive which makes Henry covet laurels is to lay them at your feet."

"The darling!" murmured Clara.

"You see your parents very naturally wished you to make a better worldly marriage. That difficulty was smoothed over, not by the merits of Henry, but the money of Sir Percival Tracey. Could you respect your husband if he were not secretly chafed at that thought? He desires to lift himself up to you even in your parents' eyes, not by a miserable pecuniary settlement effected through a kinsman, but by his own deeds. Oppose that, and you humiliate him. Never humiliate a husband. Yield to it, and you win his heart and his gratitude for ever. Man must never be put into an inferior position to his helpmate. Is not that true? Thank you, my child — (come, the word is out) — for that pressure of my hand. You understand us men. Let Henry leave you, sure that his name will be mentioned with praise in his commanding officer's report after some gallant action, looking forward to the day when, in command himself, Parliament shall vote him its thanks, and its Sovereign award him her honours; and your Henry, as you cling in pride to his breast, shall whisper in words only heard by you — 'Wife mine, your parents are not ashamed of me now! All this is your work! all results from the yearning desire to show that the man whom you had singled out from the world was not unworthy of your love!'"

"But Henry does not say those pretty things," sighed Clara, half smiling, half weeping.

"Say them? In words, of course not. What man, and especially what Englishman, does say pretty things to his wife? It is only authors, who are the interpreters of hearts, that say what lovers and heroes feel. But a look says to the beloved one more than authors can put into words. Henry's look will tell you what you, his own, his wife, have been to him in the bivouac, in the battle; and you will love and reverence him the more because he does not say the pretty things into which I mince and sentimentalise the calm Englishman's grand, silent, heartfelt combination of love with duty and with honour. My dear Clara, I speak to you as I would to my own daughter. Let your young soldier go. You and I indeed — the woman and the civilian — may talk as we will of distinctions between the defence of the island and the preservation of the empire. But a soldier is with his country's flag wherever it is placed — whether in the wilds of Caffraria or on the cliffs of Dover. Clara, am I not right? Yes! you again press my hand. After all, there is not a noble beat in the heart of man which does not vibrate more nobly still in the heart of the wife who loves him!"

Just at this time our little anchor dropped on a fairy island. There was as much bustle on board as if we had discovered a new Columbia. We landed for a few minutes to enjoy a glorious view of the lake, to which this island was the centre, and explore a curious cave, which, according to tradition, had been the dwelling of some unsocial anchorite in Gothic days.

The rocky walls of this cell were now inscribed with the names or initials of summer holiday visitors from provincial towns.

"See," said the Painter, "how instinctive to man is the desire to leave some memorial of himself wherever he has been."

"Do you acknowledge then," said Tracey, "that the instinct which roused Joseph Higgins to carve on the rock, for the benefit of distant ages, the fact, that in the year 1837 he visited this spot in company with 'Martha Brown,' is but a family branch of the same instinct which makes genius desire to write its name on the 'flammantia mœnia mundi'?"

"Perhaps," replied the Painter, "the instinct is the same; but if it be so, that truth would not debase and vulgarise the yearning of genius — it would rather elevate and poetise the desire of Joseph Higgins."

"Well answered," said I. "Has any one present a knife that he will not mind blunting? if so, I should like to carve my name under that of Joseph Higgins. It is something to leave a trace of one's whereabout twenty years hence, even in the rock of this lonely cave."

Henry produced the knife, and I carved my name under that of Joseph Higgins, with the date, and these words — "A Summer Holiday." "I have not had many holidays," said I, "since I left school; let me preserve one from oblivion." I passed the knife to Tracey.

"Nay," said he, laughing. "I have no motive strong enough to induce me to take the trouble. I have no special holiday to record — my life is all holiday."

We re-entered our vessel, and drifted along the lake — the Painter jotting down hints of scenery in his sketch-book, and Percival reading to us aloud from a volume of Robert Browning's Poems which he had brought with him. He was a great admirer of that poet, and was bent upon making Clara share his own enthusiasm. Certainly he read well, and the poems he selected seemed in harmony with the scene; for there is in Robert Browning a certain freshness and freedom of music, and a certain suggestiveness of quiet thought reflected from natural images, which fit him to be read out of doors, in English landscapes, on summer days.

When we returned from our cruise, we found our rural banquet awaiting us. We were served under an awning suspended from the trunks of two mighty elms, whose branches overhung the water. Lady Gertrude had not exaggerated the culinary skill of the *ci-devant* housekeeper. What with the fish from the lake, various sorts, dressed in different ways, probably from receipts as old as the monastic days in which fresh-water fishes received the honours due to them — what with some excellent poultry, which, kept in that wild place, seemed to have acquired a finer flavour than farmyard coops bestow — and what with fruits, not rendered malefic by walls of pastry — the repast would have satisfied more refined epicures than we were. Cool, light, sparkling wines, innocent as those which Horace promised to Tyndaris, circled freely. All of us became mirthful, even Clara — all of us except Henry, who still looked as if he were wasting time; and the Painter, who became somewhat too seriously obtrusive of his art, and could with difficulty be kept from merging the whole conversation into criticisms on the landscape effects of Gainsborough contrasted with those of Claude.

After dinner we quietly settled ourselves to our several amusements — Lady Gertrude to some notable piece of female work. Clara, after playing us a few airs on her lute, possessed herself of Tracey's volume of Browning, and pretended to read. The Painter flung himself on the grass, and contemplated with an artist's eye the curves in the bank, and the lengthening shadows that crept over the still waters. Henry, ever restless, wandered away with a rod in his hand towards a distant gravelly creek, in which the old man at the lodge assured us he had seen perch of three pounds weight.

The Librarian alone remained seated at the table, finishing very slowly his bottle of claret, and apparently preparing himself for a peaceful slumber.

Tracey and I strolled along the margin of the lake, the swans following us as we walked: they were old friends of his.

"So," said Tracey at last, "you think that my course of life has not been a wise one."

"If all men lived like you, it might be very well for a paradise, but very bad for the world we dwell in."

"Possibly; but it would be very bad for the world we dwell in if the restless spirits were not in some degree kept in check by the calm ones. What a miserable, unsafe, revolutionary state of society would be that in which all the members were men of combative ambition and fidgety genius; all haranguing, fighting, scribbling; all striving, each against the other! We sober fellows are the ballast in the state vessel: without us, it would upset in the first squall! We have our uses, my friend, little as you seem disposed to own it."

"My dear Tracey, the question is not whether a ship should carry ballast, but whether you are of the proper material for ballast. And when I wonder why a man of great intellect and knowledge should not make his intellect and knowledge more largely useful, it is a poor answer to tell me that he is as useful as — a bag of stones."

"A motive power is as necessary to impel a man, whatever his intellect or knowledge, towards ambitious action, as it is to lift a stone from the hold of a vessel into the arch of a palace. No motive power from without urges me into action, and the property inherent in me is to keep still."

"Well, it is true, yours is so exceptional a lot that it affords no ground for practical speculation of human life. Take a patrician of £60,000 a-year, who only spends £6000: give him tastes so cultivated that he has in himself all resources; diet him on philosophy till he says, with the Greek sage, 'Man is made to contemplate, and to gaze on the stars,' and it seems an infantine credulity to expect that this elegant Looker-on will condescend to take part with the actors on the world's stage. Yet without the actors, the world would be only a drop-scene for the Lookers-on. Yours, I repeat, is an exceptional case. And those who admire your mind, must regret that it has been robbed of fame by your fortune."

"Flatterer," said Tracey, with his imperturbable good-temper, "I am ashamed of myself to know that you have not hit on the truth. If I had been born to £200 a-year, and single as I am now — that is, free to choose my own mode of life — I should have been, I was about to say as idle as I am, but idle is not the word; I should have been as busy in completing my own mind, and as reluctant to force that mind into the squabbles of that mob which you call the world: in fact, I am but a type — somewhat exaggerated by accidental circumstances, which make me more prominent than others to your friendly if critical eye — of a very common and a very numerous class in a civilisation so cultivated as that of our age. Wherever you look, you will find men whom the world has never heard of, yet who in intellect or knowledge could match themselves against those whose names are in all the newspapers. Allow me to ask, Do you not know, in the House of Commons, men who never open their lips, but for whose mere intellect, in judgment, penetration, genuine statesmanship, you have more respect than you have for that of the leading orators? Allow me to ask again, Should you say the profoundest minds and the most comprehensive scholars are to be found among the most popular authors of your time; or among men who have never published a line, and never will? Answer me frankly."

"I will answer you frankly. I should say that, in political judgment and knowledge, there are many men in the back benches of Parliament, who are the most admirable critics of the leading statesmen. I should say that, in many educated, fastidious gentlemen, there are men who, in exquisite taste and extensive knowledge, are the most admirable critics of the popular authors. But still there is an immense difference in human value between even a first-rate critic who does not publish his criticisms, and even a second or third-rate statesman or author who does contribute his quota of thought to the intellectual riches of the world."

"Granted; but the distinction, between man and man, in relation to the public, is not mere intellect, nor mere knowledge; it is in something else. What is it?"

"Dr. Arnold, the schoolmaster, said, that as between boy and boy the distinction was energy, perhaps it is so with men."

"Energy! yes: but what puts the energy into movement? what makes one man dash into fame by a harum-scarum book full of blunders and blemishes, or a random fiery speech, of which any sound thinker would be heartily ashamed; and what keeps back the man who could write a much better book and make a much better speech?"

"Perhaps," said I, ironically, "that extreme of elegant vanity, an over-fastidious taste; perhaps that extreme of philosophical do-nothingness, which always contemplates and never acts."

"Possibly you are right," answered Tracey, shaming my irony by his urbane candour. "But why has the man this extreme of elegant vanity or philosophical do-nothingness? Is it not, perhaps, after all, a physical defect? The lymphatic temperament instead of the nervous-bilious?"

"You are not lymphatic," said I, with interest; for my hobby is — metaphysical pathology, or pathological metaphysics — "You," said I, "are not lympathic; you are dark-haired, lean, and sinewy; why the deuce should you not be energetic! it must be that infamous

£60,000 a-year which has paralysed all your motive power."

"Friend," answered Tracey, "are there not some men in the House of Lords with more than £60,000 a-year, and who could scarcely be more energetic if they lived on 4d. a-day and worked for it?"

"There have been, and are, such instances in the Peerage, doubtless; but, as a general rule, the wealthiest peers are seldom the most active. Still, I am willing to give your implied argument the full benefit of the illustration you cite. Wherever legislative functions are attached to hereditary aristocracy, that aristocracy, as long as the State to which they belong is free, will never fail of mental vigour — of ambition for reputation and honours achieved in the public service. It was so with the senators of Rome as long as the Roman Republic lasted; it will be so with the members of the House of Lords as long as the English Constitution exists. And in such an order of men there will always be a degree of motive power sufficiently counteracting the indolence and epicurism which great wealth in itself engenders, to place a very large numerical proportion of the body among the most active and aspiring spirits of the time. But your misfortune, my dear Tracey, has been this (and hence I call your case exceptional) — that, immeasurably above the average of our peers, both as regards illustrious descent and territorial possessions, still you have had none of the duties, none of the motive power, which actuate hereditary legislators. You have had their wealth — you have had their temptations to idleness; you have not had their responsible duties — you have not had their motives for energy and toil. That is why I call your case exceptional."

"Still," answered Tracey, "I say that I am but a very commonplace type of educated men who belong neither to the House of Lords nor the House of Commons, and who, in this country, despise ambition, yet in some mysterious latent way serve to influence opinion. Motive power — motive power! how is it formed? why is it so capricious? why sometimes strongest in the rich and weakest in the poor? why does knowledge sometimes impart, and sometimes destroy it? On these questions I do not think that your reasonings will satisfy me. I am sure that mine would not satisfy you. Let us call in a third party and hear what he has to say on the matter. Ride with me to-morrow to the house of a gifted friend of mine, who was all for public life once, and is all for private life now. I will tell you who and what he is. In early life my friend carried off the most envied honours of a university. Almost immediately on taking his degree, he obtained his fellowship. Thus he became an independent man. The career most suited to his prospects was that of the Church. To this he had a conscientious objection; not that he objected to the doctrines of our Church, nor that he felt in himself any consciousness of sinful propensities at variance with the profession; but simply because he did not feel that strong impulse towards the holiest of earthly vocations, without which a very clever man may be a very indifferent parson: and his ambition led him towards political distinction. His reputation for talents, and for talents adapted to public life, was so high, that he received an offer to be brought into Parliament, at the first general election, from a man of great station, with whose son he had been intimate at college, and who possessed a predominant influence in a certain borough. The offer was accepted. But before it could be carried out, a critical change occurred in my friend's life and in his temper of mind. He came suddenly and unexpectedly into the succession to a small estate in this county, which had belonged for several generations to a distant branch of his family. On taking possession of the property, he naturally made acquaintance with the rector of the parish, and formed a sudden and passionate attachment for one of the rector's daughters, resigned the fellowship he no longer needed, married the young lady, and found himself so happy with his young partner and in his new home, that before the general election took place, the idea of the parliamentary life, which he had before coveted, became intolerable to him. He excused himself to the borough and its patron, and has ever since lived as quietly in his rural village as if he had never known the joys of academical triumph, nor nursed the hope of political renown. Let us then go and see him to-morrow (it is a very pretty ride across the country), and you will be compelled to acknowledge that his £600 or £700 a-year of wood and sheepwalk, with peace and love at his fireside, have sufficed to stifle ambition in one whose youth had been intensely ambitious. So you see it does not need £60,000 a-year to make a man cling to private life, and shrink from all that, in shackling him with the fetters and agitating him with the passion of public life, would lessen his personal freedom and mar his intellectual serenity."

"I shall be glad to see your friend. What is his name?"

"Hastings Gray."

"What! the Hastings Gray who, seventeen or eighteen years ago, made so remarkable a speech at some public meeting (I own I forget where it was), and wrote the political pamphlet which caused so great a sensation!"

"The same man."

"I remember that he was said to have distinguished himself highly at the university, and that he was much talked of in London, for a few weeks, as a man likely to come into Parliament, and even to make a figure in it. Since then, never having heard more of him, I supposed he was dead. I am glad to learn that he only sleepeth."

Here we heard behind us the muffled fall of hoofs on the sward; our party was in movement homeward, Lady Gertrude leading the van in her pony chaise. I had to retake my place by her side; Clara and the Librarian followed in a similar vehicle, driven by Henry Thornhill, who had caught none of the great perches; I suspect he had not tried for them. Percival and the Painter rode. The twilight deepened, and soon melted into a starry night, as we went through the shadowy forest-land.

Lady Gertrude talked incessantly and agreeably, but I was a very dull companion, and, being in a musing humour, would much rather have been alone. At length we saw the moon shining on the white walls of the villa. "I fear we have tired you with our childish party of pleasure," said Lady Gertrude, with a malicious fling at my silence.

"Perhaps I am tired," I replied, ingenuously.

"Pleasures are fatiguing, especially when one is not accustomed to them."

"Satirist!" said Lady Gertrude. "You come from the brilliant excitements of London, and what may be pleasure to us must be *ennui* to you."

"Nay, Lady Gertrude, let me tell you what a very clever and learned man, a Minister of State, said the other day at one of those great public ceremonial receptions which are the customary holidays of a Minister of State. 'Life,' said he, pensively, 'would be tolerably agreeable if it were not for its amusements.' He spoke of those 'brilliant excitements,' as you call them, which form the amusements of capitals. He would not have spoken so of the delight which Man can extract from a holiday with Nature. But tell me, you who have played so considerable a part in the world of fashion, do you prefer the drawing-rooms of London to the log-house by the lake?"

"Why," said Lady Gertrude, honestly, and with a half-sigh, "I own I should be glad if Percival would consent to spend six months in the year, or even three, in London. However, what he likes I like. Providence has made us women of very pliable materials."

"Has it?" said I; "that information is new to me — one lives to learn." And here, as the pony stopped at the porch, I descended to offer my arm to the amiable charioteer.

Nothing worth recording took place the rest of the evening. Henry and the Painter played at billiards, Lady Gertrude and the Librarian at backgammon. Clara went into the billiard-room, seating herself there with her work: by some fond instinct of her loving nature, she felt as if she ought not to waste the minutes yet vouchsafed to her — she was still with him who was all in all to her!

I took down 'The Faithful Shepherdess,' wishing to refresh my memory of passages which the scenes we had visited that day vaguely recalled to my mind. Looking over my shoulder, Percival guided me to the lines I was hunting after. This led to comparisons between 'The Faithful Shepherdess' and the 'Comus,' and thence to that startling contrast in the way of viewing, and in the mode of describing, rural nature, between the earlier English poets and those whom Dryden formed upon Gallic models, and so on into the pleasant clueless labyrinth of metaphysical criticism on the art of poetic genius. When we had parted for the night, and I regained my own room, I opened my window and looked forth on the moonlit gardens. A few minutes later, a shadow, moving slow, passed over the silvered ground, and, descending the terrace stairs, vanished among the breathless shrubs and slumbering flowers. I recognised the man who loved to make night his companion.

The next day the atmosphere was much cooler, refreshed by a heavy shower that had fallen at dawn; and when, not long after noon, Percival and I, mounted on ponies bred in the neighbouring forests, were riding through the narrow lanes towards the house we had agreed to visit, we did not feel the heat oppressive. It was a long excursion; we rode slowly, and the distance was about sixteen miles.

We arrived at last at a little hamlet remote from the highroads. The cottages, though old-fashioned, were singularly neat and trim — flower-plots before

them, and small gardens for kitchen use behind. A
very ancient church, with its parsonage, backed the
broad village-green; and opposite the green stood one
of those small quaint manor-houses which satisfied the
pride of our squires two hundred years ago. On a
wide garden-lawn in front were old yew-trees cut into
fantastic figures of pyramids and obelisks and birds
and animals; beyond the lawn, on a levelled platform
immediately before the house, was a small garden, with
a sundial, and a summer-house or pavilion of the date
of William III., when buildings of that kind, for a
short time, became the fashionable appendage to country-houses, frequently decorated inside with musical
trophies, as if built for a music-room; but, I suspect,
more generally devoted to wine and pipes by the host
and his male friends. At the rear of the house stretched
an ample range of farm-buildings in very good repair
and order, the whole situated on the side of a hill,
sufficiently high to command an extensive prospect,
bounded at the farthest distance by the sea, yet not
so high as to lose the screen of hills, crested by young
plantations of fir and larch; while the midmost slopes
were, in part, still abandoned to sheepwalks; in part,
brought (evidently of late) into cultivation; and farther
down, amid the richer pastures that dipped into the
valley, goodly herds of cattle indolently grazed or
drowsily reposed.

We dismounted at the white garden-gate. A man
ran out from the farmyard and took our ponies; evidently a familiar acquaintance of Tracey's, for he said
heartily, "that he was glad to see his honour looking
so well," and volunteered a promise that the ponies
should be well rubbed down, and fed. "Master was

at home; we should find him in the orchard swinging Miss Lucy."

So, instead of entering the house, Tracey, who knew all its ways, took me round to the other side, and we came into one of those venerable orchards which carry the thought back to the early day when the orchard was, in truth, the garden.

A child's musical laugh guided us through the lines of heavy-laden apple-trees to the spot where the once famous prizeman — the once brilliant political thinker — was now content to gratify the instinctive desire *tentare aërias vias* — in the pastime of an infant.

He was so absorbed in his occupation that he did not hear or observe us till we were close at his side. Then, after carefully arresting the swing, and tenderly taking out the little girl, he shook hands with Percival; and when the ceremony of mutual introduction was briefly concluded, extended the same courtesy to myself.

Gray was a man in the full force of middle life, with a complexion that seemed to have been originally fair and delicate, but had become bronzed and hardened by habitual exposure to morning breezes and noonday suns. He had a clear, bright blue eye, and a countenance that only failed of being handsome by that length and straightness of line between nostril and upper lip, which is said by physiognomists to be significant of firmness and decision. The whole expression of his face, though frank and manly, was, however, rather sweet than harsh; and he had one of those rare voices which almost in themselves secure success to a public speaker — distinct and clear, even in its lowest tone, as a silvery bell.

I think much of a man's nature is shown by the way in which he shakes hands. I doubt if any worldly student of Chesterfieldian manners can ever acquire the art of that everyday salutation, if it be not inborn in the kindness, loyalty, and warmth of his native disposition. I have known many a great man who lays himself out to be popular, who can school his smile to fascinating sweetness, his voice to persuasive melody, but who chills or steels your heart against him the moment he shakes hands with you.

But there is a cordial clasp which shows warmth of impulse, unhesitating truth, and even power of character — a clasp which recalls the classic trust in the "faith of the right hand."

And the clasp of Hastings Gray's hand at once propitiated me in his favour. While he and I exchanged the few words with which acquaintance commences, Percival had replaced Miss Lucy in the swing, and had taken the father's post. Lucy, before disappointed at the cessation of her amusement, felt now that she was receiving a compliment, which she must not abuse too far; so she very soon, of her own accord, unselfishly asked to be let down, and we all walked back towards the house.

"You will dine with us, I hope," said Gray. "I know when you come at this hour, Sir Percival, that you always meditate giving us that pleasure." (Turning to me,) "It is now half-past three; we dine at four o'clock, and that early hour gives you time to rest, and ride back in the cool of the evening."

"My dear Gray," answered Percival, "I accept your invitation for myself and my friend. I foresaw you would ask us, and left word at home that we were not to be waited for. Where is Mrs. Gray?"

"I suspect that she is about some of those household matters which interest a farmer's wife. Lucy, run and tell your mamma that these gentlemen will dine with us."

Lucy scampered off.

"The fact is," said Tracey, "that we have a problem to submit to you. You know how frequently I come to you for a hint when something puzzles me. But we can defer that knotty subject till we adjourn, as usual, to wine and fruit in your summer-house. Your eldest boy is at home for the holidays?"

"Not at home, though it is his holidays. He is now fifteen, and he and a school friend of his are travelling on foot into Cornwall. Nothing, I think, fits boys better for life than those hardy excursions in which they must depend on themselves, shift for themselves, think for themselves."

"I daresay you are right," said Tracey; "the earlier each of us human beings forms himself into an individual God's creature, distinct from the *servum pecus*, the better chance he has of acquiring originality of mind and dignity of character. And your other children?"

"Oh, my two younger boys I teach at home, and one little girl — I play with." Here addressing me, Gray asked "If I farmed?"

"Yes," said I, "but very much as *les Rois Fainéants* reigned. My bailiff is my *Maire du Palais*. I hope, therefore, that our friend Sir Percival will not wound my feelings as a lover of Nature by accusing me of wooing her for the sake of her turnips."

"Ah!" said Gray, smiling, "Sir Percival, I know, holds to the doctrine that the only pure love of Nature is the æsthetic; and looks upon the intimate connection which the husbandman forms with her as a cold-blooded *mariage de convenance.*"

"I confess," answered Percival, "that I agree with the great German philosopher, that the love of Nature is pure in proportion as the delight in her companionship is unmixed with any idea of the gain she can give us. But a pure love may be a very sterile affection; and a *mariage de convenance* may be prolific in very fine offspring. I concede to you, therefore, that the world is bettered by the practical uses to which Nature has been put by those who wooed her for the sake of her dower: and I no more commend to the imitation of others my abstract æsthetic affection for her abstract æsthetic beauty; than I would commend Petrarch's poetical passion for Laura to the general adoption of lovers. I give you, then, gentlemen farmers, full permission to woo Nature for the sake of her turnips. Our mutton is all the better for it."

"And that is no small consideration," said Gray. "If I had gazed on my sheepwalks with the divine æsthetic eye, and without one forethought of the profit they might bring me, I should not already have converted 200 out of the 1000 acres I possess into land that would let at 30s. per acre, where formerly it let at 5s. But, with all submission to the great German philosopher, I don't think I love Nature the less because of the benefits with which she repays the pains I have taken to conciliate her favour. If, thanks to her, I can give a better education to my boys, and secure a modest provision for my girl, is it the property of gratitude to destroy or to increase affection? But you see, sir, there is this difference between Sir Percival and myself: — He has had no motive in improving Nature for her positive uses, and therefore he has been contented with giving her a prettier robe. He loves her as a *grand seigneur* loves his mistress. I love her as a man loves the helpmate who assists his toils. According as in rural life my mind could find not repose, but occupation — according as that occupation was compatible with such prudent regard to fortune as a man owes to the children he brings into the world — my choice of life would be a right or a wrong one. In short, I find in the cultivation of Nature my business as well as my pleasure. I have a motive for the business which does not diminish my taste for the pleasure."

Tracey and I exchanged looks. So, then, here was a motive for activity. But why was the motive towards activity in pursuits requiring so little of the intellect for which Gray had been characterised, and so little of the knowledge which his youth had acquired, so much stronger than the motive towards a career which proffered an incalculably larger scope for his powers? Here, there was no want of energy — here, there had been no philosophical disdain of ambition — here, no great wealth leaving no stimulant to desires — no niggard poverty paralysing the sinews of hope. The choice of retirement had been made in the full vigour of a life trained from boyhood to the exercises that discipline the wrestlers for renown.

While I was thus musing, Gray led the way towards the farmyard, and on reaching it said to me, —

"Since you do farm, if only by deputy, I must show you the sheep with which I hope to win the first prize at our agricultural show in September.".

"So you still care for prizes?" said I: "the love of fame is not dead within your breast."

"Certainly not; 'Pride attends us still.' I am very proud of the prizes I have already won; last year for my wurzel — the year before, for the cow I bred on my own pastures."

We crossed the farmyard, and arrived at the covered sheep-pens. I thought I had never seen finer sheep than those which Gray showed me with visible triumph. Then we two conversed with much animation upon the pros and cons in favour of stall-feeding *versus* free grazing, while Tracey amused himself, first in trying to conciliate a great dog, luckily for him chained up in the adjoining yard, and next, in favouring the escape of a mouse who had incautiously quitted the barn, and ventured within reach of a motherly hen, who seemed to regard it as a monster intent on her chicks.

Reaching the house, Gray conducted us up a flight of oak stairs — picturesque in its homely old-fashioned way — with wide landing-place, adorned by a blue china jar, filled with *pot-pourri*, and by a tall clock (one of Tompion's, now rare), in walnut-wood case; consigning us each to a separate chamber, to refresh ourselves by those simple ablutions with which, even in rustic retirements, civilised Englishmen preface the hospitable rites of Ceres and Bacchus.

The room in which I found myself was one of those never seen out of England, and only there in unpretending country-houses which have escaped the innovating tastes of fashion. A bedstead of the time of George I., with mahogany fluted columns and panels at the bedhead, dark and polished, decorated by huge watch-pockets of some great-grandmother's embroidery, white spotless curtains, the walls in panel, and covered in part with framed engravings a century old; a large high screen, separating the wash-stand from the rest of the room, made lively by old caricatures and prints, doubtless the handiwork of female hands long stilled. A sweet, not strong, odour of dried lavender escaped from a chest of drawers polished as bright as the bedstead. The small lattice-paned window opened to the fresh air, the woodbine framing it all round from without; amongst the woodbine the low hum of bees. A room for early sleep and cheerful rising with the eastern sun, which the window faced.

Tracey came into my room while I was still looking out of the casement, gazing on the little garden-plot without, bright with stocks and pinks and heartsease, and said, "Well, you see £600 a-year can suffice to arrest a clever man's ambition."

"I suspect," answered I, "that the ambition is not arrested, but turned aside to the object of doubling the £600 a-year. Neither ambition nor the desire of gain is dead in that farmyard."

"We shall cross-question our host after dinner," answered Tracey; "meanwhile let me conduct you to the dining-room. A pretty place this, in its way, is it not?"

"Very," said I, with enthusiasm. "Could you not live as happily here as in your own brilliant villa?"

"No, not quite, but still happily."

"Why not quite?"

"First, because there is nothing within or without the house which one could attempt to improve, unless by destroying the whole character of what is so good in its way; secondly, where could I put my Claudes and Turners? where my statues? where, oh where, my books? where, in short, the furniture of Man's mind?"

I made no answer, for the dinner-bell rang loud, and we went down at once into the dining-room — a quaint room, scarcely touched since the date of William III. A high and heavy dado of dark oak, the rest of the walls in Dutch stamped leather, still bright and fresh; a high mantelpiece, also of oak, with a very indifferent picture of still life let into the upper panel; arched recesses on either side, receptacles for china and tall drinking-glasses; heavy chairs, with crests inlaid on their ponderous backs, and faded needlework on their ample seats; — all, however, speaking of comfort and home, and solid though unassuming prosperity. Gray had changed his rude morning-dress, and introduced me to his wife with an evident husbandlike pride. Mrs. Gray was still very pretty; in her youth she must have been prettier even than Clara Thornhill, and, though very plainly dressed, still it was the dress of a gentlewoman. There was intelligence, but soft timid intelligence, in her dark hazel eyes and broad candid forehead. I soon saw, however, that she was painfully shy, and not at all willing to take her share in the expense of conversation. But with Tracey she was more at her ease than with a stranger, and I thanked him inwardly for coming to my relief as I was vainly endeavouring to extract from her lips more than a murmured monosyllable.

The dinner, however, passed off very pleasantly. Simple old English fare — plenty of it — excellent of its kind. Tracey was the chief talker, and made himself so entertaining, that at last even Mrs. Gray's shyness wore away, and I discovered that she had a well-informed graceful mind, constitutionally cheerful, as was evidenced by the blithe music of her low but happy laugh.

The dinner over, we adjourned, as Percival had proposed, to the summer-house. There we found the table spread with fruits and wine, of which last the port was superb; no better could be dragged from the bins of a college, or blush on the board of a prelate. Mrs. Gray, however, deserted us, but we now and then caught sight of her in the garden without, playing gaily with her children — two fine little boys, and Lucy, who seemed to have her own way with them all, as she ought — the youngest child, the only girl — justifiably papa's pet, for she was the child most like her mother.

"Gray," said Tracey, "my friend and I have had some philosophical disputes, which we cannot decide to our own satisfaction, on the reasons why some men do so much more in life than other men, without having any apparent intellectual advantage over those who are contented to be obscure. We have both hit on a clue to the cause, in what we call motive power. But what this motive power really is, and why it should fail in some men and be so strong in others, is matter of perplexity, at least to me, and I fancy my friend himself is not much more enlightened therein than I am. So we have both come here to hear what you have to say — you, who certainly had motive enough for ambitious purposes when you swept away so many academical prizes — when you rushed into speech and into print, and cast your bold eye on St. Stephen's. And now, what has become of that motive power? Is it all put into prizes for root-crops and sheep?"

"As to myself," answered Gray, passing the wine. "I can give very clear explanations. I am of a gentleman's family, but the son of a very poor curate. Luckily for me, we lived close by an excellent grammar-school, at which I obtained a free admission. From the first day I entered, I knew that my poor father, bent on making me a scholar, counted on my exertions not only for my own livelihood, but for a provision for my mother should she survive him. Here was motive enough to supply motive power. I succeeded in competition with rivals at school, and success added to the strength of the motive power. Our county member, on whose estate I was born, took a kindly interest in me, and gave me leave, when I quitted school as head-boy, to come daily to his house and share the studies of his son, who was being prepared for the university by a private tutor, eminent as a scholar and admirable as a teacher. Thus I went up to college not only full of hope (in itself a motive power, though, of itself, an unsafe one), but of a hope so sustained that it became resolution, by the knowledge that to maintain me at the university my parents were almost literally starving themselves. This suffices to explain whatever energy and application I devoted to my academical career. At last I obtained my fellowship; the income of that I shared with my parents; but if I died before them the income would die also — a fresh motive power towards a struggle for fortune in the Great World. I took up politics, I confess it very frankly, as a profession rather than a creed; it was the shortest road to fame, and, with prudence, perhaps to pecuniary competence. If I succeeded in Parliament, I might obtain a living for my father, or some public situation for myself not dependent on the fluctuations of party. A very high political ambition was denied me by the penury of circumstance. A man must have good means of his own who aspires to rank among party chiefs. I knew I was but a political adventurer, that I could only be so considered; and had it not been for my private motive power, I should have been ashamed of my public one. As it was, my scholarly pride was secretly chafed at the thought that I was carrying into the affairs of state the greed of trade. However, just as I was studying 'Hansard's Debates,' and preparing myself for Parliament, this estate of Oakden suddenly fell to my lot. You large proprietors will smile when I say that we had always regarded the Grays of Oakden Hall with venerating pride; they were the head of our branch of the clan. My father had seen this place in his boyhood; the remembrance of it dwelt on his mind as the unequivocal witness of his dignity as a gentleman born. He came from the same stock as the Grays of Oakden, who had lived on the land for more than three centuries, entitled to call themselves squires. The relationship was very distant, still it existed. But a dream that so great a place as Oakden Hall, with its thousand acres, should ever pass to his son — no, my father thought it much more likely that his son might be prime minister! John Gray of Oakden had never taken the least notice of us, except that, when I won the Pitt scholarship, he sent me a fine turkey, labelled 'From John Gray, Esq. of Oakden.' This present I acknowledged, but John Gray never answered my letter. Just at that time, however, as appears by the date, he remade his will, by which the succession to this property was secured to me in what must then have seemed the very improbable event of the death, without issue, of two nephews, both younger men than myself. That event, so improbable, happened. The elder nephew died, unmarried, of rheumatic fever, a few months before old Gray's decease; the other, two weeks after it: poor fellow! he was thrown from his horse, and killed on the spot. Thus I came into this property. Soon afterwards I married. The possession of land is a great tranquilliser to a restless spirit, and a happy marriage is a sedative as potent. Poverty is a spur to action. Great wealth, on the other hand, not unnaturally tends to the desire of display, and in free countries often to the rivalry for political power. The golden mean is proverbially the condition most favourable to content, and content is the antidote to ambition. Mine was the golden mean! Other influences of pride and affection contributed to keep me still. Of pride; for was I not really a greater man here, upon my ancestral acres, and my few yearly hundreds, than as a political aspirant, who must commence his career by being a political dependant? How rich I felt here! how poor I should be in London! How inevitably, in the daily expenses of a metropolitan life, and in the costs of elections (should I rise beyond being a mere nominee), I must become needy and involved! So much for the influence of pride.

Now for the influence of affection: my dear wife had never been out of these rural shades among which she was born. She is of a nature singularly timid, sensitive, and retiring. The idea of that society to which a political career would have led me terrified her. I loved her the better for desiring no companionship but mine. In fine, my desires halted at once on these turfs; the Attraction of the Earth prevailed; the motive power stopped here."

"You have never regretted your choice?" said Tracey.

"Certainly not; I congratulate myself on it more and more every year. For, after all, here I have ample occupation and a creditable career. I have improved my fortune, instead of wasting it. I have a fixed, acknowledged, instead of an unsettled, equivocal position. I am an authority on many rural subjects of interest besides those of husbandry. I am an active magistrate; and, as I know a little of the law, I am the habitual arbiter upon all the disputes in the neighbourhood. I employ here with satisfaction, and not without some dignity, the energies which, in the great world, would have bought any reputation I might have gained at the price of habitual pain and frequent mortification."

"Then," said I, "you do not think that a saying of Dr. Arnold's, which I quoted to Tracey as no less applicable to men than to boys, is altogether a true one — viz., that the difference between boys, as regards the power of acquiring distinction, is not so much in talent as in energy; you retain the energies that once raised you to public distinction, but you no longer apply them to the same object."

"I believe that Dr. Arnold, if he be quoted correctly, spoke only half the truth. One difference between boy and boy or man and man, no doubt, is energy; but for great achievements or fame there must be also application — viz., every energy concentred on one definite point, and disciplined to strain towards it by patient habit. My energy, such as it is, would not have brought my sheepwalks into profitable cultivation if the energy had not been accompanied with devoted application to the business. And it is astonishing how, when the energy is constantly applied towards one settled aim — astonishing, I say — how invention is kindled out of it. Thus, in many a quiet solitary morning's walk round my farm, some new idea, some hint of improvement or contrivance, occurs to me; this I ponder and meditate upon till it takes the shape of experiment. I presume that it is so with poet, artist, orator, or statesman. His mind is habituated to apply itself to definite subjects of observation and reflection, and out of this habitual musing thereon, involuntarily spring the happy originalities of thinking which are called his 'inspirations.'"

"One word more," said I. "Do you consider, then, that which makes a man devote himself to fame or ambition is a motive power of which he himself is conscious?"

"No; not always. I imagine that most men entering on some career are originally impelled towards it by a motive which, at the time, they seldom take the trouble to analyse or even to detect. They would at once see what that motive was if, early in the career, it were withdrawn. In a majority of cases it is the *res angusta*, yet not poverty in itself, but a poverty disproportioned to the birth, or station, or tastes, or intellectual culture of the aspirant. Thus, the peasant or operative rarely feels in his poverty a motive power towards worldly distinction; but the younger son of a gentleman does feel that motive power. And hence a very large proportion of those who in various ways have gained fame, have been the cadets of a gentleman's family, or the sons of poor clergymen, sometimes of farmers and tradesmen, who have given them an education beyond the average of their class. Other motive powers towards fame have been sometimes in ambition, sometimes in love; sometimes in a great sorrow, from which a strong mind sought to wrest itself; sometimes even in things that would appear frivolous to a philosopher. I knew a young man, of no great talents, but of keen vanity and great resolution and force of character, who, as a child, had been impressed with envy of the red ribbon which his uncle wore as Knight of the Bath. From his infancy he determined some day or other to win a red ribbon for himself. He did so at last, and in trying to do so became famous.

"In great commercial communities a distinction is given to successful trade, so that the motive power of youthful talent nourished in such societies is mostly concentred on gain, not through avarice, but through the love of approbation or esteem. Thus, it is noticeable that our great manufacturing towns, where energy and application abound, have not contributed their proportionate quota of men distinguished in arts or sciences (except the mechanical), or polite letters, or the learned professions. In rural districts, on the contrary, the desire of gain is not associated with the desire of honour and distinction, and therefore, in them, the youth early coveting fame strives for it in other channels than those of gain. But whatever the original motive power, if it has led to a continuous habit of the mind, and is not withdrawn before that habit becomes a second nature, the habit will continue after the motive power has either wholly ceased or become very faint, as the famous scribbling Spanish cardinal is said, in popular legends, to have continued to write on after he himself was dead. Thus, a man who has acquired the obstinate habit of labouring for the public originally from an enthusiastic estimate of the value of public applause, may, later, conceive a great contempt for the public, and, in sincere cynicism, become wholly indifferent to its praise or its censure, and yet, like Swift, go on as long as the brain can retain faithful impressions and perform its normal functions, writing for the public he so disdains. Thus many a statesman, wearied and worn, satisfied of the hollowness of political ambition, and no longer enjoying its rewards, sighing for retirement and repose, nevertheless continues to wear his harness. Habit has tyrannised over all his actions; break the habit, and the thread of his life snaps with it!

"Lastly, however, I am by no means sure that there is not in some few natures an inborn irresistible activity, a constitutional attraction between the one mind and the human species, which requires no special, separate motive power from without to set it into those movements which, per force, lead to fame. I mean those men to whom we at once accord the faculty which escapes all satisfactory metaphysical definition — INGENIUM; viz., the inborn spirit which we call genius.

"And in *these* natures, whatever the motive power that in the first instance urged them on, if at any stage, however early, that motive power be withdrawn, some other one will speedily replace it. Through them Providence mysteriously acts on the whole world, and their genius while on earth is one of Its most visible ministrants. But genius is the exceptional phenomenon in human nature; and in examining the ordinary laws that influence human minds we have no measurement and no scales for portents."

"There is, however," said Tracey, "one motive power towards careers of public utility which you have not mentioned, but the thought of which often haunts me in rebuke of my own inertness, — I mean, quite apart from any object of vanity or ambition, the sense of our own duty to mankind; and hence the devotion to public uses of whatever talents have been given to us — not to hide under a bushel."

"I do not think," answered Gray, "that when a man feels he is doing good in his own way he need reproach himself that he is not doing good in some other way to which he is not urged by special duty, and from which he is repelled by constitutional temperament. I do not, for instance, see that because you have a very large fortune you are morally obliged to keep correspondent establishments, and adopt a mode of life hostile to your tastes; you sufficiently discharge the duties of wealth if the fair proportion of your income go to objects of well-considered benevolence, and purposes not unproductive to the community. Nor can I think that I, who possess but a very moderate fortune, am morally called upon to strive for its increase in the many good speculations which life in a capital may offer to an eager mind, provided always that I do nevertheless remember that I have children; to whose future provision and wellbeing some modest augmentations of my fortune would be desirable. In improving my land for their benefit, I may say also that I add, however trivially, to the wealth of the country. Let me hope that the trite saying is true, that 'he who makes two blades of corn grow where one grew before' is a benefactor to his race. So with mental wealth: surely it is permitted to us to invest and expend it within that sphere most suited to those idiosyncrasies, the adherence to which constitutes our moral health. I do not, with the philosopher, condemn the man who, irresistibly impelled towards the pursuit of honours and power, persuades himself that he is toiling for the public good when he is but gratifying his personal ambition; — probably he is a better man thus acting in conformity with his own nature, than he would be if placed beyond all temptation in Plato's cave. Nor, on the other hand, can I think that a man of the highest faculties and the largest attainments, who has arrived at a sincere disdain of power or honours, would be a better man if he were tyrannically forced to pursue the objects from which his temperament recoils, upon the plea that he was thus promoting the public welfare. No doubt, in every city, town, street, and lane, there are bustling, officious, restless persons, who thrust themselves into public concerns, with a loud declaration that they are animated only by the desire of public good; they mistake their fidgetiness for philanthropy. Not a bubble company can be started, but what it is with a programme that its direct object is the public benefit, and the ten per cent promised to the shareholders is but secondary consideration. Who believes in the sincerity of that announcement? In fine, according both to religion and to philosophy, virtue is the highest end of man's endeavour; but virtue is wholly independent of the popular shout or the lictor's fasces. Virtue is the same, whether with or without the laurel crown, or the curule chair. Honours do not sully it, but obscurity does not degrade. He who is truthful, just, merciful, and kindly, does his duty to his race, and fulfils his great end in creation, no matter whether the rays of his life are not visibly beheld beyond the walls of his household, or whether they strike the ends of the earth; for every human soul is a world complete and integral, storing its own ultimate uses and destinies within itself; viewed only for a brief while, in its rising on the gaze of earth; pressing onward in its orbit amidst the infinite, when, snatched from our eyes, we say, 'It has passed away!' And as every star, however small it seem to us from the distance at which it shines, contributes to the health of our atmosphere, so every soul, pure and bright in itself, however far from our dwelling, however unremarked by our vision, contributes to the wellbeing of the social system in which it moves, and, in its privacy, is part and parcel of the public weal."

Shading my face with my hand, I remained some moments musing after Gray's voice had ceased. Then looking up, I saw so pleased and grateful a smile upon Percival Tracey's countenance, that I checked the reply by which I had intended to submit a view of the subject in discussion somewhat different from that which Gray had taken from the Portico of the Stoics.

Why should I attempt to mar whatever satisfaction Percival's reason or conscience had found in our host's argument? His tree of life was too firmly set for the bias of its stem to swerve in any new direction towards light and air. Let it continue to rejoice in such light and such air as was vouchsafed to the site on which it had taken root. Evening, too, now drew in, and we had a long ride before us. A little while after, we had bid adieu to Oakden Hall, and were once more threading our way through the green and solitary lanes.

We conversed but little for the first five or six miles. I was revolving what I had heard, and considering how each man's reasoning moulds itself into excuse or applause for the course of life which he adopts. Percival's mind was employed in other thoughts, as became clear when he thus spoke: —

"Do you think, my dear friend, that you could spare me a week or two longer? It would be a charity to me if you could, for I expect, after to-morrow, to lose my young artist, and, alas! also the Thornhills."

"How! The Thornhills? So soon!"

"I count on receiving to-morrow the formal announcement of Henry's promotion and exchange into the regiment he so desires to enter, with the orders to join it abroad at once. Clara, I know, will not stay here; she will be with her husband till he sails, and after his departure will take her abode with his widowed mother. I shall miss them much. But Thornhill feels that he is wasting his life here; and so — well — I have acted for the best. With respect to the artist, this morning I received a letter from my old friend

Lord ———. He is going into Italy next week; he wishes for some views of Italian scenery for a villa he has lately bought, and will take Bourke with him on my recommendation, leaving him ultimately at Rome. Lord ———'s friendship and countenance will be of immense advantage to the young painter, and obtain him many orders. I have to break it to Bourke this evening, and he will, no doubt, quit me to-morrow to take leave of his family. For myself, as I always feel somewhat melancholy in remaining on the same spot after friends depart from it, I propose going to Bellevue, where I have a small yacht. It is glorious weather for sea excursions. Come with me, my dear friend! The fresh breezes will do you good; and we shall have leisure for talk on all the subjects which both of us love to explore and guess at."

No proposition could be more alluring to me. My recent intercourse with Tracey had renewed all the affection and interest with which he had inspired my youth. My health and spirits had been already sensibly improved by my brief holiday, and an excursion at sea had been the special advice of my medical attendant. I hesitated a moment. Nothing called me back to London except public business, and, in that, I foresaw but the bare chance of a motion in Parliament which stood on the papers for the next day; but my letters had assured me that this motion was generally expected to be withdrawn or postponed.

So I accepted the invitation gladly, provided nothing unforeseen should interfere with it.

Pleased by my cordial assent, Tracey's talk now flowed forth with genial animation. He described his villa overhanging the sea, with its covered walks to the solitary beach — the many objects of interest and landscapes of picturesque beauty within reach of easy rides, on days in which the yacht might not tempt us. I listened with the delight of a schoolboy, to whom some goodnatured kinsman paints the luxuries of a home at which he invites the schoolboy to spend the vacation.

By little and little, our conversation glided back to our young past, and thence to those dreams, nourished ever by the young; — love and romance, and home brightened by warmer beams than glow in the smile of sober friendship. How the talk took this direction I know not; perhaps by unconscious association, as the moon rose above the forest-hills, with the love-star by her side. And, thus conversing, Tracey for the first time alluded to that single passion which had vexed the smooth river of his life — and which, thanks to Lady Gertrude, was already, though vaguely, known to me.

"It was," said he, "just such a summer night as this, and, though in a foreign country, amid scenes of which these woodland hills remind me, that the world seemed to me to have changed into a Fairyland; and, looking into my heart, I said to myself, 'This, then, is — love.' And a little while after, on such a night, and under such a moon, and amid such hills and groves, the world seemed blighted into a desert — life to be evermore without hope or object; and, looking again into my heart, I said, 'This, then, is love denied!'"

"Alas!" answered I, "there are few men in whose lives there is not some secret memoir of an affection thwarted; but rarely indeed does an affection thwarted leave a permanent influence on the after-destinies of a man's life. On that question I meditate an essay, which, if ever printed, I will send to you."

I said this, wishing to draw him on, and expecting him to contradict my assertion as to the enduring influence of a disappointed love. He mused a moment or so in silence, and then said, "Well, perhaps so; an unhappy love may not permanently affect our after-destinies, still it colours our after-thoughts. It is strange that throughout my long and various existence I should have seen only one woman whom I could have wooed as my wife — one woman in whose presence I felt as if I were born for her and she for me."

"May I ask you what was her peculiar charm in your eyes; or, if you permit me to ask, can you explain it?"

"No doubt," answered Tracey, "much must be ascribed to the character of her beauty, which realised the type I had formed to myself from boyhood of womanly loveliness in form and face, and much also to a mind with which a man, however cultivated, could hold equal commune. But to me her predominating attraction was in a simple, unassuming nobleness of sentiment — a truthful, loyal, devoted, self-sacrificing nature. In her society I felt myself purified, exalted, as if in the presence of an angel. But enough of this. I am resigned to my loss, and have long since hung my votive tablet in the shrine of 'Time the Consoler.'"

"Forgive me if I am intrusive; but did she know that you loved her?"

"I cannot say; probably most women discover if

they are loved; but I rejoice to think that I never told her so."

"Would she have rejected you if you had?"

"Yes, unhesitatingly; her word was plighted to another. And though she would not, for the man to whom she had betrothed herself, have left her father alone in poverty and exile, she would never have married any one else."

"You believe, then, that she loved your rival with a heart that could not change?"

Tracey did not immediately reply. At last he said, "I believe this — that when scarcely out of girlhood, she considered herself engaged to be one man's wife, or for ever single. And if, in the course of time, and in length of absence, she could have detected in her heart the growth of a single thought unfaithful to her troth, she would have plucked it forth and cast it from her as firmly as if already a wedded wife, with her husband's honour in her charge. She was one of those women with whom man's trust is for ever safe, and to whom a love at variance with plighted troth is an impossibility. So, she lives in my thoughts still, as I saw her last, five-and-twenty years ago, unalterable in her youth and beauty. And I have been as true to her hallowed remembrance as she was true to her maiden vows. May I never see her again on earth! Her or her likeness I may find amid the stars. No," he added, in a lighter and cheerier tone — "no; I do not think that my actual destinies, my ways of life here below, have been affected by her loss. Had I won her, I can scarcely conceive that I should have become more tempted to ambition or less enamoured of home. Still, whatever leaves so deep a furrow in a man's heart cannot be meant in vain. Where the ploughshare cuts, there the seed is sown, and there later the corn will spring. In a word, I believe that everything of moment which befalls us in this life — which occasions us some great sorrow — for which, in this life, we see not the uses — has, nevertheless, its definite object, and that that object will be visible on the other side of the grave. It may seem but a barren grief in the history of a life — it may prove a fruitful joy in the history of a soul. For if nothing in this world is accident, surely all that which affects the only creature upon earth to whom immortality is announced, must have a distinct and definite purpose, often not developed till immortality begins."

Here we had entered on the wide spaces of the park. The deer and the kine were asleep on the silvered grass, or under the shade of the quiet trees. Now, as we cleared a beech-grove, we saw the lights gleaming from the windows of the house, and the moon, at her full, resting still over the peaceful house-top! Truly had Percival said, "That there are trains of thought set in motion by the stars which are dormant in the glare of the sun" — truly had he said, too, "That without such thoughts man's thinking is incomplete."

We gained the house, and, entering the library, it was pleasant to see how instinctively all rose to gather round the master. They had missed Percival's bright presence the whole day.

Some little time afterwards, when, seated next to Lady Gertrude, I was talking to her of the Grays, I observed Tracey take aside the Painter, and retire with him into the adjoining colonnade. They were not long absent. When they returned, Bourke's face, usually serious, was joyous and elated. In a few moments, with all his Irish warmth of heart, he burst forth with the announcement of the new obligations he owed to Sir Percival Tracey. "I have always said," exclaimed he, "that, give me an opening and I will find or make my way. I have the opening now; you shall see!" We all poured our congratulations upon the young enthusiast, except Henry Thornhill, and his brow was shaded and his lip quivered. Clara, watching him, curbed her own friendly words to the artist, and, drawing to her husband's side, placed her hand tenderly on his shoulder. "Pish! do leave me alone," muttered the ungracious churl.

"See," whispered Percival to me, "what a brute that fine young fellow would become if we insisted on making him happy our own way, and saving him from the chance of being shot!"

Therewith rising, he gently led away Clara, to whose soft eyes tears had rushed; and looking back to Henry, whose head was bended over a volume of 'The Wellington Despatches,' said in his ear, half-fondly, half-reproachfully, "Poor young fool! how bitterly you will repent every word, every look of unkindness to her, when — when she is no more at your side to pardon you!"

That night it was long before I slept. I pleased myself with what is now grown to me a rare amusement — viz, the laying out plans for the morrow. This holiday, with Tracey all to myself; this summer sail on the seas; this interval of golden idlesse, refined by intercourse with so serene an intelligence, and on subjects so little broached in the world of cities, fascinated my imagination; and I revolved a hundred questions it would be delightful to raise, a hundred problems it would be impossible to solve. Though my life has been a busy one, I believe that constitutionally I am one of the most indolent men alive. To lie on the grass in summer noons under breathless trees, to glide over smooth waters, and watch the still shadows on tranquil shores, is happiness to me. I need then no books — then, no companion. But if to that happiness in the mere luxury of repose, I may add another happiness of a higher nature, it is in converse with some one friend, upon subjects remote from the practical work-day world, — subjects akin less to our active thoughts than to our dream-like reveries, — subjects conjectural, speculative, fantastic, embracing not positive opinions — for opinions are things combative and disputatious — but rather those queries and guesses which start up from the farthest border-land of our reason, and lose themselves in air as we attempt to chase and seize them.

And perhaps this sort of talk, which leads to no conclusions clear enough for the uses of wisdom, is the more alluring to me, because it is very seldom to be indulged. I carefully separate from the business of life all which belong to the visionary realm of speculative conjecture. From the world of action I hold it imperatively safe to banish the ideas which exhibit the cloudland of metaphysical doubts and mystical beliefs. In the actual world let me see by the same broad sun that gives light to all men; it is only in the world of reverie that I amuse myself with the sport of the dark lantern, letting its ray shoot before me into the gloom, and caring not if, in its illusive light, the thorn-tree, in my path take the aspect of a ghost. I shall notice the thorn-tree all the better, distinguish more clearly its shape, when I pass by it the next day under the sun, for the impression it made on my fancy seen first by the gleam of the dark lantern. Now, Tracey is one of the very few highly-educated men it has been my lot to know, with whom one can safely mount in rudderless balloons, drifting wind-tossed after those ideas which are the phantoms of Reverie, and wander, ghost-like, out of castles in the air. And my mind found a playfellow in his, where, in other men's minds, as richly cultured, it found only companions or competitors in task-work.

Towards dawn, I fell asleep, and dreamt that I was a child once more, gathering bluebells and chasing dragonflies amid murmuring water-reeds. The next day I came down late; all had done breakfast. The Painter was already gone; the Librarian had retired into his den. Henry Thornhill was walking by himself to and fro, in front of the window, with folded arms and downcast brow. Percival was seated apart writing letters. Clara was at work, stealing every now and then a mournful glance towards Henry. Lady Gertrude, punctiliously keeping her place by the tea-urn, filled my cup, and pointed to a heap of letters formidably ranged before my plate. I glanced anxiously and rapidly over these unwelcomed epistles. Thank heaven, nothing to take me back to London! My political correspondent informed me, by a hasty line, that the dreaded motion which stood first on the parliamentary paper for that day would in all probability be postponed, agreeably to the request of the Government. The mover of it had not, however, given a positive answer; he would do so in the course of the night (last night); and there was little doubt that, as a professed supporter of the Government, he would yield to the request that had been made to him.

So, after I had finished my abstemious breakfast, I took Percival aside and told him that I considered myself free to prolong my stay, and asked him, in a whisper, if he had yet received the official letter he expected, announcing young Thornhill's exchange and promotion.

"Yes," said he, "and I only waited for you to announce its contents to poor Henry; for I wish you to tell me whether you think the news will make him as happy as yesterday he thought it would."

Tracey and I then went out, and joined Henry in his walk. The young man turned round on us an impatient countenance.

"So we have lost Bourke," said Tracey. "I hope he will return to England with the reputation he goes forth to seek."

"Ay," said Henry, "Bourke is a lucky dog to have found, in one who is not related to him, so warm and so true a friend."

"Every dog, lucky or unlucky, has his day," said Percival, gravely.

"Every dog except a house-dog," returned Henry. "A house-dog is thought only fit for a chain and a kennel."

"'Ah, happy if his happiness he knew!'" replied Tracey. "But I own that liberty compensates for the loss of a warm litter and a good dinner. Away from the kennel and off with the chain! Read this letter, and accept my congratulations — *Major* Thornhill!"

The young man started; the colour rushed to his cheeks; he glanced hastily over the letter held out to him; dropped it; caught his kinsman's hand, and, pressing it to his heart, exclaimed, "Oh, sir, thanks, thanks! So then, all the while I was accusing you of obstructing my career you were quietly promoting it. How can you forgive me my petulance, my ingratitude?"

"Tut," said Percival, kindly, "the best-tempered man is sometimes cross in his cups; and nothing, perhaps, more irritates a young brain than to get drunk on the love of glory."

At the word glory the soldier's crest rose, his eye flashed fire, his whole aspect changed, it became lofty and noble. Suddenly his eye caught sight of Clara, who had stepped out of the window, and stood gazing on him. His head dropped, tears rushed to his eyes, and with a quivering, broken voice, he muttered, "Poor Clara — my wife, my darling! Oh, Sir Percival, truly you said how bitterly I should repent every unkind word and look. Ah, they will haunt me!"

"Put aside regrets now. Go and break the news to your wife: support, comfort her; you alone can. I have not dared to tell her."

Henry sighed, and went, no longer joyous, but with slow step and paling cheek, to the place where Clara stood. We saw him bend over the hand she held out to him, kiss it humbly, and then, passing his arm round her waist, he drew her away into the farther recesses of the garden, and both disappeared from our eyes.

"No," said I, "he is not happy; like us all, he finds

that things coveted have no longer the same charm when they are things possessed. Clara is avenged already. But you have done wisely. Let him succeed or let him fail, you have removed from Clara her only rival. If you had debarred him from honour, you would have estranged him from love. Now you have bound him to Clara for life. She has ceased to be an obstacle to his dreams, and henceforth she herself will be the dream which his waking life will sigh to regain."

"Heaven grant he may come back with both his legs and both his arms; and, perhaps, with a bit of ribbon or five shillings' worth of silver on his breast!" said Percival, trying hard to be lively. "Of all my kinsmen, I think I like him the best. He is rough as the east wind, but honest as the day. Heigho! they will both leave us in an hour or two. Clara's voice is so sweet; I wonder when she will sing again! What a blank the place will seem without those two young faces! As soon as they are gone, we two will be off. Aunt Gertrude does not like Bellevue, and will pay a visit for a few days to a cousin of hers on the other side of the county. I must send on before to let the housekeeper at Bellevue prepare for our coming. Meanwhile, pardon me if I leave you — perhaps you have letters to write; if so, despatch them."

I was in no humour for writing letters, but when Percival left me I strolled from the house into the garden, and, reclining there on a bench opposite one of the fountains, enjoyed the calm beauty of the summer morning. Time slipped by. Every now and then I caught sight of Henry and Clara among the lilacs in one of the distant walks, his arm still round her waist, her head leaning on his shoulder. At length they went into the house, doubtless to prepare for their departure.

I thought of the wild folly with which youth casts away the substance of happiness to seize at the shadow which breaks on the wave that mirrors it; wiser and happier surely the tranquil choice of Gray, though with gifts and faculties far beyond those of the young man who mistook the desire of fame for the power to win it. And then my thoughts settling back on myself, I became conscious of a certain melancholy. How poor and niggard compared with my early hopes had been my ultimate results! How questioned, grudged, and litigated, my right of title to every inch of ground that my thought had discovered or my toils had cultivated! What motive power in me had, from boyhood to the verge of age, urged me on "to scorn delight and love laborious days"? Whatever the motive power once had been, I could no longer trace it. If vanity — of which, doubtless, in youth I had my human share — I had long since grown rather too callous than too sensitive to that love of approbation in which vanity consists. I was stung by no penury of fortune, influenced by no feverish thirst for a name that should outlive my grave, fooled by no hope of the rewards which goad on ambition. I had reached the age when Hope weighs her anchor and steers forth so far that her amplest sail seems but a silvery speck on the last line of the horizon. Certainly I flattered myself that my purposes linked my toils to some slight service to mankind; that in graver efforts I was asserting opinions in the value of which to human interests I sincerely believed, and in lighter aims venting thoughts and releasing fancies which might add to the culture of the world — not, indeed, fruitful harvests, but at least some lowly flowers. But though such intent might be within my mind, could I tell how far I unconsciously exaggerated its earnestness? — still less could I tell how far the intent was dignified by success. "Have I done aught for which mankind would be the worse were it swept into nothingness to-morrow?" — is a question which many a grand and fertile genius may, in its true humility, address mournfully to itself. It is but a negative praise, though it has been recorded as a high one, to leave

"No line which, dying, we would wish to blot."

If that be all, as well leave no line at all. He has written in vain who does not bequeath lines that, if blotted, would be a loss to that treasure-house of mind which is the everlasting possession of the world. Who, yet living, can even presume to guess if he shall do this? Not till at least a century after his brain and his hand are dust can even critics begin to form a rational conjecture of an author's or a statesman's uses to his kind. Was it, then, as Gray had implied, merely the force of habit which kept me in movement? if so, was it a habit worth all the sacrifice it cost? Thus meditating, I forgot that if all men reasoned thus and acted according to such reasoning, the earth would have no intermediate human dwellers between the hewers and diggers, and the idlers, born to consume the fruits which they do not plant. Farewell, then, to all the embellishments and splendours by which civilised man breathes his mind and his soul into nature. For it is not only the genius of rarest intellects which adorns and aggrandises social states, but the aspirations and the efforts of thousands and millions, all towards the advance and uplifting and beautifying of the integral, universal state, by the energies native to each. Where would be the world fit for Traceys and Grays to dwell in, if all men philosophised like the Traceys and the Grays? Where all the gracious arts, all the generous rivalries of mind, that deck and animate the bright calm of peace? Where all the devotion, heroism, self-sacrifice in a common cause, that exalt humanity even amidst the rage and deformities of war, if, throughout well-ordered, close-welded states, there ran not electrically, from breast to breast, that love of honour which is a part of man's sense of beauty, or that instinct towards utility which, even more than the genius too exceptional to be classed among the normal regulations of social law, creates the marvels of mortal progress? Not, however, I say, did I then address to myself these healthful and manly questions. I felt only that I repined, and looked with mournful and wearied eyes along an agitated, painful, laborious past. Rousing myself with an effort from these embittered contemplations, the charm of the external nature insensibly refreshed and gladdened me. I inhaled the balm of an air sweet with flowers, felt the joy of the summer sun, from which all life around seemed drawing visible happiness, and said to myself gaily, "At least to-day is mine — this blissful sunlit day —

'Nimium breves
Flores amœnæ ferre jube rosae,
Dum res et ætas et sororum,
Fila trium patiuntur atra!'"

So murmuring, I rose as from a dream, and saw before

me a strange figure -— a figure, uncouth, sinister, ominous as the evil genius that startled Brutus on the eve of Philippi. I knew by an unmistakable instinct that that figure *was* an evil genius.

"Do you want me? Who and what are you?" I asked, falteringly.

"Please your honour, I come express from the N— Station. A telegram."

I opened the scrap of paper extended to me, and read these words, —

"O— positively brings on his motion. Announced it last night too late for post. Division certain — probably before dinner. Every vote wanted. Come directly."

Said the Express with a cruel glee, as I dropped the paper, "Sir, the station-master also received a telegram to send over a fly. I have brought one; only just in time to catch the half-past twelve o'clock; no other train till six. You had best be quick, sir."

No help for it. I hurried back to the house, bade my servant follow by the next train with my portmanteau — no moments left to wait for packing; found Tracey in his quiet study — put the telegram into his hands. "You see my excuse — adieu!"

"Does this motion, then, interest you so much? Do you mean to speak on it?"

"No, but it must not be carried. Every vote against it is of consequence. Besides, I have promised to vote, and cannot stay away with honour."

"Honour! That settles it. I must go to Bellevue alone; or shall I take Caleb and make him teach me Hebrew? But surely you will join me to-morrow, or the next day?"

"Yes, if I can. But heavens!" (glancing at the clock) — "not half an hour to reach the station — six miles off. Kindest regards to Lady Gertrude — poor Clara — Henry — and all. Heaven bless you!"

I am in the fly — I am off. I gain the station just in time for the train — arrive at the House of Commons in more than time as to a vote, for the debate not only lasted all that night, but was adjourned till the next week, and lasted the greater part of that, when it was withdrawn, and — no vote at all!

But I could not then return to Tracey. Every man accustomed to business in London knows how, once there, hour after hour, arises a something that will not allow him to depart. When at length freed, I knew Tracey would no longer need my companionship — his Swedish philosopher was then with him. They were deep in scientific mysteries, on which, as I could throw no light, I should be but a profane intruder. Besides, I was then summoned to my own country place, and had there to receive my own guests, long pre-engaged. So passed the rest of the summer; in the autumn I went abroad, and have never visited the Castle of Indolence since those golden days. In truth I resisted a frequent and a haunting desire to do so. I felt that a second and a longer sojourn in that serene but relaxing atmosphere might unnerve me for the work which I had imposed on myself, and sought to persuade my tempted conscience was an inexorable duty. Experience had taught me that in the sight of that intellectual repose, so calm and so dreamily happy, my mind became unsettled, and nourished seeds that might ripen to discontent of the lot I had chosen for myself. So then, *sicut meus est mos*, I seized a consolation for the loss of enjoyments that I may not act anew, by living them over again in fancy and remembrance: I give to my record the title of "Motive Power," though it contains much episodical to that thesis, and though it rather sports around the subject so indicated than subjects it to strict analysis. But I here take for myself the excuse I have elsewhere made for Montaigne, in his loose observance of the connection between the matter and the titles of his essays.

I must leave it to the reader to blame or acquit me for having admitted so many lengthy descriptions, so many digressive turns and shifts of thought and sentiment, through which, as through a labyrinth, he winds his way, with steps often checked and often retrogressive, still, sooner or later, creeping on to the heart of the maze. There I leave him to find the way out. Labyrinths have no interest if we give the clue to them.

ESSAY XXIII.

ON CERTAIN PRINCIPLES OF ART IN WORKS OF IMAGINATION.

ON CERTAIN PRINCIPLES OF ART IN WORKS OF IMAGINATION.

Every description of literature has its appropriate art. This truth is immediately acknowledged in works of imagination. We speak, in familiar phrase, of the Dramatic Art, or the Art of Poetry. But the presence of art is less generally recognised in works addressed to the reason. Nevertheless, art has its place in a treatise on political economy, or in a table of statistics. For in all subjects, however rigidly confined to abstract principles or positive facts, the principles and facts cannot be thrown together pell-mell; they require an artistic arrangement. Expression itself is an art. So that even works of pure science cannot dispense with art, because they cannot dispense with expression. What is called method in Science is the art by which Science makes itself intelligible. There is exquisite art in the arrangement of a problem in Euclid. If a man have a general knowledge of the fact that all lines drawn from the centre of a circle to the circumference are equal, but has never read the Third Book of Euclid, let him attempt to show, in his own way, that lines equally distant from the centre are equal to one another, and then compare his attempt with Euclid's theorem (Book III. Prop. 14), and he will at once acknowledge the master's art of demonstration. Pascal is said to have divined, by the force of his own genius, so large a number of Euclid's propositions, as to appear almost miraculous to his admirers, and wholly incredible to his aspersers. Yet that number did not exceed eighteen. In fact, art and science have their meeting-point in method.

And though Kant applies the word *genius* (*ingenium*) strictly to the cultivators of Art, refusing to extend it to the cultivators of Science, yet the more we examine the highest orders of intellect, whether devoted to science, to art, or even to action, the more clearly we shall observe the presence of a faculty common to all such orders of intellect, because essential to completion in each — a faculty which seems so far intuitive or innate (*ingenium*) that, though study and practice perfect it, they do not suffice to bestow — viz., the faculty of grouping into order and symmetrical form, ideas in themselves scattered and dissimilar. This is the faculty of Method; and though every one who possesses it is not necessarily a great man, yet every great man must possess it in a very superior degree, whether he be a poet, a philosopher, a statesman, a general; for every great man exhibits the talent of organisation or construction, whether it be in a poem, a philosophical system, a policy, or a strategy. And without method there is no organisation nor construction. But in art, method is less perceptible than in science, and in familiar language usually receives some other name. Nevertheless, we include the meaning when we speak of the composition of a picture, the arrangement of an oration, the plan of a poem. Art employing method for the symmetrical formation of beauty, as science employs it for the logical exposition of truth: but the mechanical process is, in the last, ever kept visibly distinct; while, in the first, it escapes from sight amid the shows of colour and the curves of grace. And though, as I have said, Art enters into all works, whether addressed to the reason or to the imagination, those addressed to the imagination are works of Art *par emphasis*, for they require much more than the elementary principles which Art has in common with Science. The two part company with each other almost as soon as they meet on that ground of Method which is common to both, — Science ever seeking, through all forms of the Ideal, to realise the Positive — Art, from all forms of the Positive, ever seeking to extract the ideal. The *beau ideal* is not in the reason — its only existence is in the imagination. To create in the reader's mind images which do not exist in the world, and leave them there, imperishable as the memories of friends with whom he has lived, and of scenes in which he has had his home, obviously necessitates a much ampler and much subtler Art than that which is required to make a positive fact clear to the comprehension. The highest quality of Art, as applied to literature, is therefore called "the Creative." Nor do I attach any importance to the cavil of some over-ingenious critics, who have denied that genius in reality *creates;* inasmuch as the forms it presents are only new combinations of ideas already existent. New combinations are, to all plain intents and purposes, creations. It is not in the power of man to create something out of nothing. And though the Deity no doubt can do so now — as those who acknowledge that the Divine Creator preceded all created things, must suppose that He did before there was even a Chaos —

yet, so far as it is vouchsafed to us to trace Him through Nature, all that we see in created Nature is combined out of what before existed. Art, therefore, may be said to create when it combines existent details into new wholes. No man can say that the watch which lies before me, or the table on which I write, were not created (that is, made) by the watch-maker or cabinetmaker, because the materials which compose a watch or a table have been on the earth, so far as we know of it, since the earth was a world fit for men to dwell in. Therefore, neither in Nature nor in Art can it be truly said that that power is not creative which brings into the world a new form, though all which compose a form, as all which compose a flower, a tree, a mite, an elephant, a man, are, if taken in detail, as old as the gases in the air we breathe, or the elements of the earth we tread. But the Creative Faculty in Art requires a higher power than it asks in Nature; for Nature may create things without life and mind — Nature may create dust and stones which have no other life and mind than are possessed by the animalcules that inhabit them. But the moment Art creates, it puts into its creations life and intellect; and it is only in proportion as the life thus bestowed endures beyond the life of man, and the intellect thus expressed exceeds that which millions of men can embody in one form, that we acknowledge a really great work of Art — that we say of the Artist, centuries after he is dead, "He was indeed a Poet," that is, a creator: He has created a form of life which the world did not know before, and breathed into that form a spirit which preserves it from the decay to which all of man himself except his soul is subjected. Achilles is killed by Paris; Homer re-creates Achilles — and the Achilles of Homer is alive to-day.

By the common consent of all educated nations, the highest order of Art in Literature is Poetic Narrative, whether in the form of the Epic or that of the Drama. We are, therefore, compelled to allow that the objective faculty — which is the imperative essential of excellence in either of these two summits of the 'forked Parnassus' — attains to a sublimer reach of art than the subjective — that is, in order to make my scholastic adjectives familiar to common apprehension, the artist who reflects vividly and truthfully, in the impartial mirror of his mind, other circumstances, other lives, other characters than his own, belongs to a higher order than he who, subjecting all that he contemplates to his own idiosyncrasy, reflects but himself in his various images of nature and mankind. We admit this when we come to examples. We admit that Homer is of a higher order of art than Sappho; that Shakespeare's 'Macbeth' is of a higher order of art than Shakespeare's Sonnets; 'Macbeth' being purely objective — the Sonnets being perhaps the most subjective poems which the Elizabethan age can exhibit.

But it is not his choice of the highest order of art that makes a great artist. If one man says "I will write an epic," and writes but a mediocre epic, and another man says "I will write a song," and writes an admirable song — the man who writes what is admirable is superior to him who writes what is mediocre. There is no doubt that Horace is inferior to Homer — so inferior that we cannot apportion the difference. The one is epic, the other lyrical. But there is no doubt also that Horace is incalculably superior to Tryphiodorus or Sir Richard Blackmore, though they are epical and he is lyrical. In a word, it is perfectly obvious, that in proportion to the height of the art attempted must be the powers of the artist, so that there is the requisite harmony between his subject and his genius; and that he who commands a signal success in one of the less elevated spheres of art must be considered a greater artist than he who obtains but indifferent success in the most arduous.

Nevertheless, Narrative necessitates so high a stretch of imagination, and so wide a range of intellect, that it will always obtain, if tolerably well told, a precedence of immediate popularity over the most exquisite productions of an inferior order of the solid and staple qualities of imagination — so much so that, even where the first has resort to what may be called the brick and mortar of prose, as compared with the ivory, marble, and cedar of verse, a really great work of Narrative in prose will generally obtain a wider audience, even among the most fastidious readers, than poems, however good, in which the imagination is less creative, and the author rather describes or moralises over what is, than invents and vivifies what never existed. The advantage of the verse lies in its durability. Prose, when appealing to the imagination, has not the same characteristics of enduring longevity as verse; — first and chiefly, it is not so easily remembered. Who remembers twenty lines in 'Ivanhoe'? Who does not remember twenty lines in the 'Deserted Village'? Verse chains a closer and more minute survey to all beauties of thought expressed by it than prose, however elaborately completed, can do. And that survey is carried on and perpetuated by successive generations.

So that in a great prose fiction, one hundred years after its date, there are innumerable beauties of thought and fancy which lie wholly unobserved; and in a poem, also surveyed one hundred years after its publication, there is probably not a single beauty undetected. This holds even in the most popular and imperishable prose fictions, read at a time of life when our memory is most tenacious, such as 'Don Quixote' or 'Robinson Crusoe', 'Gulliver's Travels' or the 'Arabian Nights.' We retain, indeed, a lively impression of the pleasure derived from the perusal of those masterpieces; of the salient incidents in story; the broad strokes of character, wit, or fancy; but quotations of striking passages do not rise to our lips as do the verses of poets immeasurably inferior, in the grand creative gifts of Poetry, to those fictionists of prose. And hence the Verse Poet is a more intimate companion throughout time than the Prose Poet can hope to be. In our moments of aspiration or of despondency, his musical thoughts well up from our remembrance. By a couple of lines he kindles the ambition of our boyhood, or soothes into calm the melancholy contemplations of our age.

Cæteris paribus, there can be no doubt of the advantage of verse over prose in all works of the imagination. But an artist does not select his own department of art with deliberate calculation of the best chances of posthumous renown. His choice is determined partly by his own organisation, and partly also by the circumstances of his time. For these last may control and tyrannise over his own more special bias. For instance, in our country, at present, it is scarcely an exaggeration to say that there is no tragic drama—

scarcely any living drama at all; whether from the
want of competent actors, or from some disposition on
the part of our public and our critics, not to accord to
a successful drama the rank which it holds in other
nations, and once held in this, I do not care to examine;
but the fact itself is so clear, that the Drama, though
in reality it is the highest order of poem, with the exception of the Epic, seems to have wholly dropped out
of our consideration as belonging to any form of poetry
whatsoever. If an Englishman were asked by a foreigner
to name even the minor poets of his country who have
achieved reputation since the death of Lord Byron, it
would not occur to him to name Sheridan Knowles —
though perhaps no poet since Shakespeare has written
so many successful dramas; nay, if he were asked to
quote the principal poets whom England has produced,
I doubt very much whether Ben Jonson, Beaumont,
Fletcher, or Otway, would occur to his mind as readily
as Collins or Cowper. We have forgotten, in short,
somehow or other, except in the single instance of
Shakespeare, that dramas in verse are poems, and that
where we have a great dramatist, who can hold the
hearts of an audience spell-bound, we have a poet
immeasurably superior, in all the great qualities of
poetry, to three-fourths of the lyrical, and still more
of the didactic versifiers who, lettered and bound as
British poets, occupy so showy a range on our shelves.
It is not thus anywhere except in our country. Ask
a Frenchman who are the greatest poets of France, he
names her dramatists immediately — Corneille, Racine,
Molière. Ask a German, he names Goethe and Schiller; and if you inquire which of the works of those
great masters in all variety of song he considers their

greatest poems, he at once names their dramas. But to return; with us, therefore, the circumstances of the time would divert an author, whose natural bias might otherwise lead him towards dramatic composition, from a career so discouraged; and as the largest emoluments and the loudest reputation are at this time bestowed upon prose fiction, so he who would otherwise have been a dramatist becomes a novelist. I speak here, indeed, from some personal experience, for I can remember well, that when Mr. Macready undertook the management of one of those two great national theatres, which are now lost to the national drama, many literary men turned their thoughts towards writing for the stage, sure that in Mr. Macready they could find an actor to embody their conceptions; a critic who could not only appreciate, but advise and guide; and a gentleman with whom a man of letters could establish frank and pleasant understanding. But when Mr. Macready withdrew from an experiment probably requiring more capital than he deemed it prudent to risk in the mere rental of a theatre, which in other countries would be defrayed by the State, the literary flow towards the drama again ebbed back, and many a play, felicitously begun, remains to this day a fragment in the limbo of neglected pigeon-holes.

The circumstances of the time, therefore, though they do not arrest the steps of genius, alter its direction. Those departments of art in which the doors are the most liberally thrown open, will necessarily most attract the throng of artists; and it is the more natural that there should be a rush toward novel-writing, because no man and no woman who can scribble at all, ever doubt that they can scribble a novel. Certainly,

it seems that the kinds of writing most difficult to
write well, are the easiest to write ill. Where are the
little children who cannot write what they call poetry,
or the big children who cannot write what they call
novels?

"Scribimus indocti doctique poemata passim,"

says Horace of the writers of his day. In our day the
saying applies in most force to that class of *poemata*
which pretends to narrate the epic of life in the form
of prose. For the *docti* as well as the *indocti* — men
the most learned in all but the art of novel-writing
— write novels, no less than the most ignorant; and
often with no better success. One gentleman wishing
to treat us with a sermon, puts it into a novel; another
gentleman, whose taste is for political disquisition, puts
it into a novel; High Church and Low Church and No
Church at all, Tories and Radicals, and speculators on
Utopia, fancy that they condescend to adapt truth to
the ordinary understanding, when they thrust into a
novel that with which a novel has no more to do than
it has with astronomy. Certainly it is in the power of
any one to write a book in three volumes, divide it
into chapters, and call it a novel; but those processes
no more make the work a novel, than they make it a
History of China. We thus see many clever books by
very clever writers, which, regarded as novels, are de-
testable. They are written without the slightest study
of the art of narrative, and without the slightest natural gift to divine it. Those critics who, in modern
times, have the most thoughtfully analysed the laws of
æsthetic beauty, concur in maintaining that the real
truthfulness of all works of imagination — sculpture,

painting, written fiction — is so purely in the imagination, *that the artist never seeks to represent the positive truth, but the idealized image of a truth.* As HEGEL well observes, "that which exists in nature is a something purely individual and particular. Art, on the contrary, is essentially destined to manifest the general." A fiction, therefore, which is designed to inculcate an object wholly alien to the imagination, sins against the first law of art; and if a writer of fiction narrow his scope to particulars so positive as polemical controversy in matters ecclesiastical, political, or moral, his work may or not be an able treatise, but it must be a very poor novel.

Religion and politics are not, indeed, banished from works of imagination; but to be artistically treated, they must be of the most general and the least sectarian description. In the record of the Fall of Man, for instance, Milton takes the most general belief in which all Christian nations concur, — nay, in which nations not Christian still acknowledge a myth of reverential interest. Or, again, to descend from the highest rank of poetry to a third rank in novel-writing; when Mr. Ward, in his charming story of 'Tremaine,' makes his very plot consist in the conversion of an infidel to a belief in the immortality of the soul, he does not depart from the artistic principle of dealing, not with particulars, but with generals. Had he exceeded the point at which he very wisely and skilfully stops, and pushed his argument beyond the doctrine on which all theologians concur, into questions on which they dispute, he would have lost sight of art altogether. So in politics; the general propositions from which politics start — the value of liberty, order, civilisation, &c. — are not only within the competent range of imaginative fiction, but form some of its loftiest subjects; but descend lower into the practical questions that divide the passions of a day, and you only waste all the complicated machinery of fiction, to do what you could do much better in a party pamphlet. For, in fact, as the same fine critic, whom I have previously quoted, says, with admirable eloquence: —

"Man, enclosed on all sides in the limits of the finite, and aspiring to get beyond them, turns his looks towards a superior sphere, more pure and more true, where all the oppositions and contradictions of the finite disappear — where his intellectual liberty, spreading its wings, without obstacles and without limits, attains to its supreme end. This region is that of art, and its reality is the ideal. The necessity of the beau-idéal in art is derived from the imperfections of the real. The mission of art is to represent, under sensible forms, the free development of life, and especially of mind."

What is herein said of Art more especially applies to the art of narrative fiction, whether it take the form of verse or prose. For, when we come to that realm of fiction which, whether in verse or prose, is rendered most alluring to us, either by the fashion of our time or the genius of the artist, it is with a desire to escape, for the moment, out of this hard and narrow positive world in which we live; to forget, for a brief holiday, disputes between High Church and Low Church, Tories and Radicals — in fine, to lose sight of *particulars* in the contemplation of *general* truths. We can have our real life, in all its harsh outlines, whenever we please; we do not want to see that real life, but its ideal image, in the fable-land of art. There is another error common enough in second-rate novelists, and made still more common because it is praised by ordinary critics — viz., an attempt at the exact imitation of what is called Nature. One writer will thus draw a character in fiction as minutely as he can, from some individual he has met in life; another perplexes us with the precise *patois* of provincial mechanics — not as a mere relief to the substance of a dialogue, but as a prevalent part of it. Now I hold all this to be thoroughly antagonistic to art in fiction — it is the relinquishment of generals for the servile copy of particulars. .... It cannot be too often repeated that art is *not* the imitation of nature: it is only in the very lowest degree of poetry — viz., the Descriptive — that the imitation of nature can be considered an artistic end. Even there, the true poet brings forth from nature more than nature says to the common ear or reveals to the common eye. The strict imitation of nature has always in it a something trite and mean: a man who mimics the cackle of the goose or the squeak of a pig, so truthfully, that for the moment he deceives us, attains but a praise that debases him. Nor this because there is something in the cackle of the goose, and the squeak of the pig, that in itself has a mean association; for as Kant says truly, "Even a man's exact imitation of the song of the nightingale displeases us when we discover that it is a mimicry, and not the nightingale." Art does not imitate nature, but it founds itself on the study of nature — takes from nature the selections which best accord with its own intention, and then bestows on them that which nature does not possess — viz., *the mind and the soul of man.*

Just as he is but a Chinese kind of painter, who seeks to give us, in exact prosaic detail, every leaf in a tree, which, if we want to see only a tree, we could see in a field much better than in a picture; so he is but a prosaic and mechanical pretender to imagination who takes a man out of real life, gives us his photograph, and says, "I have copied nature." If I want to see that kind of man I could see him better in Oxford Street than in a novel. The great artist deals with large generalities, broad types of life and character; and though he may take flesh and blood for his model, he throws into the expression of the figure a something which elevates the model into an idealised image. A porter sate to Correggio for the representation of a saint; but Correggio so painted the porter, that the porter, on the canvas, was lost in the saint.

Some critics have contended that the delineation of character artistically — viz., through the selection of broad generalities in the complex nature of mankind, rather than in the observation of particulars by the portraiture of an individual — fails of the verisimilitude and reality — of the flesh-and-blood likeness to humanity — which all vivid delineation of human character necessarily requires. But this objection is sufficiently confuted by a reference to the most sovereign masterpieces of imaginative literature. The principal characters in Homer — viz., Achilles, Hector, Ulysses, Nestor, Paris, Thersites, &c. — are so remarkably the types of large and enduring generalities in human character, that, in spite of all changes of time and manners, we still classify and designate individuals under those antique representative names. We call such or such a man the Ulysses, or Nestor, or Achilles, or Thersites, of his class or epoch. Virgil, on the contrary, has, in Æneas, but a feeble shadow reflected from no bodily form with which we are familiar, precisely because Æneas is not a type of any large and lasting generality in human character, but a poetised and half-allegorical *silhouette* of Augustus. There is, indeed, an antagonistic difference between fictitious character and biographical character. In biography, truth must be sought in the preference of particulars to generals; in imaginative creations, truth is found in the preference of generals to particulars. We recognise this distinction more immediately with respect to the former. In biography, and indeed in genuine history, character appears faithful and vivid in proportion as it stands clear from all æsthetic purposes in the mind of the delineator. The moment the biographer or historian seeks to drape his personages in the poetic mantle, to subject their lives and actions to the poetic or idealising process, we are immediately and rightly seized with distrust of his accuracy. When he would dramatise his characters into types, they are unfaithful as likenesses. In like manner, if we carefully examine, we shall see that when the Poet takes on himself the task of the Biographer, and seeks to give minute representations of living individuals, his characters become conventional — only partially accurate — the accuracy being sought by exaggerating trivial peculiarities into salient attributes, rather than by the patient exposition of the concrete qualities which constitute the interior nature of living men. Satire or eulogy obtrudes itself unconsciously to the artist, and mars the catholic and enduring truthfulness which, in works of imagination, belongs exclusively to the invention of original images for æsthetic ends.

Goethe, treating of the drama, has said, that "to be theatrical a piece must be symbolical; that is to say, every action must have an importance of its own, and it must tend to one more important still." It is still more important, for dramatic effect, that the *dramatis personæ* should embody attributes of passion, humour, sentiment, character, with which large miscellaneous audiences can establish sympathy; and sympathy can be only established by such a recognition of a something familiar to our own natures, or to our conception of our natures, as will allure us to transport ourselves for the moment into the place of those who are passing through events which are not familiar to our actual experience. None of us have gone through the events which form the action of 'Othello' or 'Phèdre;' but most of us recognise in our natures, or our conceptions of our natures, sufficient elements for ardent love or agonising jealousy, to establish a sympathy with the agencies by which, in 'Othello' and 'Phèdre,' those passions are expressed. Thus, the more forcibly the characters interest the generalities of mankind which compose an audience, the more truthfully they must represent what such generalities of mankind have in common — in short, the more they will be types, and the less they will be portraits. Some critics have supposed that, in the delineation of types, the artist would fall into the frigid error of representing mere philosophical abstractions. This, however, is a mistake which the poet who comprehends and acts upon the first principle of his art — viz., the preference of **generals** to particulars — will be the less likely to commit, in proportion as such generals are vivified into types of humanity. For he is not seeking to personate **allegorically** a passion; but to show the effects of the passion upon certain given forms of character under certain given situations: And he secures the individuality required, and avoids the lifeless pedantry of an allegorised abstraction, by reconciling passion, character, and situation with each other; so that it is always a living being in whom we sympathise. And the rarer and more unfamiliar the situation of life in which the poet places his imagined character, the more in that character itself we must recognise relations akin to our own flesh and blood, in order to feel interest in its fate. Thus, in the hands of great masters of fiction, whether dramatists or novelists, we become unconsciously reconciled, not only to unfamiliar, but to improbable, nay, to impossible situations, by recognising some marvellous truthfulness to human nature in the thoughts, feelings, and actions of the character represented, granting that such a character *could* be placed in such a situation. The finest of Shakespeare's imaginary characters are essentially typical. No one could suppose that the poet was copying from individuals of his acquaintance in the delineations of Hamlet, Macbeth, Othello, Iago, Angelo, Romeo. They are as remote from portraiture as are the conceptions of Caliban and Ariel. In fine, the distinctive excellence of Shakespeare's highest characters is that, while they embody truths the most subtle, delicate, and refining in the life and organisation of men, those truths are so assorted as to combine with the elements which humanity has most in common. And it is obvious to any reader of ordinary reflection, that this could not be effected if the characters themselves, despite all that is peculiar to each, were not, on the whole, typical of broad and popular divisions in the human family.

Turning to prose fiction, if we look to the greatest

novel which Europe has yet produced (meaning by the word novel a representation of familiar civilised life) — viz., 'Gil Blas' — we find the characters therein are vivid and substantial, capable of daily application to the life around us, in proportion as they are types and not portraits — such as Ambrose Lamela, Fabricio, the Archbishop of Grenada, &c.; and the characters that really fail of truth and completion are those which were intended to be portraits of individuals — such as Olivarez, the Duke de Lerma, the Infant of Spain, &c. And if it be true that, in Sangrado, Le Sage designed the portrait of the physician Hecquet (the ingenious author of the 'Système de la Trituration'), all we can say is, that the portrait is a coarse caricature of the original, and that Sangrado is a creation worthy of Le Sage's genius only where the author abandons the attempt at resemblance to an individual, and, in the freedom and sport of creative humour, involuntarily generalises attributes of character common to all professional fanatics. Again, with that masterpiece of prose romance or fantasy, 'Don Quixote,' the character of the hero, if it could be regarded as that of an individual whom Cervantes found in life, would be only an abnormal and morbid curiosity subjected to the caricature of a satirist. But regarded as a type of certain qualities which are largely diffused throughout human nature, the character is psychologically true, and artistically completed; hence we borrow the word "Quixotic" whenever we would convey the idea of that extravagant generosity of enthusiasm for the redress of human wrongs, which, even in exciting ridicule, compels admiration and conciliates love. The grandeur of the conception of 'Don Quixote' is its fidelity to a certain nobleness of sentiment, which, however latent or however modified, exists in every genuinely noble nature. And hence, perhaps, of all works of broad humour, 'Don Quixote' is that which most approximates the humorous to the side of the sublime.

The reflective spirit of our age has strongly tended towards the development of a purpose in fiction, symbolical in a much more literal sense of the word than Goethe intended to convey in the extract I have quoted on the symbolical nature of theatrical composition. Besides the interest of plot and incident, another interest is implied, more or less distinctly or more or less vaguely, which is that of the process and working out of a symbolical purpose interwoven with the popular action. Instead of appending to the fable a formal moral, a moral signification runs throughout the whole fable, but so little obtrusively, that, even at the close, it is to be divined by the reader, not explained by the author. This has been a striking characteristic of the art of our century. In the former century it was but very partially cultivated, and probably grows out of that reaction from materialism which distinguishes our age from the last. Thus — to quote the most familiar illustrations I can think of — in Goethe's novel of "Wilhelm Meister," besides the mere interest of the incidents, there is an interest in the inward signification of an artist's apprenticeship in art, of a man's apprenticeship in life. In "Transformation," by Mr. Hawthorne, the mere story of outward incident can never be properly understood, unless the reader's mind goes along with the exquisite mysticism which is symbolised by the characters. In that work, often very faulty in the execution, exceedingly grand in the conception, are typified the classical sensuous life, through Donato; the Jewish dispensation, through Miriam; the Christian dispensation, through Hilda, who looks over the ruins of Rome from her virgin chamber amidst the doves.

To our master novelists of a former age — to Defoe, Fielding, Richardson, and Smollett — this double plot, if so I may call it, was wholly unknown. Swift, indeed, apprehended it in 'Gulliver's Travels,' which I consider the greatest poem — that is, the greatest work of pure imagination and original invention — of the age in which he lived; and Johnson divined it in 'Rasselas,' which, but for the interior signification, would be the faulty and untruthful novel that Lord Macaulay has (I venture to opine, erroneously) declared it to be. Lord Macaulay censures 'Rasselas' because the Prince of Abyssinia does not talk like an Abyssinian. Now, it seems to me that a colouring faithful to the manners of Abyssinia, is a detail so trivial in reference to the object of the author of a philosophical romance, that it is more artistic to omit than to observe it. Rasselas starts at once, not from a positive but from an imagined world — he starts from the Happy Valley to be conducted (in his progress through actual life, to the great results of his search after a happiness more perfect than that of the Happy Valley) to the Catacombs. This is the interior poetical signification of the tale of 'Rasselas' — the final result of all departure from the happy land of contented ignorance is to be found at the grave. There, alone, a knowledge happier than ignorance awaits the seeker beyond the catacombs. For a moral so broad, intended for civilised readers, any attempt to suit colouring and manners to Abyssinian savages would have been, not an adherence to, but a violation of, Art. The artist here wisely disdains the particulars — he is dealing with generals. Thus Voltaire's Zadig is no more a Babylonian than Johnson's Rasselas is an Abyssinian. Voltaire's object of philosophical satire would have been perfectly lost if he had given us an accurate and antiquarian transcript of the life of the Chaldees; and, indeed, the worst parts in 'Zadig' (speaking artistically) are those in which the author does, now and then, assume a *quasi* antique Oriental air, sadly at variance with meanings essentially modern, couched in irony essentially French.

But the writer who takes this duality of purpose — who unites an interior symbolical signification with an obvious popular interest in character and incident — errs, firstly, in execution, if he render his symbolical meaning so distinct and detailed as to become obviously allegorical — unless, indeed, as in the 'Pilgrim's Progress,' it is avowedly an allegory; and secondly, he errs in artistic execution of his plan, whenever he admits a dialogue not closely bearing on one or the other of his two purposes, and whenever he fails in merging the two into an absolute unity at the end.

Now, the fault I find chiefly with novelists is their own contempt for their craft. A clever and scholarlike man enters into it with a dignified contempt. "I am not going to write," he says, "a mere novel." What, then, is he going to write? What fish's tail will he add to the horse's head? A tragic poet might as well say, "I am not going to write a mere tragedy." The first essential to success in the art you practise is respect for the art itself. Who could ever become a good shoemaker if he did not have a profound respect for the art of making shoes? There is an ideal even in the humblest mechanical craft. A shoemaker destined to excel his rivals will always have before his eye the vision of a perfect shoe, which he is always striving to realise, and never can. It was well said by Mr. Hazlitt, "That the city prentice who did not think the Lord Mayor in his gilded coach was the greatest of human beings would come to be hanged." Whatever our calling be, we can never rise in it unless we exalt, even to an exaggerated dignity, the elevation of the calling itself. We are noble peasants or noble kings just in proportion as we form a lofty estimate of the nobility that belongs to peasants or the nobility that belongs to kings.

We may despair of the novelist who does not look upon a novel as a consummate work of art — who does not apply to it, as Fielding theoretically, as Scott practically, did, the rules which belong to the highest order of imagination. Of course he may fail of his standard, but he will fail less in proportion as the height of his standard elevates his eye and nerves his sinews.

The first object of a novelist is to interest his reader; the next object is the quality of the interest. Interest in his story is essential, or he will not be read; but if the quality of the interest be not high, he will not be read a second time. And if he be not read a second time by his own contemporaries, the chance is that he will not be read once by posterity. The degree of interest is for the many — the quality of interest for the few. But the many are proverbially fickle, the few are constant. Steadfast minorities secure, at last, the success of great measures, and confirm, at last, the fame of great writings.

I have said that many who, in a healthful condition of our stage, would be dramatists, become novelists. But there are some material distinctions between the dramatic art and the narrative — distinctions as great as those between the oratorical style and the literary. Theatrical effects displease in a novel. In a novel much more than in a drama must be explained and accounted for. On the stage the actor himself interprets the author; and a look, a gesture, saves pages of writing. In a novel the author elevates his invention to a new and original story; in a drama, I hold that the author does well to take at least the broad outlines of a story already made. It is an immense advantage to him to find a tale he is to dramatise previously told, whether in a history, a legend, a romance, or in the play of another age or another land; and the more the tale be popularly familiarised to the audience, the higher will be the quality of the interest he excites. Thus, in the Greek tragedy, the story and the characters were selected from the popular myths. Thus Shakespeare takes his story either from chronicles or novels. Thus Corneille, Racine, and Voltaire take, from sources in antiquity the most familiarly known, their fables and their characters. Nor is it only an advantage to the dramatist that the audience should come to the scene somewhat prepared by previous association for the nature of the interest invoked; it is also an advantage to the dramatist that his invention

— being thus relieved from the demand on its powers in what, for the necessities of the dramatic art, is an unimportant if not erroneous direction of art — is left more free to combine the desultory materials of the borrowed story into the harmony of a progressive plot — to reconcile the actions of characters, whose existence the audience take for granted, with probable motives — and, in a word, to place the originality there where alone it is essential to the drama — viz., in the analysis of the heart, in the delineation of passion, in the artistic development of the idea and purpose which the drama illustrates, through the effects of situation and the poetry of form.

But in the narrative of prose fiction an original story is not an auxiliary or erroneous, but an essential, part of artistic invention; and even where the author takes the germ of his subject and the sketch of his more imposing characters from History, he will find that he will be wanting in warmth of interest if the tale he tells be not distinct from that of the history he presses into his service — more prominently brought forward, more minutely wrought out — and the character of the age represented, not only through the historical characters introduced, but those other and more general types of life which he will be compelled to imagine for himself. This truth is recognised at once when we call to mind such masterpieces in historical fiction as 'Ivanhoe,' 'Kenilworth,' 'Quentin Durward,' and 'I Promessi Sposi.'

In the tragic drama, however, historical subjects appear to necessitate a different treatment from that which most conduces to the interest of romantic narrative. There is a dignity in historical characters which scarcely permits them to be transferred to the stage without playing before the audience the important parts which they played in life. When they enter on the scene they excite a predominating interest, and we should not willingly see them deposed into secondary agencies in the conduct of the story. They ought not to be introduced at all, unless in fitting correspondence with our notions of the station they occupied and the influence they exercised in the actual world; and thus, whether they are made fated victims through their sufferings, or fateful influences through their power, still, in the drama, it is through them that the story moves: them the incidents affect — them the catastrophe involves — whether for their triumph or their fall.

The drama not necessitating an original fable nor imaginary characters, that which it does necessitate in selecting a historical subject is, the art of so arranging and concentrating events in history as to form a single action, terminating in a single end, wrought through progressive incidents clearly linked together. It will be seen that the dramatic treatment is, in this respect, opposed to the purely historical treatment; for in genuine history there are innumerable secondary causes tending to each marked effect, which the dramatist must wholly eliminate or set aside. He must, in short, aim at generals to the exclusion of particulars.

And thus, as his domain is the passions, he must seek a plot which admits of situations for passion, and characters in harmony with such situations. Great historical events in themselves are rarely dramatic — they are made so on the stage by the appeal to emotions with which, in private life, the audience are accustomed to sympathise. The preservation of the Republic of Venice from a conspiracy would have an interest in history from causes appealing to political reasoning, that would be wholly without interest on the stage. The dramatist, therefore, places the preservation of Venice in the struggle of a woman's heart between the conflicting passions, with which, in private life, the audience could most readily sympathise. According as Belvidera acts, as between her husband and her father, Venice will be saved or lost. This is dramatic treatment — it is not historical.

All delineations of passion involve the typical; because whoever paints a passion common to mankind presents us with a human type of that passion, varied, indeed, through the character of an individual and the situations in which he is placed; but still, in the expression of the passion itself, sufficiently germane to all in whom that passion exists, whether actively or latently, to permit the spectator to transfer himself into the place and person of him who represents it. Hence the passions of individuals, though affecting only themselves, or a very confined range of persons connected with them, command, in reality, a far wider scope in artistic treatment than the political events affecting millions in historical fact. For political events, accurately and dispassionately described, are special to the time and agents — they are traced through the logic of the reason, which only a comparative few exercise, and even the few exercise it in the calm of their closets, they do not come into the crowd of a theatre for its exercise. But the passions of love, ambition, jealousy — the conflict between opposing emotions of affection and duty — expressed in the breast of an individual, are not special, — they are universal. And before a dramatic audience the safety of a state is merged or ignored in the superior interest felt in the personation of some emotion more ardent than any state interest, and only more ardent because universal among mankind in all states and all times. If the domestic interest be the strongest of which the drama is capable, it is because it is the interest in which the largest number of human breasts can concur, and in which the poet who creates it can most escape from particulars into generals. In the emancipation of Switzerland from the Austrian yoke, history can excite our interest in the question whether William Tell ever existed — and in showing the large array of presumptive evidence against the popular story of his shooting the apple placed on his son's head. But in the drama William Tell is the personator of the Swiss liberties; and the story of the apple, in exciting the domestic interest of the relationship between father and son, is that very portion of history which the dramatic artist will the most religiously conserve, — obtaining therein one incalculable advantage for his effect — viz., that it is not his own invention, and therefore of disputable probability; but, whether fable or truth in the eyes of the historical critic, so popularly received and acknowledged as a truth, that the audience are prepared to enter into the emotions of the father, and the peril of the son.

It is, then, not in the invention of a story, nor in the creation of imaginary characters, that a dramatist proves his originality as an artist, but in the adaptation of a story, found elsewhere, to a dramatic purpose; and in the fidelity, not to historical detail, but to

10*

psychological and metaphysical truth, with which he reconciles the motives and conduct of the characters he selects from history, to the situations in which they are placed, so as to elicit for them, under all that is peculiar to their nature or their fates, the necessary degree of sympathy from emotions of which the generality of mankind are susceptible.

But to the narrator of fiction — to the story-teller — the invention of fable and of imaginary character is obviously among the legitimate conditions of his art; and a fable purely original has in him a merit which it does not possess in the tragic or comic poet.

On the other hand, the skilful mechanism of plot, though not without considerable value in the art of narrative, is much less requisite in the Novelist than in the Dramatist. Many of the greatest prose fictions are independent of plot altogether. It is only by straining the word to a meaning foreign to the sense it generally conveys, that we can recognise a plot in 'Don Quixote,' and scarcely any torture of the word can make a plot out of 'Gil Blas.' It is for this reason that the novel admits of what the drama never should admit — viz., the operation of *accident* in the conduct of the story: the villain, instead of coming to a tragic close through the inevitable sequences of the fate he has provoked, may be carried off, at the convenient time, by a stroke of apoplexy, or be run over by a railway train. Nevertheless, in artistic narrative, accident, where it affects a *dénouement*, should be very sparingly employed. Readers, as well as critics, feel it to be a blot in the story of 'Rob Roy' when the elder brothers of Rashleigh Osbaldistone are killed off by natural causes unforeseen and unprepared for in the previous train of events narrated, in order to throw Rashleigh into a position which the author found convenient for his ultimate purpose.

A novel of high aim requires, of course, delineation of character, and with more patient minuteness than the drama; and some novels live, indeed, solely through the delineation of character; whereas there are some tragedies in which the characters, when stripped of theatrical costume, are very trivial, while, despite the poverty of character, the tragedies themselves are immortal, partly from the skill of the plot, partly from the passion which is wrought out of the situations, and principally, perhaps, from the beauty of form — the strength and harmony of the verse. Thus, French critics of eminence have accorded to Racine, as a tragic poet, a rank equal to that of Corneille, although acknowledging the immense superiority of the latter in the treatment and conception of tragic character. The tragic drama imperatively requires passion — the comic drama humour or wit; but a novel may be a very fine one without humour, passion, or wit — it may be made great in its way (though that way is not the very highest one) by delicacy of sentiment, interest of story, playfulness of fancy, or even by the level tenor of everyday life, not coarsely imitated, but pleasingly idealised. Still mystery is one of the most popular and effective sources of interest in a prose narrative, and sometimes the unravelling of it constitutes the entire plot. Every one can remember the thrill with which he first sought to fathom the dark secret in 'Caleb Williams' or 'The Ghost-Seer.' Even in the comic novel, the great founder of that structure of art has obtained praise for perfection of plot almost solely from the skill with which Tom Jones's parentage is kept concealed; the terror, towards the end, when the hero seems to have become involved in one of the crimes from which the human mind most revolts, and the pleased surprise with which that terror is relieved by the final and unexpected discovery of his birth, with all the sense of the many fine strokes of satire in the commencement of the tale, which are not made clear to us till the close.

To prose fiction there must always be conceded an immense variety in the modes of treatment — a bold licence of loose capricious adaptation of infinite materials to some harmonious unity of interest, which even the most liberal construction of dramatic licence cannot afford to the drama. We need no lengthened examination of this fact; we perceive at once that any story can be told, but comparatively very few stories can be dramatised. And hence some of the best novels in the world cannot be put upon the stage; while some, that have very little merit as novels, have furnished subject-matter for the greatest plays in the modern world. The interest in a drama must be consecutive, sustained, progressive — it allows of no *longueurs*. But the interest of a novel may be very gentle, very irregular — may interpose long conversations in the very midst of action — always provided, however, as I have before said, that they bear upon the ulterior idea for which the action is invented. Thus we have in 'Wilhelm Meister' long conversations on art or philosophy just where we want most to get on with the story — yet, without those conversations, the story would not have been worth the telling; and its object could not, indeed, be comprehended — its object being the accomplishment of a human mind in the very subjects on which the conversations turn. So, in many of the most animated tales of Sir Walter Scott, the story pauses for the sake of some historical disquisition necessary to make us understand the altered situations of the imagined characters. I need not say that all such delays to the action would be inadmissible in the drama. Hence an intelligent criticism must always allow a latitude to artistic prose fiction which it does not accord to the dramatic, nor indeed to any other department of imaginative representation of life and character. I often see in our Reviews a charge against some novel, that this or that is "a defect of art," which is, when examined, really a beauty in art — or a positive necessity which that department of art could not avoid — simply because the Reviewer has been applying to the novel rules drawn from the drama, and not only inapplicable, but adverse, to the principles which regulate the freedom of the novel. Now, in reality, where genius is present, art cannot be absent. Unquestionably, genius may make many incidental mistakes in art, but if it compose a work of genius, that work must be a work of art on the whole. For just as virtue consists in a voluntary obedience to moral law, so genius consists in a voluntary obedience to artistic law. And the freedom of either is this, that the law is pleasing to it — has become its second nature. Both human virtue and human genius must err from time to time; but any prolonged disdain, or any violent rupture, of the law by which it exists, would be death to either. There is this difference to the advantage of virtue (for, happily, virtue is necessary to all men, and genius is but the gift of few), that we can lay down rules by the observance of which any one can become a virtuous man; but we can lay dawn no rules by which any one can become a man of genius. No technical rules can enable a student to become a great dramatist or a great novelist; but there is in art an inherent distinction between broad general principles and technical rules. In all genuine art there is a sympathetic, affectionate, and often quite unconscious adherence to certain general principles. The recognition of these principles is obtained through the philosophy of criticism; first, by a wide and patient observation of masterpieces of art, which are to criticism what evidences of fact are to science; and next, by the metaphysical deduction, from those facts, of the principles which their concurrence serves to establish. By the putting forth of these principles we cannot make bad writers good, nor mediocre writers great; but we may enable the common reader to judge with more correctness of the real quality of merit, or the real cause of defect in the writers he peruses; and by directing and elevating his taste, rectify and raise the general standard of literature. We may do more than that — we may much facilitate the self-tuition that all genius has to undergo before it attains to its full development, in the harmony between its freedom and those elements of truth and beauty which constitute its law. As to mere technical rules, each great artist makes them for himself; he does not despise technical rules, but he will not servilely borrow them from other artists; he forms his own. They are the by-laws which his acquaintance with his special powers lays down as best adapted to their exercise and their sphere. Apelles is said to have made it a by-law to himself to use only four colours in painting: probably Apelles found his advantage in that restraint, or he would not have imposed it on his pallet. But if Zeuxis found that he, Zeuxis, painted better by using a dozen colours than by confining himself to four, he would have used a dozen, or he would not have been Zeuxis.

On careful and thoughtful examination we shall find, that neither in narrative nor dramatic fiction do great writers differ on the principles of art in the works which posterity accepts from them as great — whereas they all differ more or less in technical rules. There is no great poetic artist, whether in Epic, Drama, or Romance, who, in his best works, ever represents a literal truth rather than the idealised image of a truth — who ever condescends to servile imitations of nature — who ever prefers the selection of particulars, in the delineation of character or the conception of fable, to the expression of generals — who does not aim at large types of mankind rather than the portraiture of contemporaries — or, at least, wherever he may have been led to reject these principles, it will be in performances, or parts of performances, that are allowed to be beneath him. But merely technical rules are no sooner laid down by the critics of one age, than they are scornfully violated by some triumphant genius in the next. Technical rules have their value for the artist who employs them, and who usually invents and does not borrow them. Those that he imposes on himself he seldom communicates to others. They are his secret — they spring from his peculiarities of taste; and it is the adherence to those rules which constitutes what we sometimes call his style, but more properly his manner. It is by such rules, imposed on himself, that Pope forms his peculiar cæsura, and mostly closes his sense at the end of a couplet. When this form of verse becomes trite and hackneyed, up rises some other poet, who forms by-laws for himself, perhaps quite the reverse. All that we should then ask of him is success; if his by-laws enable him to make as good a verse as Pope's in another way, we should be satisfied; if not — not. One main use in technical rules to an author, if imposed on himself, or freely assented to by himself, is this — the interposition of some wholesome impediment to the over-facility which otherwise every writer acquires by practice. And as this over-facility is naturally more apt to be contracted in prose than in verse, and in the looseness or length of the novel or romance, than in any other more terse and systematic form of imaginative fiction — so I think it a wise precaution in every prolific novelist to seek rather to multiply, than emancipate himself from, the wholesome restraints of rules; provided always that such rules are the natural growth of his own mind, and confirmed by his own experience of their good effect on his productions. For if Art be not the imitator of Nature, it is still less the copyist of Art. Its base is in the study of Nature — not to imitate, but first to select, and then to combine, from Nature those materials into which the artist can breathe his own vivifying idea; and as the base of Art is in the study of Nature, so its polish and ornament must be sought by every artist in the study of those images which the artists before him have already selected, combined, and vivified; not, in such study, to reproduce a whole that represents another man's mind, and can no more be born again than can the man who created it; but again to select, to separate, to recombine — to go through the same process in the contemplation of Art which he employed in the contemplation of Nature; profiting by all details, but grouping them anew by his own mode of generalisation, and only availing himself of the minds of others for the purpose of rendering more full and complete the realisation of that idea of truth or beauty which has its conception in his own mind. For that can be neither a work of art (in the æsthetic sense of the word) nor a work of genius in any sense of the word, which does not do a something that, as a whole, has never been done before; which no other living man could have done; and which never, to the end of time, can be done again — no matter how immeasurably better may be the *other* things which *other* men may do. 'Ivanhoe' and 'Childe Harold' were produced but the other day; yet already it has become as impossible to reproduce an 'Ivanhoe' or a 'Childe Harold' as to reproduce an 'Iliad.' A better historical Romance than 'Ivanhoe,' or a better contemplative poem than 'Childe Harold,' may be written some day or other; but, in order to be better, it must be totally different. The more a writer is imitated the less he can be reproduced. No one of our poets has been so imitated as Pope, not because he is our greatest or our most fascinating poet, but because he is the one most easily imitated by a good versifier. But is there a second Pope, or will there be a second Pope, if our language last ten thousand years longer?

ESSAY XXIV.

POSTHUMOUS REPUTATION.

POSTHUMOUS REPUTATION.

Posthumous reputation! who can honestly say that posthumous reputation, in one sense of the phrase, is of no value in his eyes? If it were only heroes and poets, those arch-cravers of renown, who cared what were said of them after death, our village burial-grounds would lack their tombstones. A certain desire for posthumous reputation is so general that we might fairly call it universal. But I shall attempt to show that, being thus universal, it springs from sources which are common in human breasts, and not from that hunger for applause which is the exceptional characteristic of the candidates for Fame. It grows out of the natural affections or the moral sentiment, rather than the reasonings of intellectual ambition.

Be a man how obscure soever — as free from the desire of fame, as devoid of the capacities to achieve it — still the thought of sudden and entire forgetfulness would be a sharp pang to his human heart. He does not take leave of the earth without the yearning hope to retain a cherished place in the love or esteem of some survivors, after his remains have been removed into the coffin and thrust out of sight into the grave. The last "*Vale*" were, indeed, a dreary word without the softening adjuration, "*Sis memor mei.*" Even criminals themselves, in that confusion of reasoning which appears inseparable from crime, reconciled, in death as in life, to names scorned by the honest (who to them, indeed, form a strange and foreign race), still hope for posthumous reputation among their comrades, for qualities which criminals esteem.

The Pirates in Byron's poem are not content to sink, without such honours as pirates afford, into the ocean that "shrouds and sepulchres their dead."

"Ours" — they exclaim, in the spirit of Scandinavian Vikings —

> "Ours the brief epitaph in danger's day,
> When those who win at length divide the prey,
> And cry — remembrance saddening o'er each brow —
> 'How had the brave who fell exulted now!'"

But if the bad cannot banish a desire to live after death in the affection even of the bad, where is the good man who, trained throughout life to value honour, can turn cynic on his deathbed, and say, "Let me in life enjoy the profitable credit for honesty, and I care not if, after death, my name be held that of a knave"?

All of us, then, however humble, so far covet posthumous reputation that we would fain be spoken and thought of with affection and esteem by those whose opinions we have prized, even when we are beyond the sound of their voices and the clasp of their hands. Such reputation may be (as with most of us it is) but a brief deferment of oblivion — the suspense of a year, a month, a day, before the final cancel and effacement of our footprint on the sands of Time. But *some* kindly reminiscence in *some* human hearts man intuitively yearns to bequeath; and the hope of it comforts him as he turns his face to the wall to die.

But if this be a desire common to the great mass of our species, it must evidently rise out of the affections common to all — it is a desire for love, not a thirst for glory. This is not what is usually meant and understood by the phrase of posthumous reputation; it is not the renown accorded to the exceptional and rare intelligences which soar above the level of mankind. And here we approach a subject of no uninteresting speculation — viz., the distinction between that love for posthumous though brief repute which emanates from the affections and the moral sentiment, and that greed of posthumous and lasting renown which has been considered the craving, not of the heart nor of the moral sentiment, but rather of the intellect, and therefore limited to those who have the skill and the strength to vie for the palm awarded to the victor only when his chariot-wheels halt and the race is done. Competitors are many; victors, alas! are few. Out of all the myriads who have tenanted our earth, the number even of eminent intellects which retain place in its archives is startlingly small. The vast democracy of the dead are represented by an oligarchy to which that of Venice was liberal. Although successive races of laborious compilers and reverential antiquarians do their utmost to preserve in dusty shelves the bones and fossils of every specimen of man which has left a vestige of its being in the layers and strata of the past, it were as well, to a lover of fame, to sleep in his grave ignored, as to be dishumed, a forlorn fragment of what he once was, and catalogued alphabetically in a Biographical Dictionary.

Let us suppose some youthful poet whose heart is now beating loud with 'the immense desire of praise,' to whom his guardian angel lifts the veil of Futurity, and saith, "Thy name shall be preserved from oblivion. Lo! its place in yon compendium of embalmed celebrities, which scholars shall compile five centuries after thy decease. Read and exult!" The poet (his name be Jones) reads as follows under the letter J:—

"JONES, DAVID, a British author in the reign of Victoria I. Wrote many poems much esteemed by his contemporaries, some few fragments of which have been collected in the recent 'Anthology' of his learned and ingenious countryman, Professor Morgan Apreece; and, though characterised by the faults prevalent in his period, are not without elegance and fancy. Died at Caermarthen A. D. 1892."

Such would be a very honourable mention — more than is said in a Biographical Dictionary of many a bard, famous in his day; and yet what poet would not as willingly be left calm in 'God's Acre,' without any mention at all? Saith Sir Thomas Brown, in his quaint sublimity of style, "To be read by bare inscriptions, like many in Grüter — to hope for eternity by enigmatical epithets or first letters of our names — to be studied by antiquarians who we were, and have new names given us, like many of the mummies, — are cold consolation unto the students of perpetuity, even by everlasting languages."*

Yet, alas! how few of us can hope for the perpetuity even of an inscription "like those in Grüter!" Nor is this all; out of those few to whom universal assent and favouring circumstance have secured high

* 'Urn Burial.'

place in the motley museum of Fame, and lengthened account in the dreary catalogue of names, how very few there are whose renown would be a thing of envy to the pure and lofty ambition of heroic youth! How few in whom the intellectual eminence conceded to them is not accompanied by such alleged infirmities and vices of character, as only allow our admiration of the dead by compelling an indulgence which we could scarcely give, even to the dearest of our friends if living!

I am not sure whether any student of perpetuity, while the white of his robe is still without a weather-stain, and his first step lightly bounds up the steep

"Where Fame's proud temple shines afar,"

would be contented to leave behind him the renown of a Bacon's wisdom, coupled with those doubts of sincerity, manliness, gratitude, and honour, which Bacon's generous advocates have so ingeniously striven to clear away. On such points, who would not rather be unknown to posterity than need an advocate before its bar?

It is not the bent of my philosophy to disparage illustrious names. I am myself predisposed rather too implicitly to revere than too harshly to criticise the statues set up in Walhalla. I do not call Alexander the Great "the Macedonian madman" — I do not fix my eyes upon all the stains that historians discover in the toga of Julius Cæsar, nor peer through the leaves of his laurel wreath to detect only the bald places which the coronal hides. I gaze with no Cavalier's abhorrence on the rugged majesty of our English Cromwell. No three in the list of the famous are perhaps more sure than these three of renown unwasted by the ages; yet, seeing all that has been said, can be said, and will be said against all three, and upon those attributes of character which I have been taught to consider more estimable than intellectual ability and power, I know not whether, after death, I would not rather have nothing said about me. It would give me no satisfaction to think that I

> "Leave a name at which the world grew pale,
> To point a moral or adorn a tale."

There is something in renown of that kind which is, after all, little better than a continuity of the ignorant gossip and uncivil slander which have so often made the great sadly wish that they were obscure. When the poet, who had achieved a fame more generally acknowledged throughout Europe than has perhaps been accorded to any poet in his own lifetime since the days of Petrarch, was on his deathbed, he did not exclaim, "I demand glory!" but sighed, "I implore peace!" Happy indeed the poet of whom, like Orpheus, nothing is known but an immortal name! Happy next, perhaps, the poet of whom, like Homer, nothing is known but the immortal works. The more the merely human part of the poet remains a mystery, the more willing is the reverence given to his divine mission. He may say with the prophet —

> "Mon empire est détruit si l'homme est reconnu."

Some kinds of posthumous renown there are indeed which the purest coveters of fame might envy. But such kinds of renown are the rarest; nor are they those which most fascinate the emulous eyes of youth by the pomps of intellectual splendour. For perhaps a certain roughness of surface is necessary to the emission of that light which most strikes the remote beholder, as it is said the moon would be invisible to us were its surface even. And the renowns of which I now speak attract less by the glare of genius than by the just proportions of moral beauty, which the genius of others hallowing and revering them (as genius ever hallows and reveres all images of moral beauty), preserves distinct and clear by the tribute of its own rays.

What English gentleman would not rejoice to bequeath a name like that of Sir Philip Sidney? what French chevalier like that of Bayard? what cosmopolitan philanthropist like that of Howard? what republican patriot like that of Washington? what holy priest like that of Carlo Borromeo? But in all these serene and beautiful renowns the intellectual attributes, though not inconsiderable, are slight in comparison with the moral. The admiring genius of others, however, invests them with the intellectual glory which genius alone can bestow. They are of those whom poets do not imitate, but whom poets exalt and sanctify. Yet in the moral attributes which secure their fame they must have been approached by many of their contemporaries never heard of. For though in intellect a man may so lift himself above his class, his land, his age, that he may be said to tower alone as well as aloft, yet the moral part of him must, almost always, draw the chief supply of its nutriment from the surrounding atmosphere. Where we recognise in any one an image of moral elevation, which seems to us at the first glance unique and transcendent, I believe that, on a careful examination, we shall find that among his coevals, or in the very nature of his times, those qualities which furnish forth their archetype in him were rife and prevalent. And if, in him, they have a more conspicuous and striking embodiment, it will be partly from circumstances, whether of birth, fortune, or favouring event, which first served to buoy up his merit to the surface of opinion, and then bear it onward in strong tide to the shore of fame; and partly from that force of will which is often neither a moral nor an intellectual property, but rather a result of physical energy and constitutional hardihood of nerve.

Again, some men have found in a grateful posterity the guardians of an enviable renown, less by any remarkable excellence of their own, than by the wrongs they have suffered in a cause which is endeared to the interests of mankind. Thus, William Lord Russell and Algernon Sidney are hallowed to English freemen so long as our history shall last. But if they had not died on the scaffold, it may be reasonably doubted whether they could still live in fame.

Seeing, then, that the prizes drawn from the funeral urn are so few, and among the few, so very few that are worth more than a blank, it is not surprising that the desire of posthumous reputation, though in itself universal, should rather contract into a yearning for affection or a regard for character, bounded to the memory of our own generation or the next, than expand into the grandiose conceit of ever-during fame. Nor do I believe that with those by whom such fame is won is the prophetic hope of it a prevalent motive power after the dreamy season of early youth. At the dawn of life, in our school and college days, we do but dimly see the line between life and death, — life seems so distinct and so long — death seems so vague and so far. Then, when we think of fame, we scarce discern the difference between the living and the dead. Then, our enthusiasm is for ideals, and our emulation is to vie with the types that express them. It is less living men we would emulate than immaterial names. In the martial sports of our playground we identify ourselves not with a Raglan or a Gortschakoff, but with a Hector or Achilles. Who shall tell us that Hector and Achilles never lived? — to us, while in boyhood, they are living still, nay, among the most potent and vital of living men. We know not then what we could not do; we fancy we could do all things were we but grown-up men. We ignore the grave. As we live familiarly with the ancients, so we associate our own life with posterity. Is our first copy of verse, on the Ruins of Pæstum — is our first theme, to the text, '*Dulce et decorum est pro patriâ mori,*' — uncommended by our tasteless master, unadmired by our envious class, we have an undefined consolatory idea that posterity will do us justice. And posterity to us seems a next-door neighbour, with whom we shall shake hands, and from whom we shall hear polite compliments — not when we are dead, but when we are grown up. We are too full of life to comprehend that there is any death except for those old folks who cannot appreciate us. Bright and illustrious illusions! Who can blame, who laugh at the boy, who not admire and commend him, for that desire of a fame outlasting the Pyramids, by which he insensibly learns to live in a life beyond the present, and nourish dreams of a good unattainable by the senses? But when a man has arrived at the maturity of his reason, and his sight has grown sufficiently disciplined to recognise the

boundaries of human life — when he has insensibly
taught his ear to detect the hollow blare of those wind-
instruments of fame which once stirred his heart like
the fife of Calliope descending from heaven to blend
the names of men with those of the Uranides, — the
greed of posthumous renown passes away with the other
wild longings of his youth. If he has not already
achieved celebrity even among his own race, his sobered
judgment reveals to him the slender chance of celebrity
among the race which follows; living claimants are
loud enough to absorb its heed. If he has achieved
celebrity, then his post is marked out in the Present.
He has his labours, his cares, his duties, for the day.
He cannot pause to dream what may be said of him
in a morrow that he will not greet. If really and substantially famous, his egotism is gone. He is moving
with and for multitudes and his age; and what he
writes, what he does, potential in his own time, must
indeed have its influence over the times that follow,
but often mediately, indirectly, and as undistinguish-
able from the influence of minds that blend their light
with his own, as one star-beam is from another. And
for the most part, men thus actively engaged in the
work which commands the gaze of contemporaries,
think as little of the fame which that work may or may
not accord among distant races to the six or seven
letters which syllable their names, as thinks a star
whose radiance reaches us, of what poets may hymn
to its honour, or astrologers assign to its effect, under
the name by which we denote the star, whether we
call it Jupiter or Saturn.

Certainly we may presume, that of all aspirants to
posthumous renown, poets are the most ardent and the

most persevering — justly so; for of all kinds of intellectual merit, the poet's is that which contemporaries may the most fail to recognise. And yet among poets since the Christian era (I shall touch later on poets of the heathen time), we cannot, I think, discover any great anxiety for posthumous renown in those who lived long enough to fulfil their mission, and have received from posterity a homage that would have sanctioned their most confident appeal to a future generation. I say, those who lived long enough to fulfil their mission; and I mean, that when their mission was fulfilled — their great works done — their care for the opinion of posterity seems to have been anything but restless and over-eager. No doubt, in youth, the longing for posthumous renown in them was strong. In youth, that yearning might dictate to Milton the first conception of some great epic which the world would not willingly let die. But when, after the toils and sorrows of his hard career, the old man returned to the dream of his young ambition, the joy of his divine task seems to have been little commingled with vain forethought of the praise it might receive from men. He himself was so grand a man, and so fully conscious of his own grandeur, that, however it may wound our vanity to own it, I do not think he cared very sensitively what we light readers or scholastic critics might say of him, for or against. The audience which he hoped to find, "fit, though few," was, according to the guess of one of his shrewdest commentators, confined much to the sect of his own Puritan brethren.

Goethe compares the joy of the poet to the joy of the bird; — the bird sings because it is its nature to sing — not because it is to be praised for singing. But

Milton's joy was high beyond the bird's — it was the joy of a sublime human soul — the joy of lifting himself above man's judgment, as a great soul ever seeks to do — high above the evil days — the dangers and the darkness with which he was encompassed round.

True, he enjoins himself not

> "Sometimes to forget
> Those other two, equalled with me in fate
> (So were I equalled with them in renown),
> Blind Thamyris and blind Mæonides."

But the brief sigh for renown, less haughtily than modestly breathed forth in the parenthetical line, soon swells into the loftier prayer with which he closes his complaint of the loss of external day —

> "So much the rather thou, celestial light,
> Shine *inward*, and the mind through all her powers
> Irradiate!"

Poor and trivial, among sublimer consolations, would have been even the assured foreknowledge of that rank among the worldly subjects of mortal kings, which Addison's elegant criticism established for Burnet's blind schoolmaster — to him who, alone among poets, had the privilege to say —

> "Into the heaven of heavens I have presumed,
> An earthly guest, and drawn empyreal air."

Again, passages in Shakespeare's Sonnets, attesting Shakespeare's sensitive pain in the thought of his equivocal worldly status and vocation, may, not illogically, be held to imply a correspondent desire for the glory to which he may have known that his genius was the rightful heir. Indeed, if in his Sonnets he may be fairly presumed to speak in his own person (as I think the probable and natural supposition), and

not, as some contend, inventing imaginary sentiments
for imaginary persons in imaginary situations — he
indulges in an exulting vaunt of the immortality his
young muse had already secured —

> "Not marble, not the gilded monuments
> Of princes, shall outlive this powerful rhyme."

But in his later days, when he attained to such reputation as the reigns of Elizabeth and James would accord to a playwriter, — and, luckier than most playwriters, and of course more prudent (for genius so complete as his is always eminently prudent, eminently practical), had saved or gained the means which allowed him to retire to New Place in Stratford — a gentleman, taking rank not with Homer and Sophocles, but with county squires — with a Master Slender, or even with a Justice Shallow, — he certainly appears to have given himself no trouble about preparing his works for us — that is, for posterity. He left them to take their chance with a carelessness that startles commonplace critics. Why so careless? — it startles me to think that critics can ask why. To an intellect so consummate as Shakespeare's, the thought of another world beyond the criticism of this world must have been very familiar; that it *was* familiar might, I think, be made clearly manifest by reference to the many passages and sentences in which, without dramatic necessity, and not always with dramatic fitness and effect, the great psychologist utters his own cherished thoughts through the lips of his imaginary creations.

Now, without straining too far lines in the Sonnets which appear to intimate his own mournful sense of humiliation in his calling of player, the age itself so austerely refused to recognise the stage as a school of morals or an ally of religion, that possibly Shakespeare, who so solemnly attests his Christian faith in the Will written a year before his death, might have had some humble doubts whether his mighty genius had conferred those vast benefits on mankind which are now recognised in the wisdom of its genial and comprehensive humanity. And thus, silent as to the works of his mind, he speaks but of the deathless nature of his soul — "I commend my soul into the hands of God my Creator, hoping, and assuredly, through the only merits of Jesus Christ my Saviour, to be made partaker of life everlasting; and my body to the earth whereof it is made."

Campbell has thought that Shakespeare made a secret and touching reference to his retirement from his own magic art, in the work which is held by so many critics, including De Quincey, to have been the last (viz., 'The Tempest'), and which Dyce esteems the most elaborately finished, of all his plays; and there is so much in the sympathy by which one great poet often divines the interior parabolic significations veiled in the verse of another, that the opinion of Campbell has here an authority which will not be lightly set aside by thoughtful critics. Certainly, if Shakespeare were at that time meditating retirement from the practice of his art, he could scarcely have been more felicitously "inspired to typify himself" than in Prospero's farewell to the enchanted isle —

"Ye elves of hills, brooks, standing lakes, and groves," &c.

It is true that it cannot be clearly proved, any more than as yet it has been satisfactorily disproved, that the 'Tempest,' performed before James in 1611, five years previous to Shakespeare's decease, really was the last drama which Shakespeare wrote; but if it were ascertained that, in his retirement at Stratford, he did, during those five intervening years, busy himself on some other play,* it would not confute the assumption that he had meant to typify himself in that farewell, and, at the time, had intended to write plays no more. Descartes at one moment seriously resolved to withdraw from philosophical pursuits, and yet revoked his resolution.

Be this as it may, one thing is certain, whether he did or did not write plays subsequent to the date of the 'Tempest,' he took no pains to secure their transmission to posterity, and evinced so little care even to distinguish those he had composed from other stock-pieces in his theatre, that it is only comparatively within a recent period that the many inferior plays assigned to his pen have been rejected from the list of his dramas; while one of the grandest of all his works, 'Lear,' is spoken of by Tate as "an obscure piece recommended to him by a friend."

My own experience of life, so far as it has extended, confirms the general views I have here taken with regard to the thirst for posthumous renown.

I have seldom known a very young man of first-rate genius in whom that thirst was not keen; and still more seldom any man of first-rate genius, who, after middle life, was much tormented by it, more especially if he had already achieved contemporaneous fame, and felt how little of genuine and unalloyed delight it bestows, even while its plaudits fall upon living ears.

* Dyce says, "I suspect that before 1613 he (Shakespeare) had entirely abandoned dramatic composition."

But, on the other hand, I daily meet with mediocre men, more especially mediocre poets, to whom the vision of a fame beyond the grave is a habitual hallucination.

And this last observation leads me to reflect on the strange deficiency of all clear understanding as to his degree of merit, which is almost peculiar to the writer of verse.

In most other departments of intellectual industry and skill, a man soon acquires a tolerably accurate idea whether what he is doing be good, bad, or indifferent; but the manufacturer of verse seems wholly unable to estimate the quality of the fabric he weaves, or perceive whether the designs he stamps or embroiders on it are really beauteous and original forms, or trite copies and graceless patterns. No matter how consummate his intelligence in other domains of mind, yet he may rank with the most stolid and purblind of self-deceivers when he has to pass judgment on his own rhymes.

Frederick the Great is certainly Fritz the Little when he abandons the tented field for the Pierian grot. Richelieu never errs in his conceptions of the powers at his command except when he plunges into rhyme — never, in his vainest moments, overrates his strength against courts and nobles and foreign armies, but is wholly unable to comprehend that he is not a match for Corneille in the composition of a tragedy.

Nay, what is still more strange, poets the most confessedly illustrious have not always been able to judge so well as the most commonplace and prosaic of their readers the relative merits of their own performances. Milton is said to have preferred his 'Paradise Regained' to his 'Paradise Lost;' Byron to have estimated his imitations of Pope at a higher value than his 'Childe Harold' or his 'Siege of Corinth;' Campbell felt for 'Theodric' a more complacent affection than he bestowed on 'Gertrude of Wyoming;' and even Goethe, who judged his own compositions with a cooler and more candid survey than any other poet ever bestowed on the beloved children of his brain, can neither by artistic critics nor popular readers be thought justified in preferring the Second Part of 'Faust' to the First.

Possibly a main cause of this offuscation of intelligence in verse-writers may be found in the delight which the composition of verse gives to the author. And Richelieu explained why he, so acute in assessing his power for governing kingdoms, was so dull in comprehending his abilities for the construction of rhyme, in the answer he once gave to Desmarets, to whom he said, wearily, "In this troubled life of mine, what do you think constitutes my chief pleasure?" Desmarets, courtier-like, replied, "The thought that you are making the happiness of France." "*Pas du tout!*" answered Richelieu, "*c'est à faire les vers.*"

Now, the mere delight of making verse was perhaps quite as great in Richelieu as in Corneille — is as great in the schoolboy poetaster as in the loftiest bard; and in the loftiest bard not less, possibly even more, when he is rapidly and painlessly writing down to his lowest level, than when piling thought on thought, with carefully selected marbles of expression, up to his highest height. If it be truly reported of Virgil that he spent the morning in pouring forth his verses, and the evening in correcting, condensing, abridging, polishing the verses thus composed, the probability is that the morning's task was one of delight, and the evening's task one of pain. But without the evening's task, possibly the morning's task might not have secured to posterity the *Monstrum sine labe*, which Scaliger has declared Virgil to be.

The verse-maker's pleasure in his verse intoxicates him. It is natural that he should think that what so pleased him to write, it ought to please others to read. If it do not please them, it is the bad taste of the day — it is the malice of coteries — the ignorance of critics. Posterity will do him justice. And thus the veriest poetaster takes refuge in the thought of posterity, with as complacent an assurance as could possibly cheer the vision of the loftiest poet. Indeed, if the loftiest poet had been sensible of pain as well as pleasure in his composition, his pain would have made him sensible of his faults; whereas the poetaster, in composing, feels only the unalloyed satisfaction of belief in his merits. And thus, having cited one traditional anecdote of the painstaking Virgil, I may add another — viz., that, far from deeming himself *Monstrum sine labe*, he considered his 'Æneid' not sufficiently corrected and perfected for the eye of posterity, and desired that it should be destroyed.

I think, then, that a poet of some thought and modesty will hesitate before he admit as a genuine, solid, well-founded consolation for any present disparagement to which he may conceive his genius unjustly subjected, that belief in future admiration, which he must share in common with the most ordinary mortals who ever composed a hemistich. He can never feel quite sure that his faith in posterity is a sound one. Granted that he have an internal conviction which appears to him a divine prescience, that posterity will reward him for the neglect of his own day; yet, if he will take the pains to inquire, he will find that an internal conviction, conceived to be a prescience just as divine, comforts the grocer's apprentice in the next street, whose hymns to Mary, or Marathon, or the Moon, have been churlishly refused admission into the Poet's Corner of a Monthly Magazine.

But, after all, a consolation for present disparagement or neglect, in the persuasion, well or ill founded, of praise awarded by a future generation, does not seem to me a very elevated source of comfort, nor do I think it would be dearly prized by a strong mind, which has matured its experiences of mortal life, and trained itself to reflect upon the scope and ends of an immortal spirit. Although most men destined to achieve large objects commence their career with a rich share of that love of approbation which is harshly called vanity, yet in masculine natures there is no property which more refines itself into vapour, and fades away out of the character, when completed, compact, rounded, solidified, by its own evolutions in the lengthened course of its orbit, than that same restless gaseous effervescence of motive power which, at the onset of the career, while the future star is still but a nebula, bubbles and seethes from the crudity of struggling forces. That passion for applause, whether we call it vanity or by some nobler name, has done its work in the organisation of the man when he has effected things that are substantially *worthy* of applause.

And here I may observe that there are three causes of satisfaction in the creation of works designed for endurance, that are often confounded with the pleasure supposed to exist in the anticipation of the fame which may eventually honour the design. 1*st*, The satisfaction of art in the consultation of the elementary requisite of artistic construction; 2*d*, The satisfaction of what I call the intellectual conscience, and shall endeavour to define; 3*d*, The satisfaction of the moral conscience.

1*st*. Durability is the requisite of all constructive art; the artist intuitively aims at it in all his ideals of form, and the aim itself constitutes one of the steadiest, nor least vivid, of the Pleasures of Art. No great architect could feel much delight in his palaces if he built them of snow; and even should he build them of marble, his anguish, as artist, would be keen if he discovered that he had committed some so great fault in mechanics, that his girders and columns were unable to support his dome, and in a few years his fabric would be a ruin. Neither could any great writer rejoice in designing works in which he knew that the principle of duration was violated or ignored. What is thus true as a source of satisfaction in art is, though in lesser degree, true also in action, if the action be that of a constructor. Strenuous endeavour, in all really great minds, aims at durability, wherever it seeks to construct.

And in proportion to a man's belief in the worthiness of labours which necessitate the sacrifice of many fugitive joys, will be his satisfaction in the adoption of principles which tend to secure the result of those labours from decay. Nor is this all. In the very habit of consulting the object of permanence for the designs which he meditates, his whole mind ascends into a higher and calmer atmosphere of intellectual enjoyment; he is less affected by the cares and troubles of the immediate hour in his positive existence, and less mortified by any shortlived envy or neglect to which his intellectual or ideal existence is subjected. As the eye finds a soothing charm in gazing on extended prospects, so does the mind take pleasure in contemplating objects remote in time:

"'Tis distance lends enchantment to the view."

2*d*. There is an intellectual as well as a moral conscience; and the content of both is serene and full in proportion as the attraction to things evanescent is counteracted by the attraction towards objects that endure. Hence genius is patient as well as virtue, and patience is at once an anodyne and a tonic — nay, more, it is the only stimulant which always benefits and never harms.

3*d*. There is a cheering pleasure to the moral conscience akin to that of beneficence, in the construction of intellectual works worthy of duration — a satisfaction which every human being not indifferent to the welfare of his kind may reasonably conceive in the design of things that may contribute to the uses and enjoyments of succeeding generations.

But all these three sources of gratification are wholly distinct from the vainer and ignobler calculations of reward for present labours in the imagined murmur of future plaudits. For, after all, perhaps the best of what a man of genius (whatever his fame may be) has accomplished, is never traced popularly or distinctly home to him. He suggests infinitely more than he can perform — what he performs is visible, what he suggests is undiscerned. Whether in science, or art, or action, he implants many an idea in other minds, which they develop in their own way, unconscious of what they owed to the originator. Can any living poet tell us, or divine himself, what he owes to Shakespeare, to Homer, or perhaps to some forgotten ballad, chanted low by an old woman's cracked voice when he lay half asleep, half awake, and the shadows of twilight crept along his nursery-floors? Let me start a great thought — let me perform a noble action — and the effects thereof may continue, impelling wave after wave of the world's moral atmosphere till the last verge of time; but that I should publish the thought or do the action from a motive of reward in human praise, would neither evince a sublime generosity of mind, nor a prudent calculation of probable results. For whether the praise be now or a thousand years hence, it would still be but human praise; and if there would be something inherently vain in my nature, and vulgar in my ambition, did I make myself a mere seeker of applause now, I do not see that I should be more magnanimous because the applause thus coveted was a deferred investment. All I can see is, that I should be less rational; for at least applause now I can enjoy — applause when I am dead I cannot.

Nor would it be a sign of a disciplined intellect to forget the unpleasant truth illustrated by so vast a majority of instances — viz., that a man who cannot win fame in his own age, will have very small chance of winning it from posterity. True, there are some half-dozen exceptions to this truth among millions of myriads that attest it; but what man of common sense would invest any large amount of hope in so unpromising a lottery!

Now, in proportion as some earnest child of genius and labour, with capacities from which renown emanates and travels as light does from a sun, nears the mystery of the grave, it is a reasonable supposition that his mind will more solemnly take into its frequent meditation the increasing interest of the mighty question to which the very thought of the grave invites all who have learned to think. Either he arrives at a firm conviction, or at least at a strong belief, one way or other — or he remains in that indecision of doubt which distrusts a guide and disdains a guess. If his conviction or belief be that which I conceive to be exceedingly rare in men of genius, — viz., that when the breath passes from his clay, his sense of being, his *Ego*, is eternally annihilated, and all of him that remain indestructible are what he in life despised as the meanest and rudest parts of him — viz., the mere elements of his material form escaping from his coffin to furnish life to some other material form, vegetable or organic, with which he can have no conscious identity, no cognate affinity, — I cannot conceive by what confusion of ideas he could rejoice in some remote honour paid to the *Ego* blotted evermore out of creation. I can understand that a man adopting this Sadducean creed might still care what h children, his friends, might think of him when absorbed in the *Néant* or, Nothingness which Danton understood by the word Death; because, though he may argue himself out of the perceptions of his soul, he has obeyed, perhaps to the last kiss of his faltering lip, the last wistful look of his glazing eye, the feelings of his heart; and it is his heart which bids him hope that the children he loves, the friends he regrets to leave, should, if but for their sakes, feel no shame in mourning him who so loved and cherished them. But an egotistical desire for mere fame continued after the *Ego* itself is annihilated — after children and friends are annihilated in their turn; a fame which, howsoever long it may endure, is but to be transmitted to races all as perishable in thought and spirit as himself, momentary animations of mere salts and minerals and gases — evanescent as May-flies on a rivulet, and obeying but instincts as limited to the earth they scarcely touch ere they quit, as are an ant's to the wants of its toilsome commonwealth; — a desire for posthumous fame, on the conditions founded on such belief, were a bloodless and imbecile vanity, to which a man worthy to win fame could scarcely bow even his human pride.

But if on this subject of spiritual immortality a man approach the grave with no conviction — no belief one way or other (simply in that state of sceptic doubt with which philosophy commences inquiry, and out of which into some definite conclusion or other it must emerge if it would solve a single secret or hazard a single guess into truth), then, I apprehend that the very coolness of his temperament would preserve him from any very eager desire for a thing so airy and barren — so unphilosophical in itself as the vague echo of a name. Minds thus cautiously hesitating before they can acknowledge the substance of proofs, are not likely to be the superstitious adorers of a phantom.

Lastly, if a man of strong mind and bright imagination has come to the firm conviction or pervading faith that he begins after death to live again in some region wholly remote from earth, with wholly new perceptions adapted to new destinations, the desire of mere renown on the spot to which for an infinitesimally brief period of his being he has been consigned, may indeed be conceived, may at moments be even keen, but it will not be constant, nor, when it stirs within him, be long indulged. For it could scarcely fail to become subordinate (in proportion to the height of his aspirations and the depth of his intellect) to the more important question — how far he has been preparing and training himself, not for renown to the name which on quitting earth he will have more cast off and done with than Pythagoras had cast off and done with that of Euphorbus, but rather for new name and new rank in that great career which only commences when earth and its names are left.

Thus the dream of fame, so warm and vivid in very early youth, gradually obtains its euthanasia, among the finest orders of minds, in a kind of serene enthusiasm for duty. The more beautiful and beautifying is the nature of the man, the more beauty that nature throws into its ideals of duty. So that duty itself loses its hard and austere aspects, and becomes as much the gracious and sweet result of impulses which mellow into habits, as harmony is the result of keys and chords fitted and attuned to music.

Among the ancients, the peculiar religious conceptions of a future life seem to have given to the desire of posthumous fame, a force, a fervour, which it could scarcely draw from any existent mode of psychological belief, whether that of a Christian or a deistical philosopher. For with either of the last this life is but an initiation — a probation; and the life hereafter is not a spectral continuance of the same modes of being, but a fresh and strange existence — immeasurably, ineffably more glorious, at least for those not condemned to lasting punishments by the Divine Judge — and (where the philosopher ventures on speculations warranted to his reason, by analogies from natural laws) a state of development and progress such as becomes the sublime notion of a being exalted from material into spiritual spheres. But the popular, and indeed (with the exception of a few segregated sages) the almost universal idea of the classic ancients as to a future state even for the Blessed, was not one of progress and development, but of a pale imitation in the sunless Elysian fields of the pursuits which had pleased on earth. It is no wonder that Horace should exult to have built in his verse a monument of himself more perennial than brass; when, in his vision of the realms of Proserpine and the chosen seats of the Pious, Sappho still wailingly sings of her mortal loves, and Alcæus, in more ample strain, chants to his golden lyre the hardships of ship-wreck and flight and war. To recall the span of life was the only occupation of eternity. The more contentious and strifeful the reminiscences invoked, the more agreeably they relieved the torpor of unwilling repose —

"Magis
Pugnas et exactos tyrannos
Densum humeris bibit aure volgus."

Putting aside the speculative conjectures of their philosophers, the notions of a future state conceived by the ancients have no representation in any of the three sections of modern doctrine at which I have superficially glanced. They did not doubt, with the modern sceptic — did not accept a natural religion, like the modern deist, nor rely upon the distinct assurances of a divine revelation, like the modern Christian. They maintained the continuance after death of an unsatisfactory, unalluring state of being, in which the mortal, conducted by Mercury to Charon's boat, was, in mind, desire, and thought, as in bodily form, but the ghost and larva of his former self. In the fields of Asphodel, nothing new, nothing more, was to be done throughout the flat waste of wearisome eternity — mortal life alone was the sphere of intellect and action. What, therefore, the mortal had done in life was all that the immortal could do throughout the endless ages. And as the instinct of immortality is not, when it be profoundly examined, the mere craving to live on, but, with all finer natures, the craving to live worthily, hereafter as here; so, to genius the life even of Elysian fields being but an objectless, unprogressive existence, the very instinct of the only immortality in any way correspondent to its powers as well as to its aspirations served to intensify the desire of perpetuity for the things achieved in the sole sphere of life wherein anything at all could be achieved. And as the brightest joy the Elysian wanderer could experience was in the remembrance of his glories past, so the fame for glories past in his life of man formed a practical idea of enduring solace, even in the notions a heathen formed of his life as spirit. Nor can even the philosopher thoroughly escape the influence of the prevalent and popular tenets of his age. And thus the old philosophers, in their rejection of vulgar fables, and their more enlightened conceptions of the destination of souls, did not, and could not, attain to the same spiritual elevation of thought as is at this day mechanically attained by even the philosophical deist, who, in rejecting Christianity, at least takes his start into speculation from the height he quits. For his idea of a soul's destination will include total change of earthly pursuits and ends — development and progress through the eternity he concedes to it.

Thus, among the ancients of the classic world, as among our Teuton or Scandinavian forefathers, the life of ghost being little more than the pale reflection of the life of man, the man not unnaturally identified his ambition with that renown amongst men, the consciousness of which would form the most vivid of his pleasures, and afford him the highest rank, in the Realm of Shadow.

It is not so to the psychologist, who associates his notion of immortal life with that of infinite progress, and lifts the hope of virtue farther and farther from the breath of man — nearer and nearer towards the smile of God.

Let us consider! Suppose you were to say to an intelligent, aspiring child, at a small preparatory school, "The reward to which you must look forward, as inducement and encouragement to all your present toils and privations, is the renown you will leave in this little school when you have left it. No matter how repugnant now your lessons, no matter how severe your floggings, no matter how cruel the boys, nor how unjust the master — is it not a sublime consolation, a sustaining joy, that, fifty years after you have gone out of these narrow walls into the spacious world on which they open, other little boys, in skeleton-jackets like your own, will point to the name you have carved on your desk, and say, 'He was one of us'?"

I suspect that the child, being intelligent and aspiring, would answer, if permitted to speak frankly, "Sir, that is all very well; but in itself such anticipation would not console me in my sufferings, nor sustain me in my trials. Certainly I should be well pleased, while I am here, to be admired by my schoolfellows and praised by my masters; that hope would encourage and animate me, as a present reward for present labours; but when you bid me look into the future for reward, my mind does not conceive it probable that it will go back to the past life in this little school — involuntarily it goes forward to that wide world, which, as you say, opens out of the school, and for which my lessons here educate and prepare me; and to win high place among those in that larger world is a dream of ambition much more inspiring, and much more comforting, than any thought of what little boys in skeleton-jackets may say of me in this little school, fifty years after I have left it, and forgotten all the troubles and torments I experienced herein."

Yet what preparatory school, as compared with the great world it leads to, can be to the child so small and insignificant as the scope of this life must seem to the man who believes himself immortal, compared with the infinity for which this life educates his soul? And if, on the other side of the grave, we allow ourselves to suppose that a departed spirit could be made aware of the renown which it has left on this — could learn that, centuries or cycles after it had quitted the poor painful little school, the name it had carved on its old worm-eaten desk was still visible, and pointed out to new-comers by the head boys with respect — we can scarcely conceive that this long-departed spirit would feel any very sensible joy.

For indeed it does happen to many of us to be told in middle life or old age, that at the little preparatory school — where, after some mental effort, we can just dimly remember that our knuckles were once rapped by an usher, and our tasks once rewarded by a badge of ribbon, or even a silver medal — little boys, little as we were then, do talk of us, do point to the name we so clumsily carved on our desk, and do say, "That fellow was one of the cleverest boys we ever had at the school." And yet I do not think that when, from time to time, such complimentary intelligence comes to us — mature men — it dwells on our minds for more than a moment or so. It may give a transient and luke-warm gratification; but the grander occupations of our mature life, in grander spheres of action, engage and absorb us, and lift our sources of joy high beyond the reminiscence of petty triumphs achieved by us when little children. Five hundred years is a long term for renown on earth, yet it is not too much to hope that five hundred years after an immortal being has left this world, he will be at least as far advanced and exalted in the measureless course of his progress — above his proudest achievements in this human life — as a man of sixty can be advanced and exalted in the development of his powers beyond the Gradus and Syntax he dog-eared fifty years ago.

Out of these reflections grows a psychological query, which, as it often occurs to me when meditating on such subjects, I venture to cast forth in suggestion. Assuming, as sufficiently borne out by evidence, the propositions herein laid down — viz., that the desire for posthumous reputation is so far common to mankind, that few of us do not desire that those we love and esteem should cherish and respect our memory for what are called our moral qualities — while the desire of renown among those not endeared to us by personal love and esteem, for qualities purely intellectual, is limited to very few, and of those few, fewer still (nor they, perhaps, the worthiest of renown) with whom the desire is either intense or habitual after the season of youth; — assuming, I say, the general truth of those propositions, may it not be possible, seeing how far the great scheme of Providence embraces general laws rather than particular exceptions, and makes most enduring the phenomena most general and least exceptional — may it not be possible that, while we retain in the next life the same or kindred instincts of affection, the same or kindred substrata of moral being, our purely intellectual attributes may undergo a complete transformation — that a wholly new order of those mental faculties which we here, in vulgar phrase, call our "talents," may grow up within altered organisations fitted to the wholly new range of destinies and duties to which we are removed and readapted? Now, when we pursue the thoughts which this query humbly starts, we are certainly compelled to allow that by far the greater number of these intellectual faculties or "talents" are specially applicable to the special order of things which belongs to this life, and for which no philosophical speculation on the next life enables us to conjecture any renewal of analogous uses.

I may have the special talents that fit me to be a great general, or a great lawyer, or a great surgeon; and for such talents, in such fitting application of them in this life, I may, in this life, obtain great renown, though, apart from the special talents for which the renown is obtained, I may be but a very ordinary mortal. Nor can I, by any stretch of imagination, suppose that any field for these special talents lies yonder — in the spiritual empyrean. There, surely, no spirit will have to consider how many other spirits he can destroy with the least destruction of life to his own spiritual followers; there, surely, no spirit can find exercise for those talents so valued here, by which witnesses are puzzled, juries dazzled, truth clipped or counterfeited by the craft of a glozing tongue; there, surely, will be no work for the surgeon's skill — no bones to set, no limbs to amputate — no discoveries in blood and tissues, such as give fame to a Harvey or a Bichat. So far as concerns the special talents which their whole intellectual organisation here was devoted to enlarge and enrich, the occupations of these Othellos — martial, forensic, clinical — would be gone.*

Do the followers of art arrogate better right of perpetuated exercise to their special talents — or may we not rather doubt if an immortal being, removed from the sphere of academies and galleries, exhibitions and patrons, would even desire to go on through eternity sculpturing and painting? Orators, to whom, here, we accord such popular renown, would find small profit from Quintilian's lessons, in realms where nothing wrong can be defended, and nothing right can be attacked. Even authors, alas! may not secure to their "talents" the scope and delight of perpetuated scribbling. For each author has his own speciality, whereby he wins, here, his fame: one is a poet, another a

* The thought here expressed is, in a previous Essay (vol. i. p. 162), applied to 'Hints on Mental Culture:' "This world is a school for the education not of a faculty, but of a man."

novelist, a third a historian, a fourth a critic, and a fifth perhaps a political pamphleteer. But out of any of these special departments of intellect subtract the special pabulum that the soil of each department requires — subtract this world of men, with men's fleeting interests and passions — and there would remain little or nothing for which the special faculty of the author is adapted. The poet, perhaps, would claim a superb exemption — he would contend for the privilege of eternal versifying, as the highest occupation of spiritual existence. But if you take from any poet to whom criticism here accords the highest order, the theses of crime and war, pity and terror, suffering and strife — you take away all that gave to his special faculty as poet its noblest exercise and its most confessed renown. He might still, it is true, describe and moralise, but it were some discouragement to that anticipation to be told by Hegel, that of all departments of poetic art, the descriptive and didactic are the lowest. And to describe and moralise as spirit in a spiritual state of being! — what special faculty in mortal poet would be fitted to describe what no mortal heart can conceive, or to moralise where no immorality is permitted? Nay, even the genius of the great preacher, who has devoted his special faculties to the holiest uses, will have surely no need to preach to immortals. It is not his talents as preacher — though here their uses are so vast — though here the renown they bequeath is so august; but rather the purity and the lovingness of motive — the moral qualities, in short, that animated the talents, dictated their uses, beautified the preacher's whole moral being — which we may reasonably conceive continued, perpetuated, developed in a world where there are no sins to denounce and no sorrows to console.

The philosophers, as the seekers after nature and explorers of the unknown, have implied, in many an eloquent page, that their special talents are those best fitted for celestial regions. But, unluckily for this assumption, it is a maxim received among philosophers themselves, from the days of Aristotle down to those of Sir William Hamilton, that philosophy ceases where truth is acknowledged. Instancing the received doctrine of gravitation, Sir William Hamilton says, "Arrived at the general fact that all bodies gravitate towards each other, we inquire no farther." Again, "The sciences always studied with keenest interest are those in a state of progress and uncertainty; absolute certainty and absolute completion would be the paralysis of any study; and the last, worst calamity that could befall man as he is at present constituted, would be that full and final possession of speculative truth which he now vainly anticipates as the consummation of his intellectual happiness." Thus the genius, and even the desire, of philosophy ceases in any state of being where truth ceases to be uncertain. The special talents of the philosopher are those which enable him keenly to detect, and cautiously to trace, a something in creation previously obscured or hidden. But let the something be made clear and acknowledged, and there is nothing left to philosophise about. So that when we come to examine, not only do the occupations for those special intellectual faculties which we call our "talents," and on which earthly renown is bestowed, seem to terminate with their special uses for their exercise on earth; but the stimulants and motives which have called forth their exercise would be withdrawn in a state of being which, according to all enlightened conjecture, must be distinguished from this by the very absence of those causes in human passion, contest, suffering, error, by which such special faculties are quickened and impelled. And seeing that, by the Divine Guide towards the future whom Christians revere, so much stress is laid on cultivating the affections of the heart, and the moral sentiments which conduce to moral improvement, while no stress is laid on the elaborate culture of purely intellectual faculties (as it was by those Greek philosophers who seem to have regarded the affections of the heart with sublime contempt, and made moral improvement the result of that scholastic wisdom into which they resolved virtue, and which not one man in a million could have the leisure to acquire or the wit to understand, so that their conception of the blessed would have been a college of lecturing sages), — this comparative silence of Christian doctrine as to heavenly reward for the intellectual faculties which win earthly renown, may have deeper reason than at first glance appears; — viz., not only because Christian promise being extended to illiterate multitudes as well as to the cultured few, only those requirements for immortal reward were enforced, with which the peasant as well as the sage could comply; but also because the foundations of our future spiritual reconstruction are in those portions of our being which are given to us in common, and not in those special faculties or talents which may be as exclusively adapted to this earth as are the instincts of the caterpillar to his state of caterpillar, and may undergo as great and entire a change as do the instincts of the insect when it abandons its creeping form and hovers in the air — a butterfly.

Possibly, at first sight, the views here suggested may seem discouraging to our human intellectual pride. "What," I may ask, "are the faculties I have so studied — whether as soldier, lawyer, surgeon, artist, author, orator — to develop and ripen here, as the finest part of my being, and to my pre-eminence in which my fellow-men accord their praise, — are those faculties to perish while I myself do not perish? No; whither goes my soul, must go my mind; whither goes my mind, must go those special faculties which my mind has the most diligently cultivated and the most largely developed." Vain presumption! Whither goes the soul, may go the mind — but a mind so wholly changed, that it no longer needs, for the purveyors of ideas, the senses of the material body, nor the inducements to special purposes and uses limited to an initiatory stage of trial.

For the rest, so long as I myself — the personal integral Ego, conscious of identity — survive, and am borne to a higher state of development, it is no extravagant supposition, that if what are now called my faculties or talents, being no longer needed, fade out from my new phase of being, they will be succeeded by other capacities and powers of which I cannot conceive nor conjecture (so foreign they will be to my present modes of thought and existence), but which may be so incomparably loftier than those I now complacently value, that could I foreknow the difference I should smile to think I had pined to carry my spark of glow-worm into the splendours of celestial light.

ESSAY XXV.

ON SOME AUTHORS IN WHOSE WRITINGS KNOWLEDGE OF THE WORLD IS EMINENTLY DISPLAYED.

ON SOME AUTHORS IN WHOSE WRITINGS KNOWLEDGE OF THE WORLD IS EMINENTLY DISPLAYED.

We all understand what is meant by "Knowledge of the World," yet it is not very easy to define the meaning. It is not identical with Knowledge of Mankind; for authors who have shown in their writings considerable knowledge of mankind, have been notable in their lives for blunders incompatible with Knowledge of the World. No one, on reading Steele's Essays in the 'Tatler' or 'Spectator,' could say, "This writer is without knowledge of mankind." No one can read Steele's biography and not wonder that a man of intellect so ready, and when in print so acute, should not acquire enough knowledge of the world to save him from those credulous imprudences and restless levities of venture which are generally confined to the raw inexperience of a novice in life. Goldsmith cannot be said, by the most disparaging of his critics, to have evinced an ignorance of mankind; and the most enthusiastic of his admirers will admit that, when it came to knowledge of the world, the author of 'the Vicar of Wakefield,' 'The Good-natured man,' and 'The Traveller,' was little better than a baby.

If Knowledge of the World be not identical with

a poet's or a thinker's Knowledge of Mankind, neither is it identical with a politician's knowledge of his time and country. For supremacy in that latter kind of knowledge has secured power to statesmen who have been considered, even by their own admirers, singularly deficient in knowledge of the world. Certainly no Minister ever better understood his time and country than the younger Pitt. The main cause of his precocious and enduring ascendancy may be found in that remarkable sympathy with public opinion, which is the most incontestable proof of a statesman's comprehension of the spirit of his age and nation. Yet his familiar friends remarked, half in complaint, half in eulogy, that he had no knowledge of the world. Mr. Wilberforce even says that he wanted knowledge of mankind. On the other hand, Mr. Fox is said to have had very great knowledge of the world. It was his superior repute for that knowledge which assigned to him rather than to Mr. Burke the leadership of the Whig party in the House of Commons. Yet, if there be one thing more than another which excluded the genius of Mr. Fox from the prizes of power, it was that defective comprehension of his time and his countrymen which made him so frequently at variance with public opinion, even when most ardently desirous of popular applause.

Knowledge of the World, so far as the phrase will bear explanation, seems to imply a knowledge of the manners and habits, the ordinary motive-springs and the conventional movements, of that society which is to the world what the surface is to the sea: and to be distinguished from knowledge of a larger and deeper kind — viz., the knowledge that interprets the laws of human nature, or comprehends the prevailing sentiment of an age and people — as the seamanship of an accomplished member of the Yacht Club is distinguished from the science of a cosmographer or the skill of an admiral. Still this knowledge of the world is not to be disparaged. There is much to envy in the brilliant owner of a yacht admirably managed and elegantly equipped; and it is not every man who has the audacious ambition to measure the waves as a Scoresby, or to rule them as a Nelson.

No common rank in social consideration is enjoyed by him who, without pretending to any other rare gifts or acquirements, possesses in high degree knowledge of the world, and the exquisite tact which is its usual concomitant. And if such knowledge be the polished addition to deeper wisdom and nobler characteristics, it will serve to render genius more consummate and virtue more alluring.

Much, it is true, has been said, in the way of satire, to depreciate, nay, even to vilify and hold up to ascetic scorn, that type of urban idiosyncrasies which is called emphatically "The Man of the World." The man of the world appears sufficiently odious in Macklin's play and Mackenzie's novel; but knowledge of the world, like any other knowledge, does not of itself necessitate participation in the follies and vices of which it is cognisant. A man of the world is not necessarily a knave because the world contains knaves, any more than he is necessarily a fool because the world contains fools. There are many more fools in the world than there are knaves, otherwise the knaves could not exist; yet the man of the world even in Mackenzie and Macklin is certainly no fool. A physician may be familiarly acquainted with diseases, yet himself be healthy; a lawyer may see through all the devices of rogues, yet himself be honest; and so a man of the world may be thoroughly aware of the world's infirmities, and thoroughly up to the world's tricks, without being himself either a Mareschal de Richelieu or a Jonathan Wild. Indeed, the legitimate result of knowledge of the world should tend to make us, on the whole, somewhat better, because somewhat juster, and being juster, somewhat kinder, than we were in those days of inexperienced presumption, when youth is inclined to be the vehement censor of such vices as it is not tempted to commit, and the flippant satirist of such virtues as it is not allured to imitate. In fact, just as it may be years before we discover the better qualities of any man, while his foibles strike us at the first glance, so it is with that aggregate of men which we call the world. Lord Melbourne, who in earlier life was somewhat predisposed towards cynical views of the world's standard of morality, said, after quitting office, "I am glad to have been First Minister, for I found that men are much better, much more honourable and sincere, than I had supposed them to be when I was in opposition." Certainly he knows very little of the world we live in nowadays, who does not become more indulgent and charitable than he was when he first started into life. And he is led into such charity and indulgence after undergoing many melancholy deceptions, and perhaps writhing under some grievous wrongs, by discovering that a man may be wise in spite of his foibles, and good in spite of his errors; that it is very rarely we find a dull man without his clever points, or a bad man without some redeeming virtue. On the other hand, greatness and goodness of a really high and noble order become more visibly great and good the more they are examined by a man who, having in himself something of great or good, can measure their proportions in the universe he inhabits with the accuracy which can only be attained by a practised eye. Stars are all small to the infant and the clown: it is the philosopher who astonishes us by the information of their magnitude. It is true that a hero may not be a hero to his *valet-de-chambre*. "Of course not," says Goethe, "for a man must be a hero to understand a hero. The valet, I daresay, would have a great respect for some man who had a superior stamp as valet." "But what," asks some juvenile Timon — "what can palliate the blackness of the perfidies which have blighted into lasting misanthropy my bloom of life?" — meaning the mournful interval between twenty-one and twenty-three. Certainly, O generous Timon, it is probable that at twenty-one you may have already found in your friend a hawk who regards you as a pigeon, and in your sweetheart an angel in nothing except the wings which have borne her away from your arms. But, granting all the infamy of those in whom, with the fondness of youth, you invested your belief in human virtue, still, if you look round, even to that limited circumference in life which your practical survey can command, all human beings have not proved themselves monsters. Perhaps your father was not altogether a rogue; perhaps your mother had some lovable quality; perhaps your little sister now and then kissed you disinterestedly; perhaps all the boys at your school were not thieves and liars. You have chanced — as we all chance, sooner or later, in going through life — on some person, male or female, who behaved very ill to you; an excellent reason for being a little more cautious whom you trust in future — no reason at all for trusting nobody. Live on, and, unless you are an incorrigible simpleton, you will find that in such society as a man of honour familiarly frequents, where he meets with one knave and traitor he meets with a hundred gentlemen as upright and loyal as himself. Nay, live on, and you will acknowledge a truth, of which, at this moment of anger, you are still more scornfully incredulous — those monsters who have behaved so atrociously to you, may in other relations of life be estimable. The parasites at whose heads Timon flung the dishes before he rushed off to his cave in the woods, had doubtless some finer trait of humanity than that of being parasites to Timon. Of those "Lords," how do we know that the first Lord was not an excellent father and husband; the second Lord a gallant warrior; the third Lord an useful member of the Areopagus?

In short, I suspect that every really skilled man of the world — as the world exists for its citizens in this nineteenth century — who, at the ripe age of forty, looks from the window of his club on the everyday mortals whom Fourier has hitherto failed to reform, has convinced himself that, considering all the mistakes in our education and rearing — all the temptations to which flesh and blood are exposed — all the trials which poverty inflicts on the poor — all the seductions which wealth whispers to the rich — men, on the whole, are rather good than otherwise, and women, on the whole, are rather better than the men.

I say "as the world exists in this nineteenth century," because it seems to me that knowledge of the world means a very different thing in one age to what it means in another. There have been times when, on the surface of society, all was putrid and loathsome; and though a knowledge of that abominable scum might have been purely scientific, and though he who knew it best might have abhorred it most, yet knowledge of the world in those days must have been, to an unvitiated taste, bitter as a draught from Marah; and any knowledge that keeps us in a perpetual state of wrath and scorn can scarcely improve our tempers or amend our hearts. Juvenal seems to have had a passably full knowledge of the world of his day, and was, we may fairly presume, conscientiously scandalised by the corruption which furnished the themes to his satire; but I very much doubt if he were made a whit better by all the stormy indignation to which the knowledge of so naughty a world transported his vehement genius. *Ridet et odit*—he laughs and hates; but the laugh of hatred is not a habit which a moralist can indulge with safety to his own moral nature. And probably Juvenal would have maintained himself in a more genuinely ethical state of mind — have been pleasanter to his friends, kinder to his slaves — have burned with more pious devotion his incense to Jove — if he had known a little less of the great world of Rome, and, when tired of its din and its smoke, sought refuge, like Horace, in Sabine shades by Bandusian founts.

If a good man find that his knowledge of the world supplies no other food to his genius than the laugh of hate, let him leave to itself the world, which he can never improve by the mere process of railing. Is it so odious? Well, he is not compelled to live in it. If he be a philosopher, he carries with him a world of his own at the sole of his foot. There never yet has been a period in history when a man so clever as Juvenal could not have been good if he pleased, no matter how wicked all other folks were. But a man certainly cannot be very good if he be always in a rage — even with the folks who are bad. In fine,

"When grief and anger in the bosom swell,
Let injured Thales bid the town farewell."

But the world of our day is not the world of Juvenal — no, nor the world of Tacitus nor Petronius (assuming, for the moment, that the Petronius Arbiter of Tacitus wrote that novel of manners which scholars generally agree that he did not write, but which was certainly written by some very clever man of the world when the world was still the Roman empire); no, nor is the world of our day the world of St. Simon, of Rochefoucauld, of Horace Walpole.

The Duc de St. Simon is partly the Tacitus, partly the Juvenal, of the old French regime. Of his style it may be said, as it was of Tertullian's, that "it is like ebony, at once dark and splendid." He stands amidst the decay of a perishing social system. The thorough rot of the old regime is clear to his sanctimonious and solemn eye, through the cracks of the satin-wood which veneers its worm-eaten substance and bungled joinery. I am far from saying that men, on the whole, were rather good than otherwise, and women, on the whole, rather better than the men, in the world which St. Simon knew; but his world was very contracted. His personal vanity served to contract it still more. Marmontel said of him, "that all which he saw in the nation was the *noblesse;* all that he saw in the *noblesse* was the peerage; and all that he saw in the peerage was himself" — an exaggerated judgment, as definitions of character condensed into sarcasms usually are, but not without a large foundation of truth. The world of a court is not a fair sample even of that mere superficies of concrete existence to which I proposed limiting our survey of what is called knowledge of the world; much less the court of an absolute monarchy. To use the Duc's own expression, no man had keener penetration than he into "*le manége des courtisans.*" But courtiers are not the people; the life of a court is not the life of a nation: it is to the nation's life what a sucker grafted on a stem is to the tree which has its roots in the soil; the flowers and fruits which it yields are those of the sucker, and not of the tree. But to the success of all grafting, these conditions are indispensable: first, that the place of juncture should be guarded from the air; secondly, that the graft should have a perfect similitude with the plant from which its nourishment is derived, in the grain of the wood, the consistency of the bark, the season for the sap. Where these conditions fail, it is a proof of the gardener's ignorance, and not of his knowledge, if, showing me a blighted quince, he tells me it is a proof of disease in the native tree — it is only a proof of disease in the alien sucker. Now, there was no similitude in bark or in wood between the courtier of Versailles and the genuine autochthon of France — the sap of the one had no natural confluence with the sap of the other: and the clay rudely plastered round the point of junction was, in the time of St. Simon, fast crumbling away, to let in, with each beam of obtrusive sunlight, the air that must kill not the tree but the graft. It is the characteristic of St. Simon, and of many other French memoir-writers less gifted, to imagine that, in showing the sickliness of the graft, they are proving the condition of the tree. They treat of the *grand monde;* but their *grand monde* is only the face of the *beau monde*, with bloom that comes not from the veins, but from carmine and pearl powder.

This defect of scope detracts from the merit of an observer still more subtle and keen than St. Simon. Rochefoucauld reduces to the dimensions of drawing-room epigram the range of a philosophy intended to illustrate the mechanism of Man by a morality drawn from the knowledge of Manners. His maxims are exquisite specimens of that kind of wisdom which might be attained in boudoirs and *petits soupers* by a French duke of brilliant wit, of sharp penetration — adorned by a style that, for neatness and finish, might have been written by Alcibiades, amusing his exile in Sparta by refining Laconic aphorisms into Attic diction.

Yet, while Rochefoucauld has no claim to original conception in the Epicurean theory tracing all the springs of our actions, good or evil, sublime or base, to that self-love of which the 'Maxims' are designed to be the brilliant Euclid, the propositions by which he illustrates his doctrine are based on experiences visibly narrow. One perceives at a glance that Rochefoucauld's men, who "in the adversity of their best friends always find something that does not displease them," were hollow-hearted intriguants for fortune, place, and favour; men who, even in the heat of civil war (the war of the Fronde) seem devoid of one patriotic sentiment, or of one ennobling opinion. Even the great Condé takes arms with the foreigner against his own country, from no conceivable motive except that he had not been treated with all the *égards* due to him at court. In such a camp as that of the Fronde, in such a court as that of France, I have no doubt that men found something not displeasing to them in the adversities of their best friends. Those men had been accustomed from childhood to think very little of their best friends where their own interests were concerned. So, when Rochefoucauld says that "there are few virtuous women who are not tired of their *métier*," I have no doubt that the saying was true as applied to the French marchionesses, to whom virtue was a *métier*. Aphorisms like these, applied to humankind in general, are only sarcasms having just that proportion of partial truth to which sarcasm is indebted for its sparkle. Nothing conveys a more inaccurate idea of a whole truth than a part of a truth so prominently brought forth as to throw the other parts into shadow. This is the art of caricature; and by the happy use of that art you might caricature the Apollo Belvidere.

To appreciate the process of thought by which Rochefoucauld arrives at his famous maxim of our secret content in the adversities of our best friends, it is necessary to glance at some of his opinions on friendship in general — as, for instance, "That which men have named friendship is only a society, a reciprocal management of interests, and an exchange of good offices: it is, in fine, only a commerce wherein self-love always proposes to itself a something to gain." Again, "It is difficult to love those whom we do not esteem, but it is not less so to love those whom we esteem much more than ourselves." Or, "We have always sufficient strength to bear the ills — of another."

Maxims thus cynical, set forth after deliberate meditation, and so carefully weighed, so laboriously polished, that every word has been a study, must either be congenial to the nature of the writer or to the social experiences from which he has drawn them; but they were not congenial to the nature of Rochefoucauld, who was esteemed, by the best judges among his contemporaries, for the chivalrous honour of his character; and therefore it is in such maxims that we see not the writer, not mankind in general, but the social attributes of the time and circle in which he lived. There are few things that more intelligibly depict the condition of any given state of society than the estimate taken of those affections of love and friendship which are the cement of all societies — but may in one age be a cement of cracking rubble or crumbling mud, and, in another age, of Parian stone.

In healthful — that is, in free — communities, there are certain public friendships in which the types of private friendship appear heroic; and, from the disinterested nature of the public friendships, private friendships insensibly acquire generosity and elevation. Certainly, in those public friendships, there is nothing that pleases men in the adversities of their best friends; for the common sympathy in great objects overpowers the egotism which either soothes a latent envy, or indulges a vain sentiment of superiority in such pleasure as can be found in contemplating the misfortunes of a friend. Shaftesbury has thus noted, among the counterpoising benefits to the evils of war, the magnanimity of the friendships which are engendered by the participation of a common peril and a common glory. It is so, if the combatants feel something sacred in the cause of the war which unites them — not if the war be a mere game of personal ambition, in which the death of your best friend may be a lucky step in your promotion. Thus, the combatant, in some war hallowed by the conviction of his conscience, and espoused by the passions of his heart, far from finding it difficult, according to Rochefoucauld's maxim, to love those whom he esteems more than himself, loves his chief exactly in proportion as he accords to that chief an esteem in which the sense of his own personality absolutely vanishes. As man must personify in flesh and blood his abstract idea of love and veneration, so the patriot soldier invests the strongest affections of his heart in some heroic chief, who seems to him most livingly to represent whatever is most divine in his enthusiastic thought. In no adversity that could befall that chief would there be a something that would not displease him. No genuine Ironside could have known any secret satisfaction had reverse befallen Cromwell — no genuine Cavalier have felt a consolatory touch of self-love when the pikemen smoked in the face of Charles. To both the Ironside and the Cavalier, the man who concentred on himself for the time the noblest affections of human friendship, was the representative of a cause — was a Cromwell or a Charles. "Yes," you will say, "but this is not friendship — it is something more and something different. It was not friendship that the Ironside felt for Cromwell, or the Cavalier for Charles." Granted; but in all which elevates and ennobles friendship into a relation beyond mere companionship, which identifies the Friend with some agency in the success of a principle that we hold to be a paramount truth — a principle that takes us literally and completely out of all cognition of our self-love, and of all which common-sense can accept as our self-interest — there enters an affection which is, more or less, like that of an enthusiast for the representative of his cause. And this comprehends the secret of that affectionate friendship which, in free States, springs up between members of the same party; so that, where party runs strong, Cicero's saying is almost painfully true, "*Idem sentire de Republica ea sola firma amicitia est*" — an aphorism which, transferred from classic Latin into homely English, means, "Sympathy in political opinions constitutes the only firm friendship." Party-spirit in our day does not run so high as it did in Cicero's — in our day we must qualify the maxim. In our day, to my judgment, a safe English politician should be many-sided, not one-sided: he should live familiarly with all classes of opinion; he should weigh deliberately and muse reflectively over all that is generous and true and wise in each class. I am not sure whether, in metaphysics, the eclectic school, adorned by the candid genius of Victor Cousin, be the deepest; but I am sure that, for the practical administration of England, the eclectic statesman will obtain the largest amount of confidence, and do the greatest amount of good. Moreover, in England, thank heaven, we are not at this moment so engrossingly politicians but what we have other fellowships besides those of politics — Literature, Art, Science — even congenialities in ordinary social tastes or sympathies, in manners and modes of living. Happy for a land is that time in which political dissensions are not the tyrannical controllers of man's intellectual, moral, spiritual being!

But party is still a noble fellowship, if it be nobly adopted; — a noble intercommunication of affection and thought: and the friendships formed by the large sympathies of party are still strong enough to give a polite contradiction to Rochefoucauld's axiom. True, in party as in literature, art, trade, there are base jealousies. Let a member of either House of Parliament, full of himself — full of the *amour propre* which Rochefoucauld so anatomically dissects — consult only his egotism; desire, if young, to shine by an oratorical display — desire, if old and hardened, to betray a colleague and indulge a spleen: certes, if he fail, in his adversity there will be something which will not displease his right honourable and noble friends. But once let a man merge his personality, however brilliant that be, in an earnest consideration of what is best for the party and the cause to which he belongs — real earnestness is so evident that it seldom admits denial in any large assembly in which the earnest speaker lifts up his truthful brow — and that man will have friends to whom his failure, or misfortunes involving failure, would convey nothing that could not displease. Those whom the misfortune does not displease will not be his friends, but his antagonists. Mr. Pitt was popularly considered a man in whom private friendships were somewhat frigid; but when his friend Lorl Melville was stricken down by a sentence of impeachment, tears, for the first time, were detected in Pitt's haughty eyes; and the shock, to a heart indomitable to foes, contributed to the causes which accelerated his death. There was not a something in Lord Melville's adversity which did not displease Mr. Pitt. Nor was the afflicted friend here the object of a hero-worship to which the worshipper renders superstitious adoration. Melville might worship Pitt — Pitt did not worship Melville. In loyal, affectionate friendship, I know not which is the stronger tie to a loyal affectionate nature — gratitude for him who serves you, or appreciation of gratitude in him whom you have served. On the whole, in proportion to the heroism of your nature, you will most devotedly sacrifice yourself to the man who has served you, and may nevertheless most fondly mourn for the misfortunes of the man whom you have had the happiness to serve; but in neither case can you find, in the misfortunes of benefactor or benefited, a something that does not displease you. Where men do feel such satisfaction in the adversities of their best friends as to justify Rochefoucauld's maxim, and lift it into the popularity of a proverb, there must be a rot in the state of society; and the cynicism of the saying condemns not the man who says it, but the society that originated illustrations so numerous as to make the saying proverbial. As I have before said, Rochefoucauld's character warrants this reflection. The author of the 'Maxims' was apparently the least selfish public man of his land and age. Saith one of his biographers, not untruly, "He gave the example of all the virtues of which he would appear to contest the existence." He ridicules bravery as a madness; and as Madame de Maintenon, who could have had no predilection for his system, curtly observes, "*il etoit cependant fort brave.*" The proofs of his bravery do not rest on Madame de Maintenon's assertion. A scorn of danger, pre-eminently French, as it became the inheritor of so great a French name to exhibit, was sufficiently shown at the siege of Bordeaux and the battle of St. Antoine. Madame de Sevigné speaks of Rochefoucauld with an admiration which she rarely bestows except on her daughter; and says that, in his last agonising illness, he thought more of his neighbour than himself. Cardinal de Retz, in the portrait he has left of the brilliant duke — a portrait certainly not flattered — tells us that this philosopher, who reduced all human motives to self-interest, did not feel (*il ne sentoit pas*) the little interests which have never been his weak point (*son foible*), and did not understand the great interests (*il ne connoissoit pas les grands*) which have not been his strong point (*son fort*); and, finally, this acute critic of contemporaneous celebrities, after assuring us that Rochefoucauld "had never been a good party-man," tells us that, in the relations of common life, Rochefoucauld was the honestest man of his age (*le plus honnête homme à l'égard de la vie commune qui eût paru dans son siècle*). And yet, though Rochefoucauld was not depraved by the world in which he lived, we may reasonably doubt if he would not have been a still better man if his knowledge of it had been somewhat less intimate. He tells us, for instance, that he was insensible to compassion. Would he have been so insensible to compassion if he had not somewhat hardened his own heart by the process of dissecting, with scientific remorselessness, the mean little hearts which furnish the subjects of his lectures on mankind? If some skilful vivisector has spent the morning in disjointing and disembowelling the curs that he submits to his philosophical scalpel, one can scarcely expect him to be seized with compassion for a hungry mastiff or a footsore pointer whom he may encounter in his evening walks.

I must crave pardon for treating at such length of the author of the 'Maxims,' and of the fallacies contained in his theory. The pardon is due to me; for we are never to forget the extent to which the fashionable philosophy of France has operated on the intellect and action of Europe; and Voltaire assures us, in his most elaborate work, that "the book which most contributed to form the taste of the French nation was the 'Maxims' of François, Duc de Rochefoucauld." That is true; — not only the taste but the mode of thought. Helvetius, preceding the Revolution, is but a learned and lengthened expositor of the philosophy contained in the 'Maxims.' Rochefoucauld was one of the founders of the Revolution, for his work was that of a leveller. His descendant, like himself a philosopher, accepted the Revolution, cheerfully renounced his titles of noblesse, and was appointed to the Presidency of the Department of Paris. It is easy to resign the titles of a duke — difficult to get rid of the honour of a gentleman. Quoth one of the patriots with whom he linked himself, "This *ci-devant* is of a virtue too troublesome" (*c'est une vertu trop incommode*). Accordingly, the descendant of the author of the 'Maxims' was doomed, and massacred in the sight, almost in the arms, of his wife and mother; — tragic and practical illustration of the dogma which the great Duke had impressed on the mind of his country; — "*Les vertus se perdent dans l'intérêt, comme les fleuves se perdent dans la mer.*" Certainly it is not in the 'Maxims' of Rochefoucauld that we would search for doctrines which make chivalry poetically heroic and democracy poetically humane.

When Alphonse Lamartine, by an immortal speech, in which there is no wit and no sparkle, struck down to his feet the red flag, we recognise intuitively the difference between the maxim-maker's knowledge of the conventional world and the poet-orator's knowledge of the universal human heart. Honour to Alphonse Lamartine for his knowledge of the heart in that moment which saved the dignity of France and the peace of Europe, no matter what were his defects in the knowledge of the world — defects by which rulers destined to replace him learned to profit! Honour to that one triumph of poetry put into action!

I have spoken of Knowledge of the World, in the current meaning of the phrase, as superficial — the knowledge of a society which is to the world what the surface is to the sea. But that definition is not always correct; for knowledge of the world in Rochefoucauld, and writers akin to him, even including La Bruyère (who, like all plagiarists of real genius, has rendered original what he plagiarised, and, copying from the skeleton-outlines of Theophrastus, has made the copy worth a million times more than the picture it honours by copying) — knowledge of the world in Rochefoucauld and La Bruyère is knowledge that cannot be called shallow — it wants breadth rather than depth. In proportion to its width it is profound. It does not skim over the sea; but it does fathom to the base of the cistern, and does ascend to the height of the spray, in an artificial fountain. On the other hand, our own Horace Walpole's knowledge of the world is much more expansive than that of St. Simon or Rochefoucauld, and is much less deep in proportion to its width. It takes a more varied survey of manners and humours, embracing more of the active and serious employments of that life which is not spent in patrician salons and royal anterooms. It sports, indeed, with the appropriate airiness of a well-born wit, over the fragile characters of its Lady Betties and Lord Jessamies; it has its familiar *entrée* into the circle set apart for princes of the blood: but it is at home in a world on the other side of the Coteries; it has a polite acquaintance with the arts which embellish our universal humanity; it has its familiar chit-chat with the grave interests and the solemn passions by whose alternate action and repulsion Freedom maintains its poise; it comprehends the truth as notable in political as in physical science — viz., that large bodies attract the smaller, and by the smaller are themselves attracted. Horace Walpole illustrates his knowledge of the world by anecdote and witticism, by the authority of his own empirical opinion, by a fancy so wanton and discursive that it cannot fail to be sometimes just; but he never fatigues himself by seeking, like Rochefoucauld, to dissect and analyse. He prides himself on being frivolous, and if he is wise, he takes care to tell you that he is only so for his own amusement. We cannot dispute his knowledge of the world in breadth of surface, as we may do that of the French Court-philosophers; but he very rarely dives to the depth which they explore, though it be but the depth of a garden fountain. Not actuated by any earnest desire of abstract truth in his survey of things, he is not likely to be scrupulously accurate in his delineations of persons; and in these his native penetration and his acquired experience are often warped and distorted by spite, spleen, party antipathies, family grudges, and still more often by the love of scandal, which is the normal characteristic of an intellectual gossip. We cannot look on his portraitures of contemporaneous characters even with the qualified respect which we attach to those in the Memoirs of St. Simon. They do not belong to a historical gallery; but they have their price as a portfolio of brilliant caricatures by an artist who might have done much better. Finally, we may doubt whether Horace Walpole's knowledge of the world conduced to his own moral wellbeing; whether if, in youth, he had immured himself in a college, like Gray — devoted himself, like Gray, to earnest study, and the patient contemplation of those forms of art which, as a fashionable virtuoso, he only deigned to regard as toys for rococo cabinets — he might not have disciplined his unquestionable genius to much nobler exercise, and cultivated into richer fertility those manly affections of which he proved, by his friendship for Conway, and his reverence for his father's memory, that he was not constitutionally barren. Remote from the world that he paints in such brilliant water-colours, he might have filled his heart and his mind with less old-maidish fondnesses than he conceived, amid swarms of human fellow-creatures, for a long-haired poodle and a Gothic reliquary.

Knowledge of the world, in the conventional sense which is given to the phrase, is rarely exhibited by poets, either in their writings or their lives. It is only intellects of a much higher order than suffices for those combinations of melodious sound, delicate fancies, or tender sentiments, by which poets can achieve lovely and immortal names — that seize and cultivate into, fruit or flower such germs of poetry as lie deep-hidden beneath the trodden soils of commonplace and matter-of-fact. Knowledge of the world, as a man of the world comprehends it, does in itself belong rather to the prose than to the poetry of life. There seems, indeed, to most poets, something antagonistic to poetic fancies, reveries, and contemplations, in the study of conventional manners — in the intimate acquaintance with the fashions and frivolities of the Court and the Town — in the analysis of the ordinary motives of prosaic characters — in the business of their idleness, the idleness of their business. It is only a poet of immense grasp and range that, seizing on all these material elements of earth, carries them aloft into his upper air, held there in solution, as the atmosphere above us holds the metals and the gases, and calling them forth at his easy will, to become tangible and visible, through luminous golden vapour; as, at the magic of the chemist, gases burst into light from the viewless space; or, in a ray of the sun, are discovered the copper and the iron which minister to our most familiar uses.

It is certainly not the least marvellous property of Shakespeare's genius that he takes up into his poetry elements that seem essentially to belong to prose, and gives them back in poetic forms, yet preserving all the practical value which plain good sense could give them in prose the most logically severe. In his aphorisms, he includes the worldly shrewdness, the fine observation of positive life, of conventional manners, which constitute the merit of the Rochefoucaulds, La Bruyères, Walpoles. Nothing can be less like their prose than his poetry; but his poetry embraces the happiest particles of the genius which places their prose among our classics. In the wide range of his characters he comprises the airy, fine gentleman, the subtle politician, the courtier, the fop — the types of those in whom the man of the world recognises the familiars from whom he derives his experience. What knowledge of the world — unsurpassed by those who are its oracles of our own day in the clubs of London and Paris — playfully blazes out in his Falstaff, his Mercutio! With what delicate and finished mastery of character, formed by the influence of the actual world, the hypocrisy of Angelo is shadowed forth and reconciled to the qualities that had made him tenacious of repute for inflexible justice and rigid virtue! Compare Shakespeare's Angelo with Molière's Tartuffe — both admirable portraitures; but the first is the portraiture by a psychologist, the second the portraiture by a satirist. There is no satire in Angelo — very little satire in Shakespeare's habitual employment of his genius; for satire is, in reality, too akin to prose views of life for Shakespeare's transmutation of prose into poetry. But whatever satire aims at in the Tartuffe is included and fused in the conception of Angelo; and so it is with Shakespeare generally. As satire consists in the exaggeration of some alleged vice or folly, to the ignoring of other components in the moral being of the individual satirised, until the individual is reduced almost to an abstraction of the idea which the satirist wishes to hold up to scorn, and a Tartuffe becomes less a hypocritical man than an allegoric personification of hypocrisy; so, on the contrary, with Shakespeare, the one dominant passion, humour, or moral quality of the character is generally softened and shaded off into various other tints; and it is through the entire system and complicated functions of the living man that the dominating idea winds and undulates — a living man, and not an automaton which an ingenious mechanician sets in movement for the purpose of exhibiting a philosophical idea that he desires to make scientifically clear to vulgar comprehension. It is for this reason that Shakespeare, in his tragedy, so remarkably preserves the intellectual freedom of his criminal characters. As Hegel well remarks, it is not the witches who lead Macbeth on to his crimes — it is the sinful desires to which the witches only give an utterance that at first dismays him; and it is also for this reason that Shakespeare is so genial in his comedy, and, being so genial, so exquisitely forgiving. That he should not only let off, but actually reward, an Angelo, is a violation of the vulgar laws of poetical justice. But Shakespeare's sovereign knowledge of the world, instead of making him cynical and austere, makes him charitable and gentle. Perhaps because he lived in a very grand age, in which, amid much that, while human nature lasts, will be eternally bad and low, there were, nevertheless, astir all the noblest elements which modern society has called into play. There was still the valiant spirit of chivalry, divested of its savage rudeness, retaining its romantic love of adventure, its unselfish loyalty, its ineffable dignity, its poetic delicacy of sentiment and high-bred courtesy of bearing. Shakespeare was the contemporary of Spenser. But there was also astir in the world — not yet divorced from the courtly graces, not yet narrowed into puritanical fanaticism — the sublime conception of a freedom for opinion and conscience, destined to create a heroism

KNOWLEDGE OF THE WORLD.

more intense and more earnest than knighthood's. Shakespeare's 'Tempest' was the precursor of Milton's 'Comus.' Shakespeare had not only the advantage of living in a very great and energetic age, but the still greater advantage, for the serene and angerless contemplation of human infirmities, of living in an age in which the conflicting passions between the old and the new heroisms of thought were not yet let loose, — when men, in their zeal for a cause or a principle, were not inflamed into a hate that destroyed all philosophical judgment of the men who differed from them. It was not only a great age, but a conciliatory age; and Shakespeare, in expressing it, is as conciliatory as he is great. This was impossible to the Poet of that after age, also great, but violently aggressive and antagonistic, which

"Was with its stored thunder labouring up."

Who could have divined in the beautiful dreamy youth of Milton the destined champion of fanatics to whom the Muses and the Graces were daughters of Belial? — who could have supposed that out of such golden platonisms, such lovely fancies, such dulcet concords of all pastoral, chivalrous, courtly, scholastic melodies, as meet and ravish us away from each ungentle thought in 'Comus' and 'L'Allegro,' 'Il Penseroso,' 'Lycidas,' 'Arcadia,' would rise the inflexible wrathful genius that became the vindicator of Charles's regicide, the eulogist of Cromwell's usurpation? Happy that, surviving the age of strife, that majestic spirit is last seen on earth, nearer in age than even in youth to the gates of heaven, and, no longer fiercest in the war of Christian against Christian, blending all the poetries of Christendom itself in that wondrous hymn, compared to which Tasso's song is but a dainty lay, and even Dante's verse but a Gothic mystery.

To return to Shakespeare. In that world which he knew so well, there were not only the Spensers, the Sidneys, the Raleighs, and the magnificent image of Elizabeth crowning all, and, to the infinite disgrace of Englishmen, of late years deposed from her throne of Gloriana, and reduced by small historians and shallow critics to the level of a Catherine of Russia; — there was also the Francis Bacon who revolutionised all the systems of practical science; and, far less known (be that also to the shame of Englishmen), the John Davies, beyond whom no metaphysician of the immaterial or spiritual school, — including its great reformers, the Scotch, with Reid — its æsthetic embellishers and logicians, with Kant — its accomplished, rhetorical, eloquent embellishers, with Victor Cousin, — has advanced, any more than Faraday, Frankhofer, Stokes, Brewster, Kirchhoff have advanced from Newton, in tracing the nature of the solar light. Contemporaneous with Shakespeare, also, were those awful politicians — far, indeed, from being scrupulously philanthropical, far from being morally spotless — Walsingham and either Cecil; but who, in practical statesmanship, who, in the knowledge of which Themistocles boasted — "the knowledge how to make small states great" — towered aloft over even a Raleigh and a Bacon. It is by the light of such an age that we can alone read adequately a Shakespeare, who, in his mere playful supererogatory knowledge of the world, comprehended them all, and fused, in his loving verse, every discord in their various wisdom.

What has most struck me in comparing, I do not

say Shakespeare's genius, for that is incomparable, but his practical wisdom, with the poets of his time, has been less his metaphysical depth and subtlety in discovering some latent truth amid the complicated folds of the human mind, than the ease with which he adapts his metaphysical acuteness to his practical views of life; in short, his knowledge of man individually, wondrous as it is, seems to me less exclusively and transcendently his own than his combination of knowledge of men individually, and of the world collectively, and his fusion of both kinds of knowledge into poetic form, which has its appropriate place in the entire composition, and is not merely a detached and occasional felicity of diction; for if we look at his contemporaries, and especially the later ones, there are few attributes they have more in common than a love for metaphysical reflection upon man in the abstract, couched in vivid poetry of expression. Passages of this kind abound in Beaumont and Fletcher; still more in the richer genius of Massinger, whose main fault, perhaps, lies in an over-fondness for metaphysical research in the creation of exceptional characters influenced by exceptional motives, and a lavish beauty of expression, which is often inharmonious to the displeasing nature of the action. This family resemblance is perhaps less salient in Jonson than in the other great dramatists of the time; but even in him it is sufficiently strong. The prevalent taste in the age of a great writer who may be regarded as its highest type, is perhaps, however, best seen in the taste of the younger generation formed in his school, and among writers of the lesser order of genius, which reflects the earlier genius that overshadows it. Daniel, Habington,

Davenant have wonderful lines here and there, combining, in the Shakespearean spirit, an abstract philosophical thought with exquisite poetry of form. Such as this description of Justice —

> "Clear-eyed Astræa
> Comes with her balance and her sword, to show
> That first her judgment weighs before it strikes."
> — Daniel's 'Goddesses.'

Or this fine discrimination between political perils —

> "Each small breath
> Disturbs the quiet of poor shallow waters,
> But winds must arm themselves ere the large sea
> Is seen to tremble."
> — Habington's 'Queen of Arragon.'

Or this striking illustration of the fear which accompanies and betokens ardent love —

> "Flame trembles most when it doth highest rise."
> — Sir W. Davenant's 'The Man's the Master.'

Observe the metaphysical depth in the lines I am about to subjoin from May,* and consider how much the thought they embody has served to furnish forth arguments in defence of miracles urged at this day:

> "Nor let us say some things 'gainst Nature be,
> Because such things as those we seldom see.
> We know not what is natural, but call
> Those acts which God does often — natural.
>
> Where, if we weighed with a religious eye
> The *power* of doing — not the *frequency* —
> All things alike in strangeness to our thought
> Would be, which He in the creation wrought;
> But in those rare and wondrous things may we
> The freedom of that great Creator see."

---

* May was about twenty-one when Shakespeare died. It was the generation preceding his own in which his youth learned to think, and it is the spirit of that epoch of thought which speaks in the verses cited — a spirit that underwent a notable change in the revolutionary epoch during which May's later manhood acted its inconsistent and passionate part.

KNOWLEDGE OF THE WORLD.

> When He at first the course of things ordained,
> And Nature within certain bounds restrained,
> That laws of seeds and seasons may be known ; —
> He did not then at all confine His own
> Almighty power! But, wheresoe'er He will,
> Works 'gainst the common course of Nature still."
> — May's 'Henry II.'

I think that every student of intellectual philosophy will allow that there must have been an immense amount of metaphysical, and even of psychological, knowledge afloat in the atmosphere of an age in which so poor a poet, in point of genius and form, as that I have quoted, could embody such refinement and depth of reasoning in verses that certainly are not inspired.

The two writers, in the full noon of the Shakespearean era, to whom we should be least disposed to look for sentences rich in abstract philosophy (always except Spenser, in whom philosophy, where found, as completely forgets its purpose, in allegorical fancies and melodious roundelays, as a bee may forget its hive amid the honeys of Hymettus), are Philip Sidney, the Court darling, and Lilye, the fashionable euphuist. Yet, even in his romance of 'Arcadia,' Sidney has depths and reaches of thought which may suffice to show what tributary rivulets were feeding the sea of Shakespeare. Lilye was pre-eminently the fashionable literary fop of his splendid age; but still Lilye, if he be compared with a fashionable novelist or play-writer of our time, in Paris or London, becomes instantly entitled to a considerable degree of respect. The 'Euphues' devoured by courtiers and maids of honour is enough to show how high a standard of intellectual eminence was required by the most frivolous portion of the reading public of that majestic day. Its pervading vice is, that it pushes into extravagant caricature Shakespeare's own greatest fault — viz., the excess of wit in verbal conceit; but strip the sense of that verbal conceit, and the substance left is robust and masculine. It abounds with materials for fine thinking, in spite of a style so opposed to good writing; and that a work in which a schoolman's erudition is employed in selecting the pithy sayings and subtle conjectures of ancient philosophers should have become the rage with light readers of fashion, is a proof how much the taste for philosophising had become the taste of the age.

In Shakespeare's day, then, the tendency to science and metaphysical speculation was marked and general, and his own fondness for it is explained by the spirit of his time. But he stands distinct from contemporaneous writers of imagination in this — that his science of man's nature in the abstract is so wondrously enriched and vivified by knowledge of the world — exhibited not only in profound aphorisms, but in vivid impersonations through created characters in every class and grade of life; and of the latter knowledge there is very little trace in his contemporaries — very little trace, I venture to think, even in Jonson and Beaumont and Fletcher. Probably his personal intimacies assisted to the perfection of his delineations of the manners and mind of the being we call gentleman — of a Bassanio, a Gratiano, a Benedick, an Orlando, a Mercutio, &c.; not to speak of the incomparable art with which he retains to Falstaff, in despite of all the fat knight's rogueries, the character of the wit who has equality with princes. Falstaff is never vulgar. And if Shakespeare, when not dealing with the destinies of tragedy, is so indulgent to his faulty characters, — not only to Angelo, the sanctimonious dissembler, but to Bertram, the faithless lover — Oliver, the unnatural elder brother — Proteus, the treacherous friend, — it is because his knowledge of the world, in its survey of mankind on the whole, softens into an artistic charity the penetration with which he detects the vice of man in the abstract. And, doubtless, I say, the age in which he lived contributed to engender and justify this charity of judgment. For in its juncture between the licence of chivalric manners and the severer morality which the Reformation and the new-born study of the sacred writings were destined to introduce, and in the struggle visible among the highest natures of the time and land between the old Northern principle of honour, and the seductive brilliancies of Italian craft — there *was*, in the characters of men of the world, a singular mixture of qualities fair and noble and qualities foul and mean, the mixture being sustained by a third element of intellectual activity or poetic grace. Without entering into the controversy as to the just estimate of Lord Bacon's character — which, I think, however, is much too harshly depreciated by Lord Macaulay — I content myself with referring to his advice to Lord Essex, in the letter of 4th October 1596, how "to win the Queen," as sufficing to show the extent to which Machiavellian policy was in 'that day admitted as blameless into English counsel. For certainly Bacon, in that letter, is altogether unconscious that he is recommending a systematic duplicity and simulation unworthy the adoption of a high-minded noble; nor is there any evidence that Essex himself, though he might reject the advice, resented it as dishonourable;

yet as certainly there is not a true gentleman nowadays who could receive such a letter from a distinguished friend without a blush for himself and his adviser; for the whole purport of the letter is to recommend this knight and soldier to seem what he is not — to make his very nature a lie. Pretend, pretend, pretend, is the moral of each wily recommendation. He is to pretend to resemble the very men whom both he and his adviser despise: "whereof I have noted you to fly and avoid, in some respect justly, the resemblance or imitation of my Lord Leicester or my Lord Chancellor Hatton; yet I am persuaded, howsoever I wish your lordship as distant as you are from them in points of form, integrity, magnanimity, and merit, that it will do you much good between the Queen and you to *allege them, as often as you find occasion, for authors and patterns;* for I do not know a readier mean to make her Majesty think you are in the right way."

Again: "Your lordship should never be without some particulars afoot which you should *seem* to pursue with earnestness and affection, and *then let them fall upon taking knowledge of her Majesty's opposition and dislike.*" He is to push this insincerity even into bad faith to his own friends and partisans, "of which (particulars) the weightiest sort may be, if your lordship *offer* to labour on the behalf of some that you favour for some of the places now void, choosing such *a subject as you think her Majesty is like to oppose unto.* And if you will say this is *conjunctum cum aliena injuria,* I will not answer, *Hæc non aliter constabunt;* but I say, commendation from so good a mouth does not peril a man, though you prevail not." A poor salvo to the conscience of a patron for holding out to trustful clients hopes that he knows are false — and a poor satisfaction to the client to receive commendation from the mouth, with the premeditated design to "be let fall" by the hand.

Again: "A less weighty sort of particulars may be the *pretence* of some journeys which, at her Majesty's request, you *might relinquish.* And the lightest sort of particulars, which are yet not to be neglected, are in your habits, apparel, wearings, *gestures*, and the like."

In short, from the greatest to the least "particular," the man is to be one pretence: "You shall *pretend* to be as bookish and contemplative as ever you were. Whereunto I add one expedient more, stronger than all the rest, and for my own confident opinion, void of any prejudice or danger of diminution of your greatness; and that is, the bringing in of some martial man to be of the Council, dealing directly with her Majesty in it, as for her service and your better assistance; *choosing, nevertheless, some person that may be known not to come in against you by any former division.* I judge the fittest to be my Lord Mountjoy or my Lord Willoughby. And if your lordship see deeplier into it than I do, that you would *not have it done in effect, you may serve your turn by the pretence of it, and stay it, nevertheless."*

Again: "The third impression is of a popular reputation, which, because it is a thing good of itself, being obtained as your lordship obtaineth it — that is, *bonis artibus* — and, besides well governed, is one of the best flowers of your greatness, both present and to come, it would be handled tenderly. The only way is to quench it *verbis,* and not *rebus;* and therefore, to take all occasions to *speak against popularity and popu-*

lar courses vehemently, and to tax it in all others — but, nevertheless, to go on in your honourable commonwealth courses as you do."

Now, judged by the morality of our day, we should say that a man following these counsels would be a contemptible hypocrite and a very dangerous citizen. But in an age where Court favour is the first object of political ambition, morality is of a more accommodating temper. To me, this letter to Essex contains the true key to Lord Bacon's character and conduct in matters relating to the world: it is, in its own way, very wise, and in any way it is very mean. It shows where Bacon's knowledge of the world was profound, and also where it ran into perilous shallows beset with rocks and shoals. It explains the rules by which he shaped his own career and sullied his own honour; how he came to rise so high, and to fall so low. It seems also to justify, on the score of wisdom, the meanness of his supplicatory attitude after his fall. I believe his self-humiliation was more a pretence than a reality; that he did for himself what he had recommended to Essex — sought to seem, rather than to be. An abject bearing was the best means to his end, which was to retrieve as far as possible the effects of his reverse. His lowliness was Ambition's ladder. The more he seemed bowed down with penitent shame, the more he converted the wrath even of his enemies into compassion. And the course he adopted in this seeming self-abasement proved its merely worldly sagacity. Step after step he began to re-arise. His fine was released — the rest of his punishment remitted — he reappeared at Court — he was readmitted to the House of Lords — his piteous importunities for his pension were successful — he got from the Government his £1200 a-year. All that his wisdom saw it possible to effect after such a reverse, he effected through the meanness which perhaps was not constitutional with him, but an essential element of that which, in dealings with the world, he conceived to be wisdom. It is not true, as Mr. Basil Montagu and others would have us believe, that he did nothing which the contemporaries who condemned him really thought wrong; but it is also not true that what he did was thought wrong in the codes of that wily Italian school of policy in which Bacon's youth had been trained. In the Cecil Correspondence, men of the greatest name and the purest repute exhibit a laxity of sentiment in what we now call honour, and a servile greediness for what were then called honours, which would not in our time be compatible with dignity of mind and elevation of character. But in that day such contrasts were compatible. Far from being worse or lower types of our kind in the age of Elizabeth than ambition exhibits now, the men of that age may rather be said to have joined meannesses which no ordinary mean man nowadays will avow, with lofty qualities of heart and intellect and courage which no man, ordinarily noble, nowadays can rival. And thus it was that, in analysing the springs of conduct, and sufficiently showing his condemnation of vice in the abstract, Shakespeare so mercifully, in his mixed characters, awards judgment on the outward fate of the offender, and so tenderly merges the hard law of poetic justice into the soft humanity of poetic love — dealing with such characters as if they were indeed his children, and he could not find it in his father's heart to devote to the avenging Furies the erring offspring he had born into the temptations of the world.

It seems to me that, among modern poets, Goethe ranks next to Shakespeare, at however wide an interval, in the combination of abstract, metaphysical speculation, and genial, easy, clement knowledge of the actual world. But this latter knowledge is perhaps even less shown in his dramas, poems, and novels — works, in short, prepared and designed for publication — than in the numerous records which his friends have preserved of his private correspondence and conversations. In the course of these Essays I have frequently quoted his sayings — perhaps somewhat too frequently; but they have been nearly always taken from such personal records — little known to English readers, and not very generally known even to Germans; and there is scarcely a subject connected with the great interests of the world — whether in art, literature, politics, or in the more trivial realm of worldly manners — on which some shrewd, wise, or playful observation of Goethe's does not spontaneously occur to me as pertinent, and throwing a gleam of new light on topics the most trite or familiar. What Goethe himself thought of the world he knew so well, and in which he won so lofty a vantage-ground of survey, is perhaps sufficiently shown in the following remark, which is made with his characteristic union of *naïveté* and irony: "The immorality of the age is a standing topic of complaint with some men; but if any one likes to be moral, I can see nothing in the age to prevent him."

I may add another of his aphorisms, which hints the explanation of his own lenient views of life: "Great talents are essentially conciliatory." And again: "Age makes us tolerant. I never see a fault which I did not myself commit."

Goethe, like Shakespeare, lived in a great and energetic time. His life comprehends that era in the intellectual history of his country which, for sudden, startling, Titan-like development of forces, has no parallel, unless it be in the outbreak of Athenian genius during the century following the Persian war. A language which, though spoken by vast populations in the central heart of Europe, had not hitherto been admitted among the polite tongues of civilised utterance — which the very kings of the Fatherland had banished from their courts — which was ignored by the *literati* of colleges and capitals, as if the Germany which gave to a sovereign the title of the Cæsars was still the savage dwelling-place of the worshippers of Herman; a language thus deemed a barbarous dialect amid the polished tongues of neighbouring populations, suddenly leapt into a rank beside those of Italy, England, France — furnishing poets, dramatists, critics, reviewers, philosophers, scholars, in dazzling and rapid fertility, and becoming henceforth and evermore a crowded storehouse of the massiest ingots of intellectual treasure, and the most finished ornaments of inventive art.

Amid these founders of a national literature, if Goethe be not indeed the earliest, he appears to be so in the eyes of foreigners, because his form is so towering that it obscures the images of his precursors; and his scope was so vast, his acquirements so various, that almost every phase of that intellectual splendour which surrounds him found on one side or other of his genius a luminiferous reflector, giving back the light which it took in. His knowledge of the world was tolerant and mild as Shakespeare's, partly from the greatness of the national epoch in which the world presented itself to his eye, partly from the prosperous fortunes which the world accorded to his taste for the elegance and the dignity of social life; and partly also from his own calm, artistic temperament, which led him, perhaps somewhat overmuch, to regard the vices or virtues of other men as the painter regards the colours which he mingles in his pallet — with passionless study of his own effects of light and shade. This want of indignation for the bad, this want of scorn for the low, this want of enthusiasm for the good, and this want of worship for the heroic, have been much dwelt upon by his adversaries or depreciators; and the charge is not without some foundation when confined to him as artist; but it does not seem just when applied to him as man. When, through his private correspondence and conversation, we approach to his innermost thoughts, we are somewhat startled to discover the extent of his enthusiasm for all that is genuinely lofty, and all, therefore, that is upright, honest, and sincere. It is this respect for a moral beauty and sublimity apart from the artistic, which made him so reverent an admirer of Lessing — this which rendered so cordial his appreciation of the heroic element in Schiller. It was this which made him so hostile to parodies and travesties. "My only reason for hating them," says he, "is because they lower the beautiful, noble, and great, in order that they may annihilate it." It is this which, in spite of his frequent and grave defects in orthodoxy, made him so thoroughly comprehend the religious truth which he has so resolutely expressed. "Art is based on a strong sentiment of religion: it is a profound and mighty earnestness; hence it is so prone to co-operate with religion." Again: "Art is a severe business; most serious when employed in grand and sacred objects. The artist stands higher than art, higher than the object. He uses art for his purposes, and deals with the object after his own fashion."

Goethe dealt with this art after his own fashion — a fashion not to be commended to any one less than Goethe. He says somewhere, "Oeser taught me that the ideal of beauty is simplicity and tranquillity." That maxim is true, but only to a certain extent — viz., so far as affects form or style; and it is only through his smaller poems, and perhaps in his dramas of 'Iphigenia' and 'Tasso,' that Goethe carries out the principle of composition it inculcates. In the works which give him his European celebrity, simplicity and tranquillity are the last qualities we detect. It is not these merits that impress the reading world in 'Werter' and 'Faust.' In truth, ideal beauty not only requires a great deal more than simplicity and tranquillity, but can exist without being either simple or tranquil. The milkmaids whom I now see out of my window are simple and tranquil, but they are certainly not beautiful. But if the tragedy of 'Othello,' as a work of art, is ideally beautiful, which no Englishman can deny, nothing can be less simple than the character of Iago, and Othello himself becomes poetically beautiful in proportion as he ceases to be tranquil. The fact is, that the intellect of poetry requires not simple but very complex thoughts, sentiments, emotions; and the passion of poetry abhors tranquillity. There is, no doubt, a poetry which embodies only the simple and the tranquil, but it is never the highest kind. Poetry is not sculpture; sculpture alone, of all the arts, is highest where the thought it embodies is the most simple, and the passion it addresses, rather than embodies, is the most tranquil. Thus, in sculpture, the Farnese Hercules rests from his labours, and bears in his arms a helpless child; thus the Belvidere Apollo has discharged his deathful arrow, and watches its effect with the calmness of a scorn assured of triumph. But neither of these images could suggest a poem of the highest order — viz., a narrative or a drama; in such poems we must have the struggle of the mind, and the restless history of the passion. But Goethe's art was not dramatic; he himself tells us so, with his characteristic and sublime candour. He tells us truly, that "tragedy deals with contradictions — and to contradictions his genii is opposed;" he adds as truly, that from the philosophical turn of his mind, he "motivates" too much for the stage. That which prevents his attaining, as a dramatist, his native rank as a poet, still more operates against Goethe as a novelist. Regarded solely as a novelist, his earliest novel, 'Werter,' is the only one that has had a marked effect upon his age, and is the only one that will bear favourable comparison with the *chefs-d'œuvre* of France and England. 'Wilhelm Meister' is the work of a much riper mind; but, as a story designed to move popular interest, it as little resembles an artistic novel as 'Comus' or 'Sampson Agonistes' resembles an acted drama. But through all the various phases of Goethe's marvellous intellect there runs an astonishing knowledge of the infirmities of man's nature, and therefore a surpassing knowledge of the world.

He cannot, like Shakespeare, lift that knowledge of the world so easily into the realm of poetic beauty as to accord to infirmity its due proportion, and no more. He makes a hero of a Claviio — Shakespeare would have reduced a Clavijo into a subordinate character; he makes of a Mephistopheles a prince of hell — Shakespeare would have made of Mephistopheles a mocking philosopher of "earth, most earthy." But knowledge of the world in both these mighty intellects was supreme — in both accompanied with profound metaphysical and psychological science — in both represented in exquisite poetical form; and if in this combination Goethe be excelled by Shakespeare, I know not where else, in imaginative literature, we are to look for his superior.

I have said that I think a Juvenal, a Rochefoucauld, a Horace Walpole, were not rendered better and nobler, and therefore wiser men, in the highest sense of the word wisdom, by their intimate knowledge of the world they lived in. This it not to be said of a Shakespeare or a Goethe. They were not satirists nor cynics. They were so indulgent that scarcely a man living dare be as indulgent as they were; and they were indulgent from the same reasons: 1st, The grandeur of the age in which they lived; 2d, The absence of all acrid and arrogant self-love, and of all those pharisaical pretensions to an austerity of excellence high above the average composite of good and evil in ordinary mortals, which grows out of the inordinate admiration for self, or the want of genial sympathy for the infirmities of others, and the charitable consideration of the influence of circumstance upon human conduct.

There is a class of writers in poetry and *belles lettres* in which what we call Knowledge of the World is more immediately recognised, because it is more sharply defined, than it is with the two great poets last mentioned. It is less fused in poetic fancy, it is less characterised by metaphysical subtlety, it is less comprehensive in its range, but it has more singleness of effect and transparency of purpose. Of this class, English literature furnishes brilliant types throughout the whole of the eighteenth century. Pope and Addison are conspicuously men of the world in their favourite modes of thought and forms of expression. Like most men of the world, it is in the school of a metropolis that they ground their studies of mankind; the urban life rather than the rural attracts their survey and stimulates their genius. Pope, indeed, is comparatively insipid and commonplace when he is the mere observer of rural nature, or the interpreter of those sentiments and emotions which rural nature excites in its familiar lovers. He is essentially the poet of capitals, and his knowledge of the world, like that of the class of poets among which he is perhaps the prince, is rather to be called knowledge of the town. *

---

* In the controversy between Bowles and his adversaries as to Pope's standard among poets, each party mistook or misapprehended the doctrine of the other. Campbell, though the briefest, is the best refuter of Bowles — not because he was the best critic or the best poet who answered him, but because he was the best poet among the critics and the best critic among the poets. Mr. Bowles says that "the true poet should have an eye attentive to and familiar with every change of season, every variation of light and shade of nature, every walk, every tree, and every leaf in her secret places. He who has not an eye to observe them, and who cannot with a glance distinguish every hue on their variety, must be so far deficient in one of the essential qualities of a poet."

Now every genuine poet and every sensible critic knows that in writing these sentences Mr. Bowles wrote something very like nonsense.

It is thus that, while the most brilliant of all the imitators of Horace, it is only to one side of Horace's genius that Pope courts comparison. Where Horace is the poet of manners, as in the Epistles and Satires, Pope may be said to surpass, in his paraphrases, the originals from which he draws inspiration. In his own Epistles and Satires he has a polish and point, a delicate finish, and an elaborate harmony of verse, which the Latin poet did not consider appropriate to that class of composition, but which the English poet has shown to be embellishing adornments. But Pope can never approach Horace in the other and diviner side of

And whether as poet or critic, Campbell has an easy victory in replying "that this botanising perspicuity might be essential to a Dutch flower-garden, but Sophocles displays no such skill, and yet he is a genuine, a great, and an affecting poet." Sophocles is no solitary instance. On the other hand, Campbell is mistaken in supposing that he meets arguments as to the real defect found in Pope by better thinkers than Mr. Bowles, in vindicating a choice of images drawn from artificial rather than natural objects. In truth, the poet illustrates from beauty wherever he finds it, in art as in nature. The defect in Pope and writers of his school is not so much in not borrowing allusion and description from solitary rural scenes, as in the town-bred affectation of patronising rural nature now and then, and want of sympathy with the romance of nature, and with the contemplative philosophy she inspires. Horace speaks of his Sabine valley with a fondness too passionate to allow of an appraiser's inventory of details: just as a lover, when he thinks of his mistress, finds words to describe the general effect of her beauty on his own heart, but no words to describe all her beauties in particular. He would not be a lover if he could specify the charms of a mistress as a horse-dealer specifies the points of a horse. The poet's eye is not "*attentive* to every variation of light and shade of nature, every walk, every tree, every leaf" — except in those moments when he ceases to be poet, and is not under the poetic influences of nature. The poetic influences of nature tend to abstract the mind of the poet from external objects, — to lull the observant faculties, while stimulating the reflective or imaginative. So that it has been said by a great critic. "The poet can no more explain how he knows so well the outward aspects of the nature which sets him a-dreaming, than he can explain the interior process by which his genius achieves its masterpieces."

the Roman's genius. He cannot pretend to the lyrical playfulness and fire, the mingled irony and earnestness, the tender pathos, the exquisite humanity, the wondrous felicity of expression, which render the Odes of Horace matchless in the power of *charm*. He cannot, in his Twickenham villa, seize and interpret the poetry of rural life and sylvan scenery, like the recluse of the Sabine farm. Pope's genius, in short, is didactic, not lyrical. He sees no Bacchus teaching song to Nymphs amid rocks remote; no cool groves, with their spiritual choirs, separate him from the populace; he has no Lucretilis for which Faunus exchanges the Arcadian hill. But as the painter of urban life, what in modern or perhaps in ancient literature can compare in elegance with the verse of Pope, unless it be the prose of Addison? No doubt, both these illustrious Englishmen were much influenced by French schools in the culture of their taste and in the formation of their style; but in their acceptation of classical models, it seems to me that they excel the French writers who served to form their taste. In the euphony and amenities of style the prose of Addison certainly surpasses that of Malebranche, whom he is said to have copied; and though Boileau may equal Pope in neatness of finish and sharpness of wit, he attains neither to Pope's habitual dignity of manner, nor to Pope's occasional sweetness of sentiment.

The English poets preceding the Restoration, when borrowing from or imitating those of other countries (I do not here speak of the models common to all generations of modern writers to be found in the ancient classics), were under Italian influences. From Spenser to Milton the study of Italian is visible in

English poets — French models seem to have been ignored. Waller is, I think, the first of our poets popularly known in whom (except in very loose adaptations of Petrarch) the Italian element vanishes; and though he cannot be said to have copied the French, yet he is allowed by their own critics to have anticipated their poets in that neatness and polish by which the French style became noted before the close of his long career. In Dryden the ascendancy of the French influence becomes notable, though rather in form than in spirit — in technical rules than in genuine principles of art; and even on him the influence is struggling and undecided. He accepts rhyme as an improvement in tragic verse; but in this attempt he was preceded by Davenant, and though he studied Corneille, and often goes beyond him in extravagance of expression, he never attained to, nor perhaps comprehended, that secret of Tragic Art which Corneille found less even in the richness of his poetic genius than in the sublimity of his moral nature. Corneille's grandeur as poet was in his grandeur as man; and whether he had written in the finest rhyme or the most simple prose, he would have equally stormed his way upon an audience so susceptible to heroic sentiment as the French ever have been. But whatever Dryden owed to the French, he remains strikingly English, and largely indebted to English predecessors, from Chaucer to Davenant. In Pope, the French element is more pervasive, and more artfully amalgamated with the English. He owed much both to Waller and to Dryden, but it was to those characteristics of either which were most in accordance with French principles of taste. He took nothing from the Italians; little from our own writers, save the two I have named; nothing from Shakespeare, though he comprehended his merit better than Dryden did; nothing from Milton, though in his own day Milton's rank among poets first became popularly acknowledged. Where he was deemed by his contemporaries to have improved upon Dryden, it was in the more complete Frenchification of Dryden's style; and where, in the finer criticism of our day, he is considered less to have improved upon than effeminised Dryden's style, it is in the over-nicety of a taste, and practice which refined, into what his French contemporaries would have called correctness, the old native freedom of rhythm and cadence, that gives to the verse of Dryden its muscular vigour and blithesome swing. But apart from the mere form of verse a change in the very essence of poetry had been made by the influence which French literature acquired in Europe in the age of Louis XIV. France had become Parisian; and thus the urban or artificial element in the representation of human life superseded the rural or natural. This it had never done in the great masters of Italian poetry. Neither in Dante, nor Petrarch, nor Tasso, nor Ariosto — though the last named exhibits the peculiar knowledge of the world which can only be acquired in the converse of capitals — is seen that terse, epigrammatic form of expression by which the poet of cities desires to reconcile "men about town" to the fatigue of reading poetry at all. As to our English poets before the time of Dryden, if they have one characteristic in common from the highest to the lowest, it is their hearty love for rural nature and a country life.

The urban influence, so strong upon Pope, operated yet more potently on the generation that succeeded him. Pope would have shrunk from confessing the frank love of urban life, with its intellectual excitements; and the scorn of rural life, with the disbelief in its calm contemplative delights, which Johnson loses no occasion to express. Yet, nevertheless, Johnson's knowledge of the world is much wider than that knowledge of the town which sparkles forth with such brilliancy in Pope. Johnson's knowledge of town life wants the intimacy with those higher ranks of society which were familiar to Pope from his youth, and only partially opened to Johnson in his maturer years. Nor did his temperament allow him to treat those trifles, which make the sum of human things in the gayer circles of a metropolis, with the easy elegance of Pope; yet, perhaps from the very defects in his comprehension of the spirit of fashionable life (I mean the spirit which, in all highly civilised capitals, ever forms the fashion of an age), Johnson excels in his conceptions of the middle class, whether of mind or station. And his knowledge of the world has a more robust character than Pope's, embracing larger views of practical human life: With all his love for the roar of Fleet Street — with all his disdain of sequestered shades, Johnson's knowledge of the world is not so much shown in delineations of urban manners, as in the seizure of catholic truths applicable to civilised men wherever they exercise their reason; and perhaps still more clearly perceptible to those in whom country life fosters habits of contemplation, than to the eager spirits that seek in urban life the arena of active contest. His true genius lay in the masculine strength of his common sense; and in spite of his prejudices, of his dogmatism, of his frequent intolerance and occasional paradox —

in spite, still more, of a style in prose strangely contrasting the cold severity of his style in verse — unfamiliar, inflated, artificially grandiose — still that common sense has such pith and substance that it makes its way to every plain solid understanding. And while all that Johnson owed to his more imaginative qualities has faded away from his reputation; while his poems are regarded but as scholastic exercises; while his tragedy is left unread; while the fables and tales scattered throughout his essays allure no popular imitation, and even 'Rasselas' is less admired for its loftiness of purpose and conception than censured for its inappropriate dialogue or stilted diction, and neglected for the dryness of its narrative and the frigidity of its characters; while his ablest criticisms, composed in his happiest style, rarely throw light upon what may be called the metaphysics of imaginative art, — his knowledge of the world has a largeness and at times a depth which preserve authority to his opinions upon the general bearings of life and the prevalent characteristics of mankind — a knowledge so expanded, by its apprehension of generical truths, from mere acquaintanceship with conventional manners, and the sphere of the town life which enthralled his tastes, that at this day it is not in capitals that his works are most esteemed as authoritative, but rather in the sequestered homes of rural book-readers. To men of wit about town, a grave sentence from Johnson upon the philosophy of the great world would seem old-fashioned pedantry, where, to men of thought in the country, it would convey some truth in social wisdom too plain to be uttered by pedants, and too solid to be laughed out of fashion by wits.

Within the period of which I speak, rose in England the Novel of Manners — a class of composition which necessitates a considerable amount of knowledge of the world. Richardson, Fielding, Smollett, Sterne, not only laid the vast foundations, but raised thereon the noble structures, of an art new to the literature of our country. All four of the writers named exhibit knowledge of the world in very high degree. In Fielding and Smollett that knowledge is the most apparent, from the astonishing vigour with which their characters are depicted and their conceptions expressed. It would be waste of words to show, what no critic has disputed — viz., Fielding's superiority to Smollett (who, nevertheless, is a giant among novelists) in philosophical treatment and dignified conception of narrative art. But Fielding is little more free than Smollett from one defect in imaginative creations, as may be seen more clearly when I shall have occasion to bring him somewhat in comparison with Sir Walter Scott — viz., the too frequent preference of conventional particulars in the selection of types of character. A proof of this may be found in the fact that Fielding, as well as Smollett, is rather national than cosmopolitan, and has had no perceptible influence on the higher forms of fiction in foreign countries. This cannot be said of Richardson and Sterne. Richardson has had, and still retains, an extraordinary influence over the imaginative literature of France; Sterne an influence not less effective over that of Germany. Goethe has attested the obligations he owed to Sterne as well as to Goldsmith. "There is no saying," he declares, with grateful enthusiasm, "how powerfully I was influenced by Goldsmith and Sterne at the most important period of my mental development." And indeed the influence of Sterne may be visibly traced in German literature to this day, wherever its genius cultivates the "Humoristic." The fact is, that while, in the conduct of story, not only Sterne, who very seldom aims at that merit, but even Richardson, who never loses sight of it, is many degrees inferior to Smollett and Fielding, yet in conception of character and in delicacy of treatment we recognise in the former two a finer order of art.

The conceptions of character in Lovelace, Clarissa, Clementina, are founded in the preference of generals to particulars; that is, they are enduring types of great subdivisions in the human family, wholly irrespective of mutations in scene and manners. The knowledge of the world manifested in the creation and completion of such characters is subtler and deeper than Smollett or even Fielding exhibits in his lusty heroes and buxom heroines. Despite the weary tediousness of Richardson's style, the beauties which relieve it are of a kind that bear translation or paraphrase into foreign languages with a facility, which is perhaps the surest test of the inherent substance and cosmopolitan spirit of imaginative writings. The wit and hardihood of Lovelace, the simplicity and *naïveté* of Clarissa, the lofty passion of Clementina, find an utterance in every language, and similitudes in every civilised race.

And what lavish and riotous beauty beyond that of mere prose, and dispensing with the interest of mere fiction, sporting with the Muse like a spoiled darling of the Graces, charms poets and thinkers in the wayward genius of Sterne! Though his most exquisite characters are but sketches and outlines, Mr. Shandy, Uncle Toby, Corporal Trim, and the mysterious shadowy

Yorick, — though his finest passages in composition are marred and blurred by wanton conceit, abrupt impertinence, audacious levity, ribald indecorum, — still how the lively enchanter enforces and fascinates our reluctant admiration! Observe how little he is conventional, how indifferent he is to the minute study of particulars, how typical of large generals are his sketches of human character. There is no reason why Uncle Toby, Corporal Trim, Yorick, might not be Frenchmen or Germans, born at any epoch or in any land. Who cares for the mere date and name of the battles which Uncle Toby fights over again? Any battles would do as well — the siege of Troy as well as the siege of Namur.

And both in Richardson's elaborate development of Lovelace's character, and throughout all the lawless phantasies of Tristram Shandy, what surprising knowledge of the world is displayed! — only in Lovelace it is more the world of the town, and therefore Lovelace more pleases the wits of the world of Paris, which is the arch-metropolitan town of Europe; while in Tristram Shandy it is more the boundless world of men, in town or country alike — that world which has no special capital; and therefore Tristram Shandy pleases more the thinkers of the German family, because Germany is a world without a special capital, and every German principality or province has its own Uncle Toby and Yorick.

The close of the last century gave birth to the finest prose comedy in the English, or perhaps any other, language. In abstract wit, Congreve equals, and, in the opinion of some critics, even surpasses, Sheridan; but Congreve's wit is disagreeably cynical. Sheridan's wit has the divine gift of the Graces — charm. The smile it brings to our lips is easy and cordial; the smile which Congreve wrings forth is forced and sardonic. In what is called *vis comica*, Farquhar, it is true, excels Sheridan by the rush of his animal spirits, by his own hearty relish of the mirth he creates. Sheridan's smile, though more polished than Farquhar's, has not less ease; but his laugh, though as genuine, has not the same lusty ring. It is scarcely necessary, however, to point out Sheridan's superiority to Farquhar in the quality of the mirth excited. If in him the *vis comica* has not the same muscular strength, it has infinitely more elegance of movement, and far more disciplined skill in the finer weapons at its command; and whatever comparison may be drawn between the general powers of Sheridan for comic composition and those of Farquhar and Congreve, neither of the two last-named has produced a single comedy which can be compared to the 'School for Scandal.' Even Molière, in prose comedy, has no work of so exquisite an art; where Molière excels Sheridan, it is where he writes in verse, and comes to the field in his panoply of poet. Like the 'Tartuffe' of Molière, the 'School for Scandal' does not borrow its plot from previous writers. Both are among the very few great dramas in which the author has invented his own fable, and perhaps, for this very reason, there are in both much the same faults of situation and *dénouement*. For in both, while the exposition is admirable, the *dénouement* is feeble; and in both there is a resort to a melodramatic contrivance in producing a critical effect in comic situation — viz., the concealment of a personage important in the conduct of the more serious interest of the plot, whether under a table or behind a screen, and preparing the audience for the laugh which is sure to follow the discovery. This is a kind of effect which can be so cheaply produced that there is scarcely a playwright at the Porte St. Martin or the Surrey Theatre who does not press it into his service. But as it does not belong to the legitimate modes of revealing character through purely intellectual processes of self-revelation, and is rather among the resources of stage-trick, I doubt whether it be worthy of place in the masterpieces of comic art. The dramatist who declines to invent his own story, usually pauses long and meditates deeply over the dramatic elements of any fable which he means to adapt to the stage, and is much more alive to faults and merits of situation and *dénouement* in the story he does not invent, than those of a story which he cannot see clearly before him till, in fact, he has told it.

Though Joseph Surface is a systematic hypocrite, he has very little likeness to Tartuffe. Tartuffe is not a comic character* — he is almost tragic, for he creates terror; the interest he gives to the play is, in our vague consciousness of a power intense, secret, and unscrupulous. Joseph Surface is almost as mysterious as Tartuffe; for, unlike Shakespeare's villains, and like Tartuffe, he does not betray himself to the audience by soliloquy. But in Joseph's mysteriousness there is no element of terror: he always remains essentially comic, though of the highest and most refined order of

---

* Marmontel, whose criticisms abound with finesse of observation, observes that "not one of the principal personages in the 'Tartuffe' is comic in himself. They all become comic by their opposition."— Marmontel upon 'Comedy.'

comedy. No doubt the outlines of his character were suggested by Fielding's portrait of Blifil, as those of Charles Surface have their ruder original in Tom Jones. But Joseph is, what Blifil is not, an exceedingly polished member of polite society — the type of those civil, well-mannered, sentimental impostors whom we meet every day in the most brilliant circles, political and social. Lady Teazle is a more vivid and lifelike female character than the ladies in 'Tartuffe;' but Orgon's wife has a touching chastity of sentiment to which Sir Peter's makes no pretence. I once heard a distinguished critic contend that the interest in Lady Teazle, and, through her, in the whole progress of the play, might have been advantageously heightened if her alleged inexperience had been more genuinely artless — if she had not joined with such gusto in the slanders which delight her fashionable friends, and seemed the sharpest-tongued pupil in the whole School of Scandal; and that the plot would have also gained in elevation of interest if Sir Peter's position, which is in itself one that touches the human heart, had been somewhat more raised in the scale of intellectual dignity. But I think we shall find, on reflection, that for the purpose of pure prose comedy any such changes tending to poetise character and situation would have been for the worse. Had our sentiment for Lady Teazle been a whit more tender, and our sympathy for Sir Peter been a whit more respectful, the peril Lady Teazle incurs from the sleek temptations of Joseph would have become almost tragically painful. We could never have quite forgiven her for subjecting herself to it — it is her frivolity of character, in fact, that alone justifies our indulgence. And had Sir Peter established a higher and graver place in our affectionate esteem, I doubt whether we should have had the same good-humoured pleasure in his final reconciliation with the helpmate by whom the honour of his name had been so carelessly risked, to be so narrowly saved.

The surpassing merits of the "School for Scandal" become the more brilliant the more minutely they are scanned, and the more fairly the faults of the play are put in juxtaposition with its beauties. Its merits are not so much to be sought in the saliency of any predominating excellence as in the harmonious combination of great varieties of excellence, in a unity of purpose sufficiently philosophical for the intellect of comedy, but not so metaphysical as to mar the airy playfulness of comic mirth. The satire it conveys is directed, not to rare and exceptional oddities in vice or folly, but to attributes of human society which universally furnish the materials and justify the ridicule of satire. It is one of the beauties of this great drama, that its moral purpose is not rigidly narrowed into the mere illustration of a maxim — that the outward plot is indeed carried on by personages who only very indirectly serve to work out the interior moral. Sir Peter, Charles Surface, the Uncle, are not pupils in the "School for Scandal" — nor do they share in its tasks; and by this very largeness of plan the minor characters acquire a vitality they would otherwise want. Without Charles and Sir Peter, a Backbite and a Candour would be mere abstractions symbolised by the names they bear. But once admit the more spontaneous flesh-and-blood characters of Sir Peter and Charles, and the personifications of abstract satire take vital substance and warmth by the contact; and wherever we look throughout the range of our worldly acquaintances we recognise a Sir Benjamin Backbite and a Mrs. Candour. I think it the originality and charm of the plot itself, that the members of the School of Scandal rather constitute the chorus of the drama than its active agents. And with what ease the marvellous wit of this marvellous comedy grows like a mother tongue out of the ideas which the author wants to express! What large knowledge of the world that wit epitomises in its epigrams! How naturally its *bons-mots* idealise the talk of our *salons* and drawing-rooms! There, refined by genius, is the dialogue of fashionable wits so long as fashion has rank in polite cities.

Campbell observes "that Dryden praises the gentlemen in Beaumont and Fletcher as the men of fashion of the times;" and Campbell adds, "it was necessary that Dryden should call them the men of fashion of the times, for they are not, in the highest sense of the word, gentlemen."

This is true of Beaumont and Fletcher. Of Congreve we may say that in no times could his heroes have been "gentlemen." Farquhar is happier. Sir Harry Wildair is a gentleman of fashion, but regarded as a young *ci-devant* actor who had obtained a commission in the army, which he did not long keep, would naturally regard a gentleman of fashion — at a distance — to bow to him, not to live with him. Sheridan's gentlemen are drawn by the pen of one who could not more have flattered a Sir Harry Wildair than by calling him "My dear fellow."

In Sheridan's comedy, knowledge of manners — knowledge of the world — is consummate, and, especially in the "School for Scandal," illustrated through enduring types. Like the other great writers of his day, his knowledge is concentred in town-knowledge. But town-knowledge, though not the first requisite in the world-knowledge of a poet or philosopher, is precisely the knowledge which we seek in the writer of comedy who, selecting prose for his medium of expression, gives us in substance the prose of life, and not its poetry. Comedy — at least prose comedy — must be gregarious and urban.

In fine, there are very few works in the literature of England, of which, as compared with the analogous literature of other countries, we have a right to be more proud than the 'School for Scandal.' If, in the poetry of the drama, we can challenge Europe to produce a rival to Shakespeare, so, in the essential prose of the drama, — in the comedy that dispenses with poetry altogether — that embodies, through forms the most exquisitely appropriate to its purpose, the idealised objects of comedy, — we may challenge Europe to show us a performance equal to the 'School for Scandal.'

We must now turn back to glance at the greatest of the French authors in whom this knowledge of the world has been displayed, not as court satirists, but as men who combine the calm lore of the philosopher with the impartial human heart of the poet. And here I cannot refuse his due rank to the Father of Modern Essay. Montaigne owes his immortality — owes his enduring influence upon thought — to that knowledge of the world which is wholly independent of change in manners.

Montaigne is in one respect the antipodes of Shakespeare; in another respect he is the French writer I would crave leave most to place in comparison with Shakespeare.

Montaigne is the antipodes to Shakespeare, inasmuch as he is intensely subjective, obtrusively personal. So, as a narrator of his own personal experiences and opinions, he ought to have been; just as Shakespeare, where a dramatist, could not have been obtrusively personal, even where writing his own most haunting thoughts. But where Montaigne is to be likened to Shakespeare is in the similar result at which, through so antagonistic a process, he arrives. Though apparently only studying himself, he himself has a nature so large that it comprehends mankind. Never did one man in his egotism more faithfully represent the greatest number of attributes common to the greatest number of men. His grasp comprehends materials for thought that it might task a thousand sages to work up into systems. His fineness of vision seizes on subtleties in character and mysteries in feeling that might open new views of the human heart to a thousand poets: and all with the same seeming artlessness which deceived even Milton himself as to the art of Shakespeare. No essay yet written is so artful as one of Montaigne's great essays, just as no drama yet written is so artful as one of Shakespeare's great dramas. The proof of art in both is the delight that they give to artists who have done their best to consider how to write a drama or how to write an essay.

Montaigne's way of viewing life, men, and manners was, as I have elsewhere said, emphatically that of the lyrical poet — viz., through a medium of personal feeling rather than scientific reasoning. He has a poet's instinctive repugnance to system; whereas a scientific reasoner has to system an almost unconquerable attraction. He gives us his impressions of men and things, troubling himself very little with the defence of his impressions; and his survey of the world is the more comprehensive because it is taken from a height and at a distance: he has seen the world, and mixed in its pleasures and pursuits; he means still to do so as an inquirer; every year he hopes to mount his horse; to ride into foreign lands, and wander through foreign cities. But when he *writes* of the world, it is in his old Gascon Tower — it is in a chamber which his nearest of kin are forbidden to enter, and in which his only comrades are books. He complacently tells us he has got together a thousand volumes — a great library for that day; but as most of those volumes must have been the books of a very different day, they only serve to enforce his own opinions and illustrate his own experience. It is his own human heart, as he has tested it through his own human life, that he first analyses and then synthesises. And out of that analysis and that synthesis, he dissects into separate members, and then puts together again, the world.

From Montaigne we pass to Molière, whose study of the humours of men necessarily embraced those views of the world of men which afford theme and subject to the Comic Poet. Knowledge of the world in him is not, therefore, spontaneously poured forth as in Montaigne; it is trained to the purposes of comic art, and considered with an eye accustomed to stage effect; so that where most philosophical it is somewhat too sharply limited to satire; and where most sportive, somewhat too wantonly carried away into farce. But Molière is one of that rarest order of poets whose very faults become sacred in the eyes of admirers. He is not only revered as a master, but beloved by us as a friend. Of all the French dramatists, he is the only one whose genius is as conspicuous to foreign nations as it is to his own. Like Shakespeare, he is for all time and for all races. A piercing observer of the society around him, he selects from that society types the least socially conventional. His very men of fashion are never out of the fashion. Where most he excels all that is left to us of the comedy of the ancients is where his invention most escapes from its influence, and reveals those truths of a poetry almost tragic, which lie half in light, half in shadow, on the serious side of humour. Here, the comedy of the 'Misanthrope' is without rival as to conception of character and delicacy of treatment, though in point of dramatic construction and vigour of style the 'Tartuffe' has been held to surpass it. "The exposition of 'Tartuffe,'" says Goethe, "is without its equal — it is the grandest and best of its kind."

Of all the many kinds of knowledge possessed by Voltaire, knowledge of the world was, perhaps, that for which he was most remarkable. It was that knowledge which secured to him so vast an audience and so lofty a position; and the aptitude for such kind of knowledge was inborn with him — made three parts of his *ingenium* or native genius. While little more than a boy, this son of a notary lifted himself to that social rank which he ever afterwards maintained as a vantage-ground to his sway over the millions. The brilliant *protégé* of Ninon de l'Enclos, the favourite wit of

Philippe the Regent, before the beard was dark on his chin; other neophytes of inferior birth admitted into the circles of social greatness usually wither away in that chilling atmosphere: their genius accommodates itself to the trifles which make up the life of idlers — their spirit bows itself to dependence; they contribute to the amusement of princes, yet are the last persons to whom princes accord the solid rewards of fortune.

But, from the first, Voltaire put to profit the personages out of whom a mere man of genius could have extracted nothing beyond praise and famine. Before he was twenty, he learned, in the society of a Vendôme and a Conti, how to flatter the great without meanness — how to maintain equality with them, yet not seem to presume — and how to put them to use with the air of doing them a favour. Ninon de l'Enclos took a fancy to this brilliant boy; Ninon de l'Enclos took a fancy to a great many brilliant boys, much more adapted to strike the eye and the senses of an antiquated beauty than the spindleshanked son of the notary Arouet; but Ninon distinguished young Arouet from other brilliant boys in this — she left him two thousand francs. The youth destined to convulse nations, knew by intuition that a man who would raise himself into a Power should begin by securing a pecuniary independence. It has been said of some writers that, from the first, they always tenderly nursed their fame. Voltaire did not do that; he sported with his fame, but he always tenderly nursed his fortune.

He early foresaw that his future life would be, as he defined it later, a combat; and accordingly took care betimes to provide himself with the sinews of war. By skilful speculations in the commerce of Cadiz, and in the purchase of corn in Barbary — still more happily by obtaining, through what we should now call a job, an interest *dans les vivres de l'armée d'Italie*, which brought him in 800,000 francs — he established a capital, which, as he invested it in life-annuities, yielded an income far above that enjoyed by the average number of the half-ruined nobles of France.

In the course of his long life Voltaire was, of course, more than once in love; but only once, and then, when the heyday of youth was over, did he form that kind of attachment which influences a man's existence. We may doubt the strength of his passion, but the prudence with which he selected its object is incontestable. He chose a *marquise* of good fortune, with a luxurious *château* and scientific predilections. Thus, far from finding in love the impoverisher of fortune and the disturber of philosophy, this wise man of the world made love fill his Exchequer and provide his Academe.

With Madame du Chastelet he shared the delights of an excellent table, the refined relaxations of a polished society; with Madame du Chastelet he shared also the study of the problems in Newton's 'Principia;' and when death bereaved the philosopher of his well-selected helpmate, the tender mathematician bequeathed him a better consolation than any to be found in Boethius — she left him a handsome addition to his already handsome fortune.

According to astrology, Venus and Saturn are friendly stars to each other; the one presides over love, the other over heritages. Voltaire, as thorough man of the world, united both in his First House. And thus, even in that passion which usually makes fools of the wisest, Voltaire pursued the occupations of wisdom, and realised the rewards of wealth.

Throughout his whole career the great writer exhibited in his own person that supreme knowledge of the world which constitutes the characteristic excellence of his works. And when he retired at last to his palace at Ferney, it was with the income of a prince, and the social consideration paid to a king.

Perhaps, however, while knowledge of the world constitutes the characteristic excellence of Voltaire's writings, it also contributes to their characteristic defect. Genius may be world-wide, but it should not be world-limited. Voltaire never escapes "this visible diurnal sphere." With all his imagination he cannot comprehend the enthusiasm which lifts itself above the earth. His Mahomet is only an ambitious impostor, whom he drags on the stage as a philosophical expositor of the wiles and crimes of priestcraft. With all his mastery of language he cannot achieve the highest realms of poetic expression or passionate eloquence; he is curbed by what he had learned in the polite world to call "good sense" and "good taste." His finest characters exhibit no delicate shades, no exquisite subtleties, like those of Shakespeare and Goethe. His finest verses are but sonorous declamations, or philosophical sentences admirably rhymed. Like Goethe, he is fond of "motivating," and the personages of his fictions always act upon philosophical principles; but, unlike Goethe, he is jejune as a metaphysician, and sterile as a psychologist. His plays — even some of those now unread and unacted — are masterpieces of mechanical construction; the speeches they contain are often as full of pith and of sound as if they had been aphorisms of Seneca versified by Lucan. But his personages want not only the lifelike movement of flesh and blood, but that *spirituality of character* (if I may use the term) which is not put into play by springs merely intellectual, and which, as it is most evident in all higher types of man, is essential to the representations of such types in the drama. If we compare those parts in his tragedies which are considered the most striking with the heroic parts conceived and embodied by Corneille, they often satisfy better our logical judgment: what they do is more within the range of prose probabilities — what they say is more conformable to the standard of prose commonsense. But they do not, like Corneille's, seize hold of the heart through its noblest emotions — carry the soul aloft from the conventional judgments of the mind in its ordinary dealings with ratiocinated prose life, and utter, in the language of men, sentiments which men never could utter if they were not immortals as well as men. The grandest of all our instincts is also that which is the most popularly stirred — viz., the struggle of thought from the finite towards the infinite. And this is the reason why the heroic in character and sentiment is always popularly comprehended on the stage — and why, through whatever varying phase it be exhibited, it is, when genuine, among those evidences of the spiritual nature of abstract man, which, by a common sympathy, all races of men appreciate and seek to preserve.

Voltaire himself seems complacently to mark the limit which divides his genius from that of a Shakespeare or a Goethe, in a knowledge of this world, so sharply closed that it rejects all that divining conjecture of the worlds beyond it, to which their knowledge of this world leads them so restlessly upward. His views of the poetry of life are thus always taken from some side of its material prose. In his genius, whether as poet or philosopher, every genuine poet, or every earnest thinker, recognises a want which he finds it difficult to express. Certainly Voltaire has the art of a poet, certainly he is not without the science of a thinker; but poetry is not all art — thought is not all science. What Voltaire seems most to want is the warmth of soul which supplies to poetry the nameless something that art alone cannot give, and to thought the free outlets into belief and conjecture which science would cease to be science if it did not refuse to admit. Be this as it may, Voltaire's knowledge of this world, as exhibited whether in his life or his writings, was exceedingly keen and sharp; and for any knowledge of a world beyond this, Voltaire is the last guide a man of bold genius would follow, or a man of calm judgment consult.

It is strange that the two contemporary writers in whom knowledge of the world is most conspicuously displayed, should have depreciated, if not actually despised, each other. Le Sage had the temerity to ridicule Voltaire at a period, indeed, of that author's life when his *chefs-d'œuvre* had not yet raised him above ridicule. Voltaire, in turn, speaks of Le Sage with the lofty disdain of slighting commendation — as a writer not altogether without merit, allowing 'Gil Blas' the praise of being 'natural,' but dismissing it as a literal plagiarism from the Spanish. Yet perhaps all Voltaire's books put together do not contain so much knowledge of the world, artificial no less than natural, as that same 'Gil Blas'; and Voltaire, with his practical mastery of his own language, ought to have been the first to perceive that, whatever 'Gil Blas' might owe to the Spanish, a book more thoroughly French in point of form and style, more original in all that constitutes artistic originality, is not to be found in the literature of France.* The form, the style, is indeed singularly at variance with the marked peculiarities of Spanish humour. Compare the style of 'Gil Blas' with that of Cervantes or Quevedo, and the radical distinctions between the spirit of the French language and that of the Spanish become conclusively apparent. The language of Spain is essentially a language of proverbs; every other sentence is a proverb. In proverbs, lovers woo; in proverbs, politicians argue; in proverbs, you make your bargain with your landlady or hold a conference with your muleteer. The language of Spain is built upon those diminutive relics of a wisdom that may have existed before the Deluge, as the town of Berlin is built upon strata amassed, in the process of ages, by the animalcules that dwell in their pores. No servile translation, nay, no liberal paraphrase from a Spanish wit (such as Le Sage's masterpiece has been deemed by his detractors), would not immediately betray its Spanish origin. But there is not a vestige of the ineffaceable characteristic of the Spanish language in the idiomatic ease of Le Sage's exquisite French. The humour of Spain, as may be expected from a language of proverbs, is replete with hyperbole and metaphor; it abounds with similes or images that provoke your

* At a later period of his life, Le Sage published a translation of the very novel of which 'Gil Blas' was said to be the servile copy. This was probably his best mode of refuting the charge against him.

laughter by their magnificent extravagance. Take, for instance, the following description of the miserly schoolmaster in Quevedo's 'Paul the Sharper.' I quote from an old translation (1741), admirable for raciness and gusto: —

"The first Sunday after Lent we were brought into the house of Famine, for 'tis impossible to describe the penury of the place. The master was a skeleton — a mere shotten herring, or like a long slender cane with a little head upon it, and red-haired; so that there needs no more to be said to such as know the proverb — 'that neither cat nor dog of that colour are good.' His eyes almost sunk into his head, as if he had looked through a perspective glass, or the deep windows in a linendraper's shop. His beard had lost its colour for fear of his mouth, which, being so near, seemed to threaten to eat it for mere hunger. His neck as long as a crane's, with the gullet sticking out so far as if it had been compelled by necessity to start out for sustenance. . . . . He walked leisurely, and whenever he happened to move anything faster, his bones rattled like a pair of snappers. As for his chamber, there was not a cobweb in it — the spiders being all starved to death. He put spells upon the mice for fear they should gnaw some scraps of bread he kept. His bed was on the floor, and he always lay on one side for fear of wearing out the sheets."

The humour of this passage is extraordinary for riot and redundance. Can anything less resemble the unforced gaiety, the easy, well-bred wit of 'Gil Blas'? Nor is it only in form and style that 'Gil Blas' is pre-eminently French; many of its salient anecdotes and illustrations of manners are suggested by Parisian life, and the whole social colouring of the novel is caught from a Parisian atmosphere. In truth, the more we examine the alleged evidences of Le Sage's plagiarism, the more visible the originality of his 'Gil Blas' becomes. It is the same with all writers of first-rate genius. They may seize what they did not inherit with an audacity that shocks the moral nerves of a critic, yet so incorporate in their own dominion every rood of ground they annex, that the result is an empire the world did not know before. Little wits that plagiarise are but pickpockets; great wits that plagiarise are conquerors. One does not cry "Stop thief!" to Alexander the Great when he adds to the heritage of Macedon the realms of Asia; one does not cry "Plagiarist!" to Shakespeare when we discover the novel from which he borrowed a plot. A writer's true originality is in his form — is in that which distinguishes the mould of his genius from the mintage of any other brain. When we have patiently examined into all Lawrence Sterne's alleged thefts, collated passages in Burton's 'Anatomy' with passages in 'Tristram Shandy,' the chief amaze of a discerning critic is caused by the transcendent originality with which Sterne's sovereign genius has, in spite of all the foreign substances it laid under contribution, preserved unique, unimitating and inimitable, its own essential idiosyncrasy of form and thought. True, there are passages in 'Tristram Shandy' taken almost literally from Burton's 'Anatomy.' But can any book be less like another than Burton's 'Anatomy' to 'Tristram Shandy'? When you have shown us all the straws in a block of amber, and proved to our entire satisfaction that the amber had imbedded the straws, still the amber remains the amber, all the more curious and all the more valuable for the liberty it took with the straws.

But though 'Gil Blas' be in form and colouring decidedly French, the knowledge of life it illustrates is so vast that, in substance, it remains to this day the epitome of the modern world. Amid all mutations of external manners, all varying fashions of costume, stand forth in immortal freshness its large types of civilised human nature. Its author is equally remarkable for variety of character, formed by the great world, and for accurate insight into the most general springs of action by which they who live in the great world are moved. Thus he is as truthful to this age as he was to his own. His Don Raphael and his Ambrose Lamela are still specimens of the two grand divisions in the genus Rogue, the bold and the hypocritical — as familiarly known to the police of London and Paris as they were to the Brotherhood of St. Hermandad; his Camilla is still found in Belgravia or Brompton; his Don Gonzales is still the elderly dupe of some artful Euphrasia. Who has not met with his Archbishop of Grenada?

Though the satire in 'Gil Blas' can be very keen, as when the author whets its blade to strike at actors and doctors, yet, for the most part, it is less satire than pleasantry. No writer, with power equal to Le Sage over the springs of ridicule, more rarely abuses it to the service of libel and caricature.

Le Sage's knowledge of the world is incomparably more wide than that of Rochefoucauld — nay, even of Voltaire; partly because the survey extends to regions towards which the first scarcely glanced, and partly because it is never, as with the second, dwarfed to a system, nor fined away into the sharp point of a scoff.

The humanity of 'Gil Blas' himself, however frail and erring, is immense, indulgent, genial. He stands by Olivarez in the reverse of fortune, and to his ear the fallen minister confides the secret of the spectre which haunts the solitude of foiled ambition; but he is found at the side of Fabricio, in the hospital at Madrid, and hears the poor poet assure him that he has so thoroughly abjured the ungrateful Muse, that at that very moment he is composing the verses in which he bids her farewell. He is not always in cities, though his sphere of action be in them: he can enjoy the country; his sketches of rural landscape are delicious. When he comes to settle in his pleasant retreat of Llirias, who does not share his delight in the discovery of a fourth pavilion stored with books? and, who does not admire the fidelity to human nature with which the author seizes on his hero's pause from the life of towns, to make him find for the first time the happy leisure to fall in love?

Since 'Gil Blas' I know not if France has produced any one novel remarkable for knowledge of the world, though, taking all together, the mass of recent French novels certainly exhibits a great deal of that knowledge. Perhaps it may be found, more than in any other French novelist of his brilliant day, in that large miscellany of fictions which M. de Balzac has grouped together under the title of 'La Comédie Humaine;' but it is not within my intention to illustrate the criticism contained in this essay by contemporaneous examples. The criticism of contemporaries is the most unsatisfactory of all compositions. The two most popular writers of the last generation — Scott and Byron — naturally engaged the analytical examination of some of the finest intellects of their time; and yet, if we turn back to the pages of our quarterly reviews, and read again what was there said of Byron's new poem or Scott's new tale, we are startled to see how shallow and insipid, how generally indiscriminate in praise or in censure, reviewers so distinguished contrived to be. Large objects must not only be placed at a certain distance from the eye that would measure them, but the ground immediately around them must be somewhat cleared. We may talk, write, argue, dispute, about the authors of our own day; but to criticise is to judge, and no man can be a judge while his mind is under all the influences of a witness. If I feel impressed with this conviction in treating of contemporary foreign authors, I must feel impressed with it yet more strongly in treating of the contemporary writers of my own country.

We stand even too near to the time of Walter Scott to escape the double influence — firstly, of the action which, during his life, he exercised on the literature of Europe; and secondly, of the reaction which always follows the worship paid to a writer of dazzling celebrity when his career is closed and his name is no longer on every tongue. Among the rising generation, neither Scott nor Byron, according to the invariable laws to which the fluctuations of fame are submitted, can receive other than the languid approbation with which persons speak of a something that has just gone out of fashion without having yet acquired the veneration due to antiquity. In proportion as a taste in authorship, architecture, in the arts of embellishment— down even to those employed on furniture and dress— has been carried to enthusiasm in its own day, is the indifference with which it is put aside for some new fashion in the day that immediately succeeds. Let time pass on — and what was undervalued as rococo, becomes again, if it have real merit, the rage as classic. I am not, therefore, at all surprised when a young lady, fresh from the nursery, tells me that all Lord Byron ever wrote is not worth a stanza by a Mr. Somebody, of whom, out of England, Europe has never heard; nor does it amaze me, when a young gentleman, versed in light literature, tells me he finds Scott, as a romance-writer, heavy, and prefers the novels of a Mr. or Miss Somebody, whose very name he will have forgotten before he is forty. When suns set, little stars come in fashion. But suns re-arise with the morrow. A century or two hence, Byron and Scott will not be old-fashioned, but ancient; and then they may be estimated according to their degree of excellence in that art, which is for all time, and not, as now, according to their place in or out of the fashion, which is but of a day. Milton and Shakespeare were for a time out of fashion. So indeed was Homer himself. If, then, the remarks upon Walter Scott, which I very diffidently hazard, convey no criticism worthy the subject, his admirers will have the satisfaction of believing that he will find ample work for much better critics than I am, five hundred years hence. And, first, it appears to me that one cause of Sir Walter Scott's unprecedented popularity as a novelist, among all classes and in all civilised lands, is to be found in the ease and the breadth of his knowledge of the world. He does not pretend to much metaphysical science or much vehement eloquence of passion. He troubles himself very little with the analysis of mind, with the struggle of conflicting emotions. For that reason, he could never have obtained, in the highest walks of the drama, a success correspondent to the loftiness of his fame as a tale-teller. The drama must bare to an audience the machinery of an intellect or the world of a heart. No mere interest of narrative, no mere skill of situation, can, for a play that is to retain a permanent hold on the stage, supply the want of that wondrous insight into motive and conduct which attests the philosophy of Shakespeare, or that fervent oratory of passion which exalts into eloquence almost superhuman the declamatory verse of Corneille. Scott could neither have described nor even conceived the progress of jealousy in Othello. He could not have described nor even conceived that contrast between Curiace and either Horace, father or son, in which is so sublimely revealed the secret of the Roman ascendancy. But, as an artist of Narrative and not of the Drama, Scott was perhaps the greater for his omissions. Let any reader bring to his recollection that passage in the grandest tragic romance our language possesses — the 'Bride of Lammermoor' — in which, the night before the Master of Ravenswood vanishes from the tale, he shuts himself up in his fated tower, and all that is known of the emotions through which his soul travailed, is the sound of his sleepless heavy tread upon the floor of his solitary room. What can be grander in narrative art, than the suppression of all dramatic attempt to analyse emotion and reduce its expression to soliloquy? But that matchless effect in narrative art would have been impossible in dramatic. On the stage, the suffering man must have spoken *out* — words must have been found for the utterance of the agonised heart. If Scott here avoided that resort to language as the interpretation of passion which Shakespeare in a similar position of one of his great characters would have seized, Scott is the more to be admired as a master in the art he undertook, which was not subjected to dramatic necessities, and permitted him to trust, for the effect he sought to convey, to the imagination of the reader; as in the old Greek picture, Agamemnon's grief in the sacrifice of his daughter was expressed, not by depicting his face, but by concealing it behind his mantle.

Still, throughout all his greatest romances, a discerning critic will notice how sparingly Scott dissects the mechanism of the human mind; how little the inclinations of his genius dispose him either towards the metaphysical treatment or the poetical utterance of conflicting passions. And it is for that reason that his stories, when dramatised, are melodramas, and cannot, with justice to himself, be converted into tragedies. The nearest approach he has made to metaphysical analysis or passionate eloquence, and therefore to the creation of a great dramatic part, is in one of his later and least popular romances, "The Fair Maid of Perth." The conception of a young Highland chief— not without noble qualities, bound by every motive of race, of pride, of love, to exhibit the vulgar personal courage which a common smith possesses to extreme, and failing from mere want of nerve — is, in point of metaphysical knowledge poetically expressed, both new and true; and in point of dramatic passion might be made on the stage intensely pathetic. But Scott does not do full justice to his own thoughtful conception. It is a magnificent idea, not perfected by the originator, but out of which some future dramatist could make an immortal play — which no dramatist ever could out of those gems of narrative romance, 'Ivanhoe' and 'Kenilworth.' But if Scott did not exhibit a depth and subtlety proportioned to the wide scope of his genius, in the dissection of the human mind or the delineation of human passion, he carried knowledge of the world — knowledge of manners, of social life in general — to an extent which no previous British novelist has ever reached; and so harmoniously, so artistically, poetised that knowledge, that it is not one of the merits in him which would most strike an ordinary critic. For Scott did not deal with the modern world of manners — his great fictions do not touch upon our own time, nor invite our immediate recollections of what we have witnessed. His art is all the greater for not doing so; and so is his knowledge of the world, as the world is ever in human societies. In 'Ivanhoe,' for instance, there are many defects in mere antiquarian accuracy. Two or three centuries are massed together in a single year. But the general spirit of the age is made clear to popular apprehension, and stands forth with sufficient fidelity to character and costume for the purpose, not of an antiquarian, but of a poet. And it is the author's knowledge of the world, as the world is ever, which enables him to give such interest, charm, and vitality to his portraitures of manners so unfamiliar to our own. The great types of character he selects are those which could have occurred to no writer who had not acquired a very large acquaintance with mankind in his own time, and who had not made that acquaintance aid him, whether in the philosophical or the poetical transcript of an era dim-seen through our chronicles. Is there, throughout all prose fiction (except elsewhere in his own), anything comparable, in the union of practical truth with poetised expression, to Scott's portraitures of the Saxon Cedric, Athelstane, Wamba, Gurth, and the Norman De Bracy, Front de Bœuf, Prince John, Cœur de Lion? With what consummate knowledge of real life even the gentle insipid virtues of Ivanhoe are indicated as the necessary link between the Saxon and Norman! It is ever thus to this day. The man who yields to what must be — who deserts the superstitious adherence to what has been for an acquiescence in what is — has always, when honourable and sincere, a something in him of an Ivanhoe or a Waverley.

Knowledge of the world never forsakes Walter Scott, and in him it is always idealised up to the point of dramatic narrative, and no further. His kings speak according to all our popular associations with those kings — his nobles are always nobles, idealised as poetry should idealise nobles — his peasants, always peasants, idealised as poetry should idealise peasants; but in both noble and peasant, no idealising process destroys what I may call the practical side of truth in character. Scott's kings may be a little more kingly than a leveller finds them; still their foibles are not disguised, and they are never stilted and over-purpled. His peasants may be a little wittier and sharper than a fine gentleman discovers peasants to be; still they are not falsified into epigrammatists or declaimers. His humanity, like Shakespeare's, is always genial and indulgent. Hence, despite his strong political opinions, the wondrous impartiality with which, as an artist, he brings out the grand heroic features which belong to the chosen representatives of either party. It is true that he exalts overmuch the Cavalier accomplishments of Claverhouse, but then he brings into fuller light than history reveals the Roundhead grandeur of Burley. It is true that the cruelty of the one vanishes overmuch, according to strict history, in graceful, lovable curves of chivalric beauty; but it is also true that the ferocious fanaticism of the other vanishes amid the awe man always feels for conscientious convictions and indomitable zeal. Claverhouse in Scott is more beautiful than he was in life — Burley more sublime; in both the author is artistically right. For, if I do not err in the doctrine I have elsewhere laid down — that the great artist seeks generals and not particulars, avoids, in art, the exact portraitures of individuals, and seeks, in selecting individuals, great representative types of humanity — then the Claverhouse of Scott is to be regarded, not as Claverhouse alone, but as the idealised type of the haughty Cavalier, with his faults and merits; and Burley is not Burley alone, but the type, also idealised, of the fanatical Roundhead, with all the heroism of his zeal, even when maddened by the extravagances of his sect. A man of Walter Scott's opinions must have been, indeed, a large-minded man of the world — and an artist, sovereign in the impartiality of art, before he could have given to Balfour of Burley that claim to moral reverence which no writer on the Cavalier side of the question ever before gave to a Roundhead. Compare Hudibras to Walter Scott, and at once you see the distinction between the satirical partisan and the world-wise poet, who, seeking through the world whatever of grand or beautiful his wisdom can discover, exalts, indeed, but never mocks, beauty or grandeur wherever he finds it; and is himself unconscious, in the divine impartiality of art, that he has sometimes placed the most enduring elements of grandeur on the side to which, in the opinions of his own actual life, he is most opposed. Does Homer more favour the Greeks or Trojans? — that is a fair dispute with scholars. But the secret of his preference is really locked within his own breast. Certainly he must (whether he was one Homer or a minstrelsy of Homers) have had a partisan's preference for one or the other. But if the Trojan, how impartially he compels our admiration of Achilles! — if the Greek, how impartially he centres our tenderness and sympathy upon Hector! Such impartiality is the highest exposition of knowledge of the world, and also of poetic art. Both these seeming opposites meet at the same point in the circle of human intellect — viz., that respect for humanity in which are merged and lost all the sectarian differences of actual individual life. Only where this point is reached do we have knowledge of the world or poetic art at its grandest apogee. And this truth is, perhaps, best shown by a reference to historians. History, in its highest ideal, requires an immense knowledge of the world; it requires also something of the genius and heart of a poet, though it avoids poetical form — that is, the difference between an accurate chronicler and a great historian is to be found partly in knowledge, not only of dry facts, but of the motives and practical conduct of mankind, and partly in the seasonable eloquence, not of mere diction, but of thought and sentiment, which is never to be found in a man who has in him nothing of the poet's nature. Yet a historian may possess a high degree of both these essentials, but failing of the highest, at which both should conjoin — viz., *impartiality* — the world cannot accept him as an authority. For this reason, while admiring their brilliant qualities as writers on history, no just-thinking man can ever recognise the authority of a historian in Hume or Macaulay. Scott, though a writer of romance, and having in his actual life political opinions quite as strong as those of Macaulay or Hume — yet, partly from a frank commune with the world in all its classes and divisions, partly from the compulsion of his art, which ordained him to seek what was grand or beautiful on either side of conflicting opinion, conveys infinitely fairer views of historical character than either of those illustrious writers of history. Scott, in a romance, could not have fallen into such Voltairean abasements of the grand principle of religious faith as those into which Hume descends when he treats of the great Puritans of the civil wars. Nor could Scott, in a romance, have so perverted the calm judicial functions of history as Lord Macaulay has done in that elaborated contrast between James II. and William and Mary, which no pomp of diction can reconcile to the reader's sense of justice and truth. The more the character of James (not as king only, but as man) is remorselessly blackened — in order to heighten, by that effect of contrast which is the favourite artifice of forensic rhetoric, the effulgence of light so lavishly thrown around every phase of frosty character in William — the more it offends us to find only the oratorical advocate where, seated in the tribunal of history, we had looked for the impartial judge. And here our reason is the more fortified against abuse of eloquence by the instincts of the universal human heart. Political reasons abound to justify a people for deposing a despotic and bigoted king, and placing on his throne, to the exclusion of the son who, according to customary right, would succeed to the vacancy, his daughter and the foreign prince she had married. But it is a vain endeavour to show that the ambitious prince and the heartless daughter were paragons of disinterested goodness and exquisite feeling. So long as human nature is human nature, it will be out of the power of genius to render William and Mary amiable and lovely characters in the eyes of those who learn at their own hearthstones to believe that whatever punishment a man, be he king or peasant, may deserve, it is not for his own daughter, nor for his daughter's husband, to be alike the punishers and the profiters by the punishment.

Scott, then, has a merit rare among even great historians — artistic impartiality. He has a merit, too, rare among even great novelists — a knowledge of the world exhibited through such types of character as are not effaceable by the mutations of time and manners. There is, in this last, a remarkable distinction between Scott and Fielding, though Fielding describes the manners of his own time, and Scott those of earlier ages; and yet, largely as Fielding's knowledge of the world was displayed, that knowledge is still more comprehensive in Scott. In Scott there is a finer insight into those elements of social manners which are permanent, not fleeting — general, and not particular. And his survey of the society of past times owed its breadth and its verisimilitude to his perceptions and experience of society in his own time. He gives us innumerable examples of the class of gentleman and gentlewoman; and they are always truthful to the enduring ideals of that class—ideals which no change of time or scene can render obsolete. But Fielding is not happy in the portraits of his ladies and gentlemen. There is no age of manners in which a Tom Jones would not be somewhat vulgar, and a Lady Bellaston an offensive libel on womanhood; while, in his most striking and famous characters, taken from lower grades of life, Fielding lavishes his glorious humour and his rich vitality of creative power too much on forms that are not large types of mankind, but eccentric individuals growing out of a special period in manners, which, nevertheless, they are too exceptional to characterise. And when, but a few years afterwards, we look round to see the likeness of these images, we cannot discover them. Thus, regarded in itself, what a creation of humorous phantasy is Parson Adams! But probably, not even in that day, nor in any day, was Parson Adams a fair type of the English country clergyman; and if it were so, it would still not be one of those types of a class which remain unalterable in its main essentials. No human being that reminds us of Parson Adams could we now discover. In a lesser degree the same remark may be applied to Squire Western, and even to Partridge. This fault in Fielding's more broadly humorous characters, if a fault (as, with profound reverence to that magnificent writer, I conceive it to be), is, at all events, not committed by Scott. Though many of his more broadly humorous characters have the disadvantage, for cosmopolitan acceptation, of expressing themselves in a Scotch dialect, only partially known to the English, and scarcely possible to translate into a foreign language without loss to their subtler traits of personality, still they suggest parallels and likenesses among human beings in whatever society we are thrown. As long as the world lives there will be Major Dalgetties and Andrew Fairservices. I am here opposing characters in either novelist which may be said to exemplify knowledge of the world; where another knowledge is required — a knowledge more appertaining to metaphysical philosophy, and requiring a depth of reflection which Scott very seldom exhibits — Fielding achieves characters which Scott could not have analysed with the same skill; and in those characters Fielding creates types of generalities that are never obsolete. Witness the masterly exposition of cant in Blifil — witness the playful but profound satire on scholastic disputations in the bold sketches of Thwackum and Square — witness also that sublime irony upon false greatness which, in 'Jonathan Wild,' exemplifies the most refined reasonings through the rudest parables, and in the wild poetry of its burlesque approaches the dignity of the heroic which it mocks. In "Jonathan Wild,' Fielding is Fielding *plus* Lucian and Swift, and rivalling at times even the point and polish of Voltaire.

There was, however, this difference between Scott and Fielding in their treatment even of humorous character: Fielding, where greatest — as in Blifil, Thwackum, Square, Jonathan Wild — is satirical. He debases, to a certain degree, high conceptions of humanity, in pulling down the false pretences of impostors. Decorum itself, that necessary accompaniment to social virtue, does not quite escape the contempt with which we regard Blifil as its spurious representative. The laugh at Thwackum and Square leaves a certain ridicule on the highest inquiries of intellectual philosophy; and, however happily false heroism may be burlesqued and bantered in 'Jonathan Wild,' still the aspirations of youth would fall to a level injurious to the grandeur of the people from which that youth sprang, if the boy could regard as the true parallels to thieves and pickpockets a Julius Cæsar or an Alexander the Great. But Scott, like Shakespeare, deals very sparingly in satire; in his employment of humour he never debases any of those ideals, the reverence for which improves or exalts society. If his humorous characters examined alone provoke a smile at their cowardice or selfishness, beside them there always soar great images of valour and generosity. And in this distinction I think he shows both the superior beauty of his poetic art, and the more dispassionate and objective survey of mankind which belongs to his knowledge of the world. Certainly Scott, like Shakespeare and Goethe, had the advantage of living in a very noble age, and in an age which, on the whole, was eminently conciliatory. An age that enabled a writer to regard Napoleon and Wellington as his contemporaries, was one which made heroism familiar to the common talk of the day. But it was also a conciliatory age. Even in the midst of the European war many circumstances tending to soften violent dissensions between honest and thoughtful minds were in operation. There had grown up a spirit of tolerance in religious opinions which was almost wholly new in our modern era; for the tolerance which Voltaire demanded for the propagandists of Deism he certainly denied to the preachers of Christianity. Out of all the crimes and the madness of the latter days of the French Revolution there had arisen, almost unconsciously, a greater respect for humanity — a deeper conviction of that consideration and tenderness which Governments owe to the masses they govern; and, on the other hand, the attempt to erase from modern societies the veneration due to their own ancient foundations, and substitute instead (for men the most innovating never can get rid of the homage due to antiquity of some kind) a spurious, ignorant, superstitious worship of old heathen republics, had awakened a desire to revive and recur to the genuine antiquity of our own northern Christian races. The first idea of this revival was caught by Chauteaubriand in his 'Génie du Christianisme' — a work which, despite a thousand faults of sentimental exaggeration and inflated style, seized hold on the age, because it fulfilled a want of the age, and had, at its first publication, directly — has now, when few read the work, indirectly — an immense effect on the sentiment of Europe. Endowed with a higher poetic genius adopting a form infinitely more popular, and guided by a taste far more masculine than Chateaubriand's, Scott rose to unite the reverence to what is best in our own genuine antiquity with what is best in our own genuine modern modes of thought. And this is really the chief merit of his affluent genius, and the main cause of his ascendant popularity throughout Europe, — that he was at once conservative and liberal in the noblest sense of either hackneyed word. Conservative in his conception and portraiture of those great elements of the Christian Past which each Christian community of Europe has employed in its progressive development;

liberal in the respect he shows to all that can advance our human destinies throughout the future — to valour, to honour, to conscience. Though his intellect did not lead him to philosophise, his grand all-comprehending human heart achieved the large results of philosophy. Here is his advantage over Byron, who had, in remarkable degree, the temperament which leads men to philosophise, but wanted the discipline of intellect which is necessary for the attainment of philosophy. But great poets never philosophise in vain; and even in philosophy Lord Byron achieved a purpose not designed by himself. With many defects of hasty, and even slovenly composition, and with notions of criticism as loose and inaccurate as were all his notions of abstract reasoning, Lord Byron expressed a something, in form more charming, despite its faults, than the world had yet known, which the world had long wanted to hear expressed, and for which, at that especial day, the world desired an utterance. For if there be a truth in the world everlastingly general, and therefore eternally poetical, it is the absolute futility and hollowness of earthly objects and sensual pleasures, — in fact, that this world is a grand thing if held in reference to another, and a miserable thing if not. Byron's poetry is the expression of that truth more palpably, more to the conception of ordinary readers, than it had been hitherto expressed, except by the Preacher. And such is human nature, that if anything is to be said with effect against the pleasures of the world, we must have it said by some one who could command them. We laugh when we read an anecdote of a French poet who, at the age of sixty, calls on the ladies of his acquaintance to tell them that he has renounced his worship to the goddess of Love: We should not laugh at, but rather feel an interest in the young poet — probably not half so good a poet as the old one — who declared that he abjured the same goddess at the age of twenty-eight. When Molière produced his 'Misanthrope,' it was supposed that he designed to portray himself as Alceste. The play was not, at first, successful. What more natural than that a poor player should be a misanthrope? But a rumour spread that Alceste was meant for a great duke, and then the popular interest was excited. What more extraordinary than that a great duke should be a misanthrope? So with Byron's verse. A truth profound, and, in itself, intensely religious, was flung forth without religious sentiment — nay, rather in daring scepticism — by a man who possessed all which the world adulates, and who mourned or mocked its nothingness; — the young noble, of lofty birth, and of a beauty so rare that only two types of masculine beauty, which painters display, can match it — viz., those of Napoleon and Raffaelle! Here was a picture which brought out with striking force the moral, imbedded in the midst of poetry, perhaps more striking to a thoughtful mind because it was not enforced by an austere preacher, but came as a wail from the lips of a sceptic. What Goethe has said of Byron I believe to be true — viz., "He was essentially a born poet." He had very little art, very little of the ordinary knowledge which is essential to most writers, whether in prose or verse. One has but to read his Letter in defence of Pope against Bowles, to perceive that he had never learned the elementary laws of criticism. His book-learning was not only inferior to that of Dryden, or even of Pope, but to that of any modern writer of mark in any country, with the solitary exception of Burns. And even when we speak of him as a born poet, we must allow that his earliest poems do not equal in merit Pope's imitation of Horace at the age of fourteen. But poetry is not like music. In music a great composer shows what is in him while he is a child — in poetry the born poet may long linger before he chances on his rightful utterance. Byron did not linger long — he chanced on an utterance that enthralled Europe before he was twenty-seven. Of all our great poets since Milton, Byron and Scott are at once the most recognised by foreign nations, and yet owe the least to foreign poets. They owed nothing to the French, yet of all our poets they are those whom the French most condescend to imitate. If the French now study Shakespeare, it is because Scott and Byron allured them to study English.

The extent to which I have already taxed, in this Essay, the patience of readers the gentlest — if, indeed that patience has not long since refused to pay the impost — will not permit me the mention of some modern writers whose claims to knowledge of the world, as shown in their pages, ought not to be ignored. But the title of my Essay implies selection, and selection must be always arbitrary. Not having room for all, I must be contented with representative examples. I regret even more than the omission of some modern writers, that I cannot widen the scope of my criticism by adequate reference to the ancient — viz., the Latin and Greek. But even the fragments left to us of Publius Syrus, who is said to have been the special delight of Julius Cæsar, the most consummate man of the world who ever lived, would justify a critical essay as lengthened as this. Those fragments consist but in apothegms, many of which, ascribed to Syrus, are probably attributable to others; yet the very imputation to him of sayings so exquisite, attests his rank as the sayer of exquisite things. And the sentences thus collectively fathered upon him, evince a solidity and a splendour of intellect surpassing all which we can discover in Terence and Plautus, and proving, not so much the amazing combination of wit and sagacity in the writer — since we are not sure that they all belong to the writer assigned — as the amazing civilisation of the age out of which they grew, whosoever the writer might be. And it is these fragments, so little familiar to even the learned, that Sydney Smith, telling us how the 'Edinburgh Review' came to be started, says, "We took our present grave motto from Publius Syrus, of whom none of us, I am sure, had ever read a single line;" — it is these fragments which, when I am treating of the knowledge of the world, bring before me the obligations in that science, and in the literature familiarising it, which we at this day owe to the Greek and Latin authors. Is there one of their merits which more serves to keep them everlastingly in vogue, and more emphatically distinguishes their genius from that of other antique races, whether Oriental or Northern, than the tone and air of highly civilised European gentlemen in a highly civilised European world?

The secret of what is called classic taste consists in the harmonious combination of manliness of sentiment with elegance of form. If I could sum up the general spirit of ancient literature by one brief definition, I should say that it was the expression of a nature highly poetical, highly imaginative, chastened by a commune with men of admirable common sense, accustomed to the strictness of scholastic reasoning, and ripened by intercourse with the living world. In societies not characterised by the collisions and checks of a highly accomplished society fastidiously alive to vulgarity of language and to bombast in sentiment, the fancy even of genius, the reason even of pure intellect, is apt to run riot. Both the one and the other will tend to forsake what we call the Practical, and, in forsaking it, to depart from the true Ideal; for the true Ideal is the noble chivalrous lover of the Practical — loth to quarrel with its earthly partner, ever seeking not to divorce, but to raise to its own rank that less highborn bride, to which, for better or for worse, it is necessarily allied.

Now, when we speak, in our formal schools, of classic taste, and solemnly commend to our youthful listeners a study of the classic authors, we cannot, unless we are the most servile of pedants, mean to imply any other check upon the divine freedom and play of imagination, so bold in the classic poets, than that which, even in the Homeric dawn of classical literature, the knowledge of man in his highest state of intellectual refinement at the time in which the Poet lived, imposed on his phantasies. If Homer created, as Herodotus implies he did, the gods whom Greece worshipped, and who have long since perished, he also represented, in more unalterable types, the men whom we still behold. But what, I apprehend, we mean to inculcate on our pupils in commending to them the study of the classics, is that soundness of taste and judgment which is formed by intercourse, not with one single writer or another, but with a literature extending over many centuries, and on the whole representing that harmonious union of imagination and reasoning which forms the predominant characteristic of ancient classical literature. In this union Shakespeare, indeed, is more classic than the classics to whom his romance is said by Formalists to be opposed. But in style or form there is a necessity for a common standard of taste, which it is the privilege of dead languages to bestow. Howsoever we English admire Shakespeare, we should hesitate before we commended his form and style as a model. In truth, we should dislike or rebuke the writer who presumed to imitate the form of Shakespeare. We should cry "off" to the mimics who aped his walk. A language dead, and therefore eternally settled, has alone the prerogative of suggesting to all living races ideals of form which are cosmopolitan, not national — which can be tamely copied by none, yet afford standards of taste to all.

Now, while the classic poets authorise the highest flights to which healthful imagination can soar — while they throw open the gates of the supernatural, admitting familiar companionship with deities and nymphs and fauns and satyrs — enlarging the realm of fable to boundaries as remote from this world of fact as the wildest romance can desire — they still, regarded as a class, a general body, preserve sufficient affinities with human nature to secure what may be called the truthfulness of art to the inventions of their fancy. They rarely forsake the Practical, as Goethe understood the word, when he applies it to the genius of the ever-idealising Schiller — meaning thereby the strong sense which *practicalises* the ideal to the common sympathies and comprehension of multitudes: while the classic prose-writers — though the severest of them, as historians or philosophers, sometimes desert reason for fancy with a licence we should be sorry nowadays to concede to guides in philosophy and authorities in history — still embody a mass of solid truths, social and moral, which makes them perennially modern in what we call knowledge of the world.

Classic literature, in short, is so essentially characterised by that liberal suavity which Cicero terms "urbanitas," in contradistinction to whatever is narrow-minded, rude, underbred, superfine, and provincial — so thoroughly the literature of gentlemen in whatsoever phase of society or period of time the stem of humanity can put forth the flower of gentleman — that the most polished communities of Europe to this day concur in the superstitious belief that there is something wanting in the tone, spirit, breeding, by which gentlemen are distinguished, in the man who, whatever his birth or his talents, is utterly ignorant of the classics.

In public life, especially, such ignorance appears to make itself felt. An orator in whom it exists rarely fails to say something that jars on the taste or alienates the sympathy of an audience in which gentlemen form the majority. The audience do not detect why — do not pedantically exclaim, "This orator knows nothing of Greek and Latin!" they rather mutter, "This orator does not know gentlemen;" or, "He has mixed very little with the great world."

Cicero finely observes, "*Inter hanc vitam perpolitam humanitate, nihil tam interest quam jus atque vis.*" And it is *jus atque vis* which seem, as a whole, to form the style by which classic literature expresses — *vitam perpolitam*.

Probably knowledge of the world in its widest and healthiest development, is not often exhibited by writers in states of society in which there do not exist at once a tolerant freedom of opinion, if not of institutions — as the former freedom, at least, existed in France even under the old regime — and the polished language which that opinion acquires from the converse of a class raised above the mercantile business of life.

Free institutions necessarily tend to the wider range and securer privilege of free opinions. The Greek eupatrid or the Roman patrician, who had to court the votes of his phyle, or of his clients, could not fail to acquire a large and liberal acquaintanceship, not only with the selfish interests, but with the nobler motive-springs of impassioned multitudes, such as is shown in Thucydides or Cicero: and as all knowledge becomes, as it were, atmospheric, and once admitted into the common air of a place, is generally inhaled; so even poets, aloof from the arena of politicians, caught that generous influence from the very breath they drew in, and express it in their pages. But still the tone of a society refined by aristocratic distinctions, is apparent in the elegance with which the classic writers utter the sentiments popular with the crowd.

But if, in forms of government which exclude free political institutions, though admitting great latitude of literary speech, knowledge of the world is apt to become too narrowed to that of a privileged circle, so, on the other hand, in forms of government so popular as to exclude admitted differences of rank, I know of no writers in whom knowledge of the world is a conspicuous attribute. The United States of America have produced authors remarkable for number and excellence, considering the briefness of period during which the American Republic has existed — remarkable even for national originality, considering the disadvantage of writing in a language appropriated already to enduring masterpieces in the parent State. But while in science and philosophical discussion, in theology, in poetry, and prose fiction, democratic America is rich in works which command just admiration, the main fault of her authorship, and indeed of her statesmanship, in dealing with foreign countries, has been the want of that *comity* — that ineffably urbane wisdom which has its expression in good breeding, and without which knowledge of the world has the air of a clever attorney in sharp practice. The absence of a fixed and permanent order of refined society, with its smile at the bombast and balderdash that captivate the vulgar, seems to lessen the quick perception of genius to the boundaries between good taste and bad; so that, when I read the printed orations of American statesmen, I find a sentence of which a Grattan might have been proud followed by a tawdry claptrap of which even a Hunt would have been ashamed. The poets of this grand Anglo-Saxon family, escaping from the popular life, and following the muse in the retirement of their groves or their closets, eliminate from their graceful verse knowledge of the world altogether; they often philosophise on man in the abstract, but they neither depict in their drama nor adorn in their lyrics, nor moralise, in their didactic vein, upon the actual world, which the ideal world surrounds with a purer atmosphere, but from which it draws up the particles it incorporates in its rays of light, or the vapours it returns in dews. Shakespeare places alike a Miranda and a Stephano in the Enchanted Isle which has Caliban and Ariel for its dwellers; and Horace invokes now a Tyndaris, now a Mæcenas, to the cool of the valley resonant with the pipe of Faunus.

Perhaps, of all American writers, in Washington Irving the polite air of the man of the European world is the most seen; but then, of all American writers, Washington Irving is the one who most sedulously imitated, and most happily caught, the spirit of European writers, formed under aristocratic as well as popular influences; — of all American writers he is thus the least American. In fact, European life — whether among the ancients, as in Athens or Rome, or among the modern civilised races — struggles perpetually for the political ascendancy of the people, but ever also seeks to preserve a superior social influence to a class in which the sense of honour is an ancestral duty — the observance of polished manners a traditional charge. And if ever, in any one of the great nations of Europe, such a class should wholly disappear, that nation will lose its distinctive European character.

Knowledge of the world, in its widest signification, is the knowledge of civilised humanity; and its artistic expression will be consummate in proportion as its range comprehends what is most general in humanity, and its tone represents what is most refined in civilised manners. By knowledge of the world we mean something more than knowledge of a class, whether the class comprise the idlers of May Fair or the operatives of Manchester. But in the mind of a great artist selecting either May Fair or Manchester for his scene and his characters, there is no demagogue's hatred of idlers, and no coxcomb's contempt of workmen. Both classes represent sections of humanity which go back to the earliest date of human records, and may possibly endure to their last.

I started with saying that knowledge of the world, where the world's condition is not unhealthful, though it may be below the average morality of sages, and must comprehend a survey of error, vice, crime, as well as of truth, virtue, innocence, does not necessarily vitiate the student of it, any more than the study of the human frame vitiates the pathologist. Only where the society to which the range of the observer is confined is thoroughly corrupt would it, almost of necessity, infect the moral health of its philosophical student, whether by acquiescence in its example, as may be the case with natures too yielding and soft, or by scorn and wrath at the example, as would be the case with natures too irascible and severe. For, as I have before said, however justly provoked scorn and wrath may be, no mind can be habitually in a state of scorn and wrath without some deterioration of the qualities essential to virtue. "*Ira, pessimus consultor.*" It would be difficult to reconcile any notions or theories of human goodness with creeds from which indulgence, charity, tolerance, philanthropy are excluded as unworthy compromises with human evil.

Now, our world at this epoch, though I do not desire to flatter, is certainly not one which would justify Thales in bidding farewell to it. If we consult history in an unprejudiced, unsuperstitious spirit, I do not think we shall find that the world, regarded as a whole, has ever been much better than it is now, and in many important respects it has been much worse. I speak more especially of the world in my own country, which at this moment is certainly a more humane, peaceable, orderly, moral, decorous, yet good-natured world, than it ever seems to have been, from the date of the last George up to that of the first William. If I look back to the chronicles of the eighteenth century — nay, if I look back only so far as the year in which I left college — I am startled at the visible improvement. I do not say that those rare individuals who stand forth as the landmarks of time were not possibly much greater, and, considering the temptations that begirt them, much better than individuals nowadays. I honour the reverence to noble tombs too implicitly to believe that any living great man can equal a dead great man. A dead great man is a shrined ideal of excellence; a living great man is a struggling fellow-mortal. The one is Hercules assoiled from mortal stain when separated from mortal labour, who has ascended from the fire-pile to the Nectar Hall of Olympus; but the other is the Hercules who, if at one time he is valiantly slaying the Hydra and calmly braving the very Powers of Orcus, is seen at another time the effeminate slave of Omphale, or the frenzied murderer of Iphitus. But the progress of society has very fallacious milestones in the monuments we erect to apotheosised individuals. Whatever my admiration for Alexander — and, in spite of Mr. Grote, it is intense — Alexander's march through Asia affords me no gleam of intelligence as to the advance of his Macedonian people in the theories of political government or ethical doctrine.

What I see in England, comparing this century with the last — or comparing even the date in which I now write with the date in which I wrote first — is the advancement of numbers, the more general culture of intellect, the milder constructions of law, the greater tenderness to suffering and erring humanity, the more decent respect to domestic sanctities, the more intellectual — not unreasoning — acquiescence in religious truths. — And, therefore, looking at the world as reflected in the microcosm of my own country, — through all gradations of society, from the palace to the cottage — and through all sections of opinion, from that of the pulpit to that of a club, — it seems to me that a writer of our day and land, aspiring to fame for knowledge of the world, would view that world not with the abhorrence of Juvenal, not with the despair of venerable Bede, but with as indulgent a charity as that which makes Shakespeare and Goethe so lovably mild and so genially wise. Still, the world is the world, and it is not Utopia. Even in our own England, no doubt, there is much that is very bad, and we varnish it over by what in vernacular vulgarism is called "cant;" while out of England there are many things which revolt our English preconceived opinions.

There is therefore quite enough material left for either Muse, the tragic or the comic — quite enough left for the grave reproof of philosophy, or the light ridicule of satire. But the writer in either of these developments of his natural genius who shall seek to win general and permanent repute for his knowledge of the world we live in, will find that the same greater mildness of manners which would render us shocked at the judgments our courts of law passed on offenders a century ago, would also indispose us to allow to writers the truculent sentences upon human error which then were considered the just denunciations of outraged virtue.

Whether the world be better, as I believe, or worse, as some fond worshippers of the past maintain, it is quite clear that the world does not nowadays think it can be improved by the old-fashioned modes of hanging and branding and pillorying, or of scoffing and scolding and snubbing, which it so cheerfully accepted as salutary mortifications from the hands and tongues of our ancestors.

And in the writer to whom we accord knowledge of the world in this our day of it, we shall expect to find that large toleration which has grown out of a wisdom more lenient, and that well-bred urbanity of tone which succeeds to the boorishness of vituperation, in proportion as the refinement of intellectual and social culture has become more diffused throughout the various ranks of the public.

ESSAY XXVI.

READERS AND WRITERS.

READERS AND WRITERS.

READING without purpose is sauntering, not exercise. More is got from one book on which the thought settles for a definite end in knowledge, than from libraries skimmed over by a wandering eye. A cottage flower gives honey to the bee, a king's garden none to the butterfly. Youths who are destined for active careers, or ambitious of distinction in such forms of literature as require freshness of invention or originality of thought, should avoid the habit of intense study for many hours at a stretch. There is a point in all tension of the intellect beyond which effort is only waste of strength. Fresh ideas do not readily spring up within a weary brain; and whatever exhausts the mind not only enfeebles its power, but narrows its scope. We often see men who have over-read at college, entering upon life as languidly as if they were about to leave it. They have not the vigour to cope with their own generation; for their own generation is young, and they have wasted the nervous energy which supplies the sinews of war to youth in its contests for fame or fortune.

Study with regularity, at settled hours. Those in the forenoon are the best, if they can be secured. The man who has acquired the habit of study, though for only one hour every day in the year, and keeps to the one thing studied till it is mastered, will be startled to see the way he has made at the end of a twelvemonth.

He is seldom over-worked who can contrive to be in advance of his work. If you have three weeks before you to learn something which a man of average quickness could learn in a week, learn it the first week, and not the third. Business despatched is business well done, but business hurried is business ill done.

In learning what others have thought, it is well to keep in practice the power to think for one's self: when an author has added to your knowledge, pause and consider if you can add nothing to his.

Be not contented to have learned a problem by heart; try and deduce from it a corollary not in the book.

Spare no pains in collecting details before you generalise; but it is only when details are generalised that a truth is grasped. The tendency to generalise is universal with all men who achieve great success, whether in art, literature, or action. The habit of generalising, though at first gained with care and caution, secures, by practice, a comprehensiveness of judgment, and a promptitude of decision, which seem to the crowd like the intuitions of genius. And, indeed, nothing more distinguishes the man of genius from the mere man of talent, than the facility of generalising the various details, each of which demands the aptitude of a special talent; but all of which can be only gathered into a single whole by the grasp of a mind which may have no special aptitude for any.

Invention implies the power of generalisation, for an invention is but the combining of many details known before, into a new whole, and for new results.

Upon any given point, contradictory evidence seldom puzzles the man who has mastered the laws of evidence; but he knows little of the laws of evidence who has not studied the unwritten law of the human heart. And without this last knowledge a man of action will not attain to the practical, nor will a poet achieve the ideal.

He who has no sympathy never knows the human heart; but the obtrusive parade of sympathy is incompatible with dignity of character in a man, or with dignity of style in a writer. Of all the virtues necessary to the completion of the perfect man, there is none to be more delicately implied and less ostentatiously vaunted than that of exquisite feeling or universal benevolence.

In science, address the few; in literature, the many. In science, the few must dictate opinion to the many; in literature, the many, sooner or later, force their judgment on the few. But the few and the many are not necessarily the few and the many of the passing time: for discoverers in science have not unoften, in their own day, had the few against them; and writers the most permanently popular not unfrequently found, in their own day, a frigid reception from the many. By the few, I mean those who must ever remain the few, from whose dicta we, the multitude, take fame upon trust; by the many, I mean those who constitute the multitude in the long-run. We take the fame of a Harvey or a Newton upon trust, from the verdict of the few in successive generations;

but the few could never persuade us to take poets and novelists on trust. We, the many, judge for ourselves of Shakespeare and Cervantes.

He who addresses the abstract reason, addresses an audience that must for ever be limited to the few; he who addresses the passions, the feelings, the humours, which we all have in common, addresses an audience that must for ever compose the many. But either writer, in proportion to his ultimate renown, embodies some new truth, and new truths require new generations for cordial welcome. This much I would say meanwhile, Doubt the permanent fame of any work of science which makes immediate reputation with the ignorant multitude; doubt the permanent fame of any work of imagination which is at once applauded by a conventional clique that styles itself "the critical few."

ESSAY XXVII.

ON THE SPIRIT OF CONSERVATISM.

ON THE SPIRIT OF CONSERVATISM.

IN every political state which admits of the free expression of opinion, it is a trite commonplace to say that there will always be two main divisions of political reasoners — viz., a class predisposed to innovate; a class predisposed to conserve. But there will be also two other divisions of reasoners, sometimes blended with, often distinct from, those that have just been defined — viz., a class predisposed to all theories that strengthen the power of the body governed; and a class predisposed to all doctrines that confirm the authority of the body governing. Prevalent with the one is a passion for political liberty, which, when carried to extreme, is fanatical; prevalent with the other is a reverence for civil order, which, when carried to extreme, is superstitious. It does not necessarily happen that the class most predisposed to conserve is identical with the class most inclined to confirm the sway of the governing body; nor that the class most predisposed to innovate should be that most inclined to strengthen the body governed. There are times when political liberty is clearly with the conservative side, and its loss is insured by the triumph of the innovating. Cæsar was an innovator, Brutus a conservative. But the cause of freedom was certainly with Brutus, and not with Cæsar. In democratic republics, we may, indeed, fairly assume that the liberties their institutions comprise are opposed to innovation. Thus, the American constitution presents a check to all tamperings with its main principles, which no existent constitutional monarchy has secured. The constitution of the United States cannot be legally altered by the votes of a mere majority. Such alteration requires the votes of two-thirds of the Assembly. So, more or less, in every community where a considerable degree of political freedom is possessed by the people, experiments which seem to involve any hazards to the duration of the liberties existing, though proffered as extensions and accelerants of their action, may be regarded, by the most devoted friends of a people's freedom, with the same disfavour with which the trustee for the enjoyers of a solid estate would listen to proposals to hazard punctual rents and solid acres for shares in a company which offers 20 per cent and the chances of bankruptcy.

It is with liberty as with all else worth having in life. The first thing is to get it, the next thing is to keep it, the third thing is to increase what we have. But if we are not without common prudence, our wariness in speculation is in proportion to the amount of the property we already possess. In desperate circumstances it is worth hazarding a shilling to gain a plum. In affluence it is not worth hazarding a plum to gain a shilling.

"Nothing venture, nothing have," says, not unwisely, the young dare-devil who can scarcely be worse off than he is. "Venture all and have nothing," says, at least as wisely, the middle-aged millionaire, besieged by ingenious projectors, who, proving to his complete satisfaction that English funds yield but a small interest, invite him to exchange his stock in consols for shares in the wonderful diamond-mines just discovered in the Mountains of the Moon.

Why do English funds yield us but $3\frac{1}{2}$ per cent, when we can get twice as much in the Spanish, and almost thrice as much in the Turkish? Simply because though the interest is smaller, the capital is more secure.

The capital of English freedom is the accumulation of centuries; and the interest derived from it, as compared with that of younger free states, is to be computed at the difference between the rent of soil lately wrung from the wilderness, and that which is paid for the building-ground of cities.

I am, and, as long as I live, I believe I shall be, a passionate lover of freedom. Individually, freedom is the vital necessity of my being. I cannot endure to cripple my personal freedom for anything less than my obligation to duty. What I, as man, thus prize for myself, I assume that each community of men should no less ardently prize.

Now, a man will develop his uses, and tend towards the nearest approach to the perfectibility of his being, in proportion as freedom and duty so harmonise in his motives and actions, that, in his ordinary course of life, he can scarcely distinguish one from the other. If I desire and will to do that which I ought to do, and desire and will not to do that which I ought not to do, my freedom and my duty are practically one — my restraints are in reality the essential properties of my own nature. If, for instance, the principle of honour has became part and parcel of my mind, I cannot pick pockets — the law against picking pockets is no restraint on me. If the law permitted me to do so, I still should not and could not pick a pocket.

As it is with a man, so it is with a state — that state will be the best in which liberty and order so, as it were, fuse into each other, that the conditions prescribed by order are not felt as restraints on liberty.

And as with a man, so with a state; the amalgamation of freedom and duty is the unconscious result of habit — the custom of liberty incorporates with its motives and actions the custom of order.

Any violent or sudden change in the conditions of this marriage-bond between freedom and duty must inflict a shock on their union. If the habitual use of my freedom in certain directions has always led me to a definite course of duties, you cannot abruptly alter those duties but what you must impair my freedom.

Thus where the mind of a nation has been so formed by its institutions that all the restraints imposed by law are made by custom consentaneous to the normal operations of liberty, you cannot raise up new institutions, enforcing restraints to which liberty is unfamiliar, but what you sow the seeds of a quarrel between liberty and order.

Hence even a mere change of dynasty, though in itself it may be the best for liberty and order in a later generation, will often sever liberty from order for the generation on which it is brought to bear.

The introduction of the Guelphs to the exclusion of the Stuarts was no doubt a fortunate event for the ultimate destinies of the British nation. But, for the then living race, it shocked the liberty of those who honoured the old line, and imperilled order to those who preferred the new.

Although the laws went on the same under George the Guelph as under Anne the Stuart — although scarcely one in ten thousand of those whom the change disaffected could have been worse off or better off for the name of the king on the throne — still what was loyalty to one part of the people seemed treason to the other part. The result was rebellion in those who conceived that their liberty of choice in the election of their sovereign was aggrieved; and, so far as we can judge, that rebellion would have been successful if Charles Edward had marched upon London instead of retreating from Derby. Had the rebellion been successful, those over whom it triumphed would have thought their liberty aggrieved. Time is the only reconciler — that is, change ceases to interrupt the union of liberty and order when it ceases to be felt as change, and when custom has again brought about the union which the infringement of custom had severed.

But where, instead of a dynasty, it is a change of institutions, affecting all the habitual relationships between duty and freedom in the minds of citizens, the danger, if less violent, is likely to prove more mortal to the wellbeing of the community. Freedom, and all its noblest consequences in the development of intellectual riches, may, we will say for the sake of argument, be equally operative under a constitutional monarchy or a well-educated democracy. But if all the habits of political thought and motive have been formed under the one, they could not be transferred to the other without that revolution of the entire system which no organised body can long survive. If I were an American, I should regard as the worst affliction that could befall my country the substitution for democracy, with all its faults, of a constitutional monarchy, with all its merits; because my countrymen would have been accustomed to associate their elementary ideas of liberty with republican institutions: So, being an Englishman, I should regard it as the worst affliction that could befall my countrymen, to substitute for constitutional monarchy a democratic republic; because all their habits of mind are formed on the notion that liberty, on the whole, is safer, and the dignity of life is higher, where the institutions essential to the duration of constitutional monarchy make the representatives of the public interests other than the paid servants of a class that must of necessity be the least educated and the most excitable.

The favourite reproach to a conservative policy is, that it is not in favour of progress. But there is nothing in a conservative policy antagonistic to progress: on the contrary, resistance to progress is destructive to conservatism.

Political conservatism can but seek the health and longevity of the political body it desires to conserve. To a state, progress is as essential as exercise is to a man. But a state has this advantage over a man, that while it is in robust health its mere exercise must, of necessity, be progress. If Science is always experimenting, if Art is always inventing, if Commerce is always exchanging, if looms are always at work, the state cannot fail to make progress; whereas I, as individual man, cannot say that my habitual walk is always in the direction of a journey towards objects yet unreached, or my habitual occupation in my study necessarily conducive to the discovery of a new truth.

A nation's habitual employment, while the nation is in health, is, then, of necessity reproductive; a man's is not.

Therefore a true conservative policy is for a nation the policy of progress, because without exercise the body politic would languish and die; and with exercise it must, if in health, augment the resources which furnish strength against external enemies, and, by widening the markets of labour, interest a wider range of citizens in the maintenance of domestic order.

But progress does not mean transformation; it means the advance towards the fullest development of forces of which any given human organisation, whether it be a man's or a society's, is capable. What is progress in one state may be paralysis to another. Each state is an integral unity; it has, when free, not otherwise — as man, when free, not otherwise — the powers within itself to improve all the faculties which it takes from birth. It cannot, any more than a man can do, alter its whole idiosyncrasies into those of another organised unity which you present to it as a model.

Suppose you had said to Shakespeare, "Friend, you have considerable talents; do not throw them away on the contemptible occupation of a play-writer. Be a philosopher. Look at your contemporary Bacon: how much higher is his fame and his station than yours! You are ambitious of progress — be a Bacon!"

If Shakespeare had listened to your advice he would not have been a Shakespeare, and it is my belief that he would not have been a Bacon. If, on the other hand, you had said to Bacon, "Friend, you have very great genius, especially in the study of nature. But see how all schools of philosophy perish. You are destroying the authority of Aristotle, to be destroyed yourself by some other bold guesser hereafter. Poets alone are sure of immortality; they are the truest diviners of nature. You put down Aristotle, but who can put down Horace? He who writes prose builds his temple to Fame in rubble; he who writes verse builds it in granite. Write poems — poetry is clearly a progress from prose. Write a tragedy out of one of those novels on your table, 'Romeo and Juliet,' or 'Othello.'"

Had Bacon taken your advice, he would not have been a Bacon: my belief is that he would never have been a Shakespeare. It is the same with states; the more highly they are gifted in one development of faculties, the less it would be progress to turn aside to another. Each leading state in civilised Europe has its idiosyncrasies; its real progress is in developing those idiosyncrasies; its real annihilation of its own highest attributes would be to exchange its own for the idiosyncrasies of another state.

Conservatism, rightly considered, is the policy which conserves the body politic in the highest condition of health of which it is capable, compatible with longevity. I make that reserve, because a man who has passed the elastic season of youth may attain to a higher condition of muscular strength by putting himself under a trainer, or scaling the Swiss mountains; but in so doing he may sow the germs of some malady which will shorten his life.

Conservatism accepts cheerfully the maxim of Bentham, "the greatest happiness of the greatest number," provided it may add this indispensable condition, "for the longest period of time." The greatest happiness of the greatest number may consist, for the moment, in the greatest number having their own way in something which will be their greatest misery in the long-run. The greatest number in the reign of King James the First thought it was especial happiness to put to death the old women whom they believed to be witches. The greatest happiness of the greatest number on board a ship may be, for the moment, to get at the rum-barrels, and shoot down the captain who stands in their way. But it is not for the greatest happiness of any population, in the long-run, to admit sanguinary superstitions into their criminal code, nor for the greatest happiness of a crew, in the long-run, to get drunk and to murder their captain.

Duration is an essential element of all plans for happiness, private or public; and conservatism looks to the durable in all its ideas of improvement.

But duration means the duration of a something definite in politics; that something is the body politic

— the Nation. A conservative party must be national, or it is nothing.

Now, in politics there are two grand theories, each antagonistic to all principles mean and selfish. The one theory is Philanthropy, the other Patriotism — a care for the whole human race, or a care for the whole community to which we belong. The tendency of the more popular party will be towards the first, the tendency of the less popular party towards the last. In the popular sentiment of masses, the cause of fellow-men creates more enthusiasm than the interests of fellow-countrymen. Oligarchies, on the other hand, have small regard for mankind in the concrete, but are capable of great enthusiasm for a state. It is difficult to conceive more passionate devotion for a state than was shown by the oligarchies of Sparta and Venice. In communities which admit to the masses a large share of political power, a conservative statesman must consult that sentiment of universal philanthropy which in itself is noble — but not at the hazard of the state, which must be his first care. Masses could easily be led to a war against some absolute sovereign oppressing his subjects — oligarchies in alliance with the sovereign might assist him to oppress his subjects. The conservative statesman of a free country remains neutral. It is not for the good of his country to lavish blood and treasure on the internal quarrels of other countries. By here consulting Patriotism, he in truth advances Philanthropy, for it is to the benefit of all nations that each nation should settle its own quarrels for itself.

Patriotism is a safer principle, both for a state and the human race, than Philanthropy. Sancho Panza administering his island is a better model than Don Quixote sallying forth to right the wrongs of the universe.

Philanthropy, like glory, is a circle in the water,

"Which never ceaseth to enlarge itself,
Till by broad spreading it disperse to nought."

But an enlightened love of country comprehends the objects of Philanthropy, without making Philanthropy its avowed object. That is to say, a man who has an enlightened love for his country will seek to identify its interests with a just and humane policy — with scrupulous faith in the fulfilment of engagements — with a respect, as inviolably preserved toward weak as toward strong powers — not only of the law, but of the comity, of nations; and thus, in a word, he will strive to render the wellbeing of the state to which he belongs conducive to the catholic and enduring interests of the varied communities of mankind. But just as an individual would become an intolerable plague to his neighbours if he were always interfering with their domestic affairs, though with the best intentions; so a weak state would become ridiculous, and a strong state tyrannical, if, under the pretext of general philanthropy, it sought to force its own notions of right or wrong, of liberty or order, upon states not subjected to its sovereignty. As it is only through self-development that any community can mature its own elements of happiness or grandeur, so non-intervention is in truth the policy not more of wisdom than of respect for humanity, without which love for humanity is an intermeddling mischief-maker. Nevertheless, where the internal feuds of any one nation assume a character so formidable as to threaten the peace of other nations, intervention may become the necessity of self-preservation. But the plea of self-preservation should be irrefragably a sound one, and not, as it usually is, an excuse for self-aggrandisement, in profiting by the dissensions which the intermeddler foments for his own crafty ends.

It has been a question frequently discussed of late, and by no means satisfactorily settled, how far non-interference in the domestic feuds of other nations admits of the frank expression of opinion — the freedom of remonstrance — the volunteered suggestion of a policy. But in free communities it would be utterly impossible for a minister to refrain from conveying to a foreign government the public sentiment of his country. The popular chamber would not allow him to be silent where a popular cause seemed at stake. To express opinions — to address remonstrances — are acts in themselves perfectly compatible with friendship, provided the tone be friendly. But for one government to volunteer, in detail, schemes of policy for the adoption of another independent government, is seldom a prudent venture. It is too calculated to wound the dignity of the state advised, not to provoke an answer which wounds the dignity of the state advising. Exceptions may arise, but they should be regarded with great caution. For there is scarcely an exception that does not engender on both sides those resentments of mortified self-esteem which, if they do not suffice to create war at once, render states more disposed to find excuses for war later.

Political freedom is, or ought to be, the best guarantee for the safety and continuance of spiritual, mental, and civil freedom. It is the combination of numbers to secure the liberty of each one.

Therefore, as each community is a life in itself, so each community, to be free, should be independent of others.

Every state, to be independent, must contain the elements of a power sufficient, under all existent circumstances, without it and within, to maintain itself.

It may not, if a small and weak state, be able in itself to stand against any one powerful aggressive neighbour; but it may so enlist the interests of all its neighbours, that if one attacks it, all the others will combine to defend it. This is the case of Switzerland. All Europe has this interest in Switzerland — that it would be unsafe for Europe that Switzerland should be engulfed either by Austria or by France. The interest of Europe guarantees the independence of Switzerland.

Alliances tending to check any one state from invading others are the natural precaution of a conservative policy. The choice of such alliances, the conditions to which they pledge us, are questions not of principle, but of expediency; they belong not to all time, but to each time, bringing forth its own mutable causes of apprehension. And here for statesmanship there can be no precise rule, because in time there is no exact precedent.

To sum up: — The true conservative policy in any given state is in self-preservation; and self-preservation does not confine itself to the mere care for existence, but extends to all that can keep the body politic in the highest state of health and vigour: therefore progress and development of forces are essential to self-preservation. But according to a conservative policy, such progress and such development will always be encouraged with a due regard to the idiosyncratic character of a state, such as it has been made by time and circumstance — to the institutions which have not only become endeared to it by custom, but have contributed to consolidate the national unity by forming and systematising the national spirit and mind. A conservative policy in England will favour peace, if only because England is essentially a commercial commonwealth, and its real sinews of strength are in its financial resources. War exposes commerce to hazard, and financial resources to an indefinite drain. It is true that foreign wars, however unpopular, never or rarely produce intestine rebellion; but the financial distress which follows a war the most popular, is the most dangerous cause of revolutions. Nevertheless, a commercial community cannot accept peace at all hazards, because no commerce would be long safe under a flag dishonoured or despised. A conservative policy in England would vigilantly guard our maritime power, and spare no cost necessary to maintain a navy superior to that of any other single European Power; but it would regard with great jealousy any attempt to maintain, in England itself, more than the well-disciplined nucleus and framework of a standing army. It has to conserve political liberty as the most precious of all heirlooms; and a nation once reconciled to the maintenance of large standing armies, submits its liberties to the mercy of accident. A state must, for durability, as I have said, conserve its special national character, and the national character of England will be lost whenever it shall see with apathy large standing armies within its own shores. One of the obvious advantages of military colonies is the facility they afford for maintaining therein such military strength as may be necessary for the protection of the empire, without quartering large bodies of troops in England, to the danger of freedom; and therefore it is a very shallow view of Imperial policy, to ascribe solely to our colonial wants the military forces kept in colonies, and exclaim, "See what those colonies cost us!" If we had no troops in colonies, we must either be without adequate military force, or we must obtain such adequate military force at the risk of freedom, by collecting and converging it into garrisons at home.

Prudence in the administration of finance is the characteristic virtue of a conservative policy; for every form of government in which the expenditure habitually exceeds the income, is doomed to undergo a vital change. The more hopelessly the finances are disordered, the more violent in all probability the change will be. Thus, despotic governments may become democratised, and republican institutions may become monarchical.

Lastly, the statesman who would maintain a conservative policy for England has always to bear in mind that any state which attains to a wealth, an influence, a grandeur disproportioned to its native population, or the extent of its native dominion, owes its rank rather to causes that may be called complicated and artificial than to causes simple and natural. The prosperity and power of France recover with a bound after numerous shocks upon internal order and commercial credit. But a single one of such shocks might suffice to destroy for a century, perhaps for ever, the rank of England among first-rate Powers; and therefore, English statesmen have to consider many political questions, not only on their own abstract merits, but with due regard to their collateral bearings upon the national wellbeing. It is for this reason, perhaps, that in England a truly conservative politician, though without any undue apprehension of revolutionary tendencies among the bulk of the population, would seek to preserve the preponderating electoral power among the middle classes; because with them there is, upon the whole, a larger amount of education and forethought than could be reasonably expected from numbers subsisting upon manual labour. But as free nations are governed either by the preponderance of numbers or by the ascendancy of cultivated intelligence, so a conservative policy, if it do not maintain itself in power by the first, must seek to conciliate and identify itself with the second. It should have no fear of the calm extension of knowledge; its real antagonist is in the passionate force of ignorance. As it seeks to develop in the state whatever is best for the state's preservation in its highest form of integral unity, so certainly it should befriend and foster all the intellectual powers which enrich and adorn a state — seeking, irrespectively of class, to honour and ally itself with all that ennobles the people it guards. It should be the friend of commerce, of art, of science, of letters, and should carefully keep open every vista by which merit can win its way to distinction; for the best mode to aristocratise the sentiment of a population is to revere, as the finest element of aristocracy, every merit which, conquering obstacles of birth and fortune, rises up into distinction, and adds a new dignity to the nation itself.

www.ingramcontent.com/pod-product-compliance
Lightning Source LLC
Chambersburg PA
CBHW030739230426
43667CB00007B/778